Machine Code Programming on the *Psion Organiser*

Bill Aitken

Kuma Computers

First Published 1990
Second Edition, revised and enlarged, 1990
Kuma Computers Ltd
12 Horseshoe Park
Pangbourne
Berkshire. RG8 7JW
Tel 0734 844335. Fax 0734 844339

Printed in Great Britain

ISBN 0-7457-0138-8

Acknowledgment

To Psion PLC for providing some of the technical information which made the publication of this book possible.

Other books available from Kuma:

Using and Programming the Psion Organiser II
by Mike Shaw

File Handling and Other Programs for the Psion Organiser II
by Mike Shaw

Z88 Magic
by Gill Gerhardi, Vic Gerhardi and Andy Berry

The Amstrad PC1640 Programmers Databook
by John Hawthorne

Foreword

Firstly, thank you for buying my book! I hope that it is all you expect and that it leads you into a very rewarding area of study. I have tried to pitch it somewhere in the middle between extremely dry and too funny for words. Whereas I have tried very hard indeed to ensure that the material contained within these covers is free from error, owing to the detailed nature of the subject matter, it is always possible that Murphy's Law will prevail. I would therefore welcome any comments from readers on either this publication or any future one they would like to see.

In writing a book, as in accepting Oscars, there is always a host of people to be thanked, without whom... Firstly, there is my long-suffering wife Maggie, who was beginning to feel that she was the head of a one-parent family. Thanks for all the support, especially through the last year.

Secondly, there is Tim Moore of Kuma who has been patience and encouragement personified. Despite the fact that the book was planned to take eight months and went on for more than twice that amount, he has been very supportive.

So, enjoy the read, make sure you keep backups of all your datafiles and long may the dreaded TRAP keep from your screen.

Bill Aitken

Contents

Chapter 1

The Ancestry of the Psion Organiser

1: The Ancestry of the Psion Organiser

TRAINING OBJECTIVE:

At the end of this chapter, you will be able to describe the development of the modern computer in general terms.

ENABLING OBJECTIVES:

To enable you to do this, you must be able to:

a. List the major land marks in computer development.

b. State the meaning of the word *software*

c. State the meaning of the word *hardware*

d. State the meaning of the term *high level language*

INTRODUCTION

1.0 In writing this book, I have tried to strike a balance between the style of presentation and the depth of content. You, the reader, may well already be an expert in writing machine code programs on other computers. For you, the book is intended as a reference work, to be dipped into as need dictates. On the other hand, many of you will have bought the Organiser for its business facilities and thereafter enjoyed the challenge of writing programs in the Organiser Programming Language (OPL). Now, you are looking to secure the benefits of speed and flexibility machine code can give but you do not yet possess the familiarity with computer structure which this type of programming demands. The chapters which follow are designed with this latter kind of reader in mind. They start, therefore, right back at basics - the development of the modern computer.

THE BEGINNINGS

1.1 I suppose the real beginnings of computers could be traced back to those ingenious clock-makers of the late Middle Ages, for they developed the mechanical basis which formed the foundation on which computers were built. But what about the Abacus and similar calculators? - do they not form part of the history of computers? Well, it all depends on your definition of a computer. Basically, I go for the one which runs "A computer is a device which will store and carry out, at some future time, a linked sequence of instructions". You can see how your Organiser fits in to this description. You have typed in your programs in OPL and watched the computer store them. You decide when to tell the machine to RUN the instructions. That being so, an Abacus could be seen really as a calculator and not as a computer in the true sense of the word - more of a distant relative rather than an ancestor, much in the same way as Apes and Man are related in an evolutionary sense but not descended one from the other.

1.2 Carrying on this separate branch of the computer family tree, the calculator was further developed in the 17th century by Pascal. He was a tax collector and to help him work out his sums, he developed a gear wheel calculator. Admittedly, it could only add and subtract but within 50 years the basic design had been modified by Leibnitz to enable multiplication and division. This sort of machine was to remain in use, with minor modifications, into the 1970s when it was replaced by its now familiar electronic cousin. But at the same time as Pascal was working on the calculator, another type of machine was being developed in parallel - the automata.

1.3 Automata were a completely different breed of machine, for they could carry out a pre-determined, sometimes complex, series of instructions. You've all seen the sort of thing I mean - music boxes for example were automata. The barrel with the spikes which tripped the notes as it rotated was, in effect, a sort of program. The 18th century was known for its little mechanical singing birds which moved and twittered away at the turn of a key. But the most exciting application of this technology came when a Frenchman by the name of Jacquard designed a weaving loom which could alter its pattern according to the program which was fed into it via a linked series of punched cards. Change the pattern of holes on the cards and you could have an entirely new weave to the tapestry produced. Other versions of this type of thing carried on in the shape of pianolas - the pianos which played music using rolls of punched paper. Famous musicians actually played the machines which produced the rolls. Their every nuance could be reproduced on card. All this meant that we could have a machine which could store instructions and execute tasks but how could this be combined with the mathematical abilities of the calculator?

CHARLES BABBAGE

1.4 Babbage took the concept of the Jacquard Loom one step further in the 19th century. He combined the programmable aspect of the loom with the gear-wheel and ratchet concept of the mechanical calculator by trying to build his "Analytical Engine" (the very name has 19th century written all over it!). Sadly, his design was too much for the engineering tolerances of the day and the machine failed to materialize.

1.5 So, that was it until the 1940s. The impetus given by World War II to the development of computers was enormous, mainly for use in cryptography and ballistic calculations. The British developed a series of machines called Colossus for the former application, while the Americans came up with ENIAC for the latter. The Germans were also active in the field and a designer
actually suggested a machine that worked in binary. Fortunately for us, bureaucracy won and the machine was not given the attention it deserved.

1.6 These computers were designed specifically for military applications and as such were not particularly useful after the War. But a rash of more general purpose machines sprouted in their wake, such as the EDSAC 1 at Cambridge. This new breed was largely mathematically orientated but it wasn't long before the business world realised the implications of computerization and so, the UNIVAC was born in the early 1950s. IBM started to pay attention at about this time too.

1.7 To say that these early computers were difficult to operate is something of an understatement. They ran on valves. Consequently, you could fry eggs on them and they needed vast cooling plants just to keep them working. Some were enormous in comparison with their capabilities and contained thousands of hand-soldered joints which would often give intermittent faults while the valves went "ping" and blew like light bulbs. They made their own fun in those days.

1.8 What turned everything around was the invention of transistors in the late 40s. After a period of refinement, they were used in computers for the first time during the early part of the next decade. Each was 1000 times smaller than a valve and streets ahead in terms of reliability. So, computers started to be taken more seriously as a useful tool. Consequently, their development went into overdrive. However, whereas in the past users could twiddle the controls of the computer themselves, the increasing complexity of the machines now coming into being meant that the day of the gifted amateur was over. Machines costing thousands of pounds simply couldn't be allowed to hang about while you worked out in your own mind what you wanted to do with them. The running costs alone were astronomical and to make the best use of these machines, they had to be used round the clock. Users began to be kept at arms length from computers. The only people allowed to touch the control panels were the computer operators. This interposed an impermeable layer of bureaucracy between the user and the machine and built in a high degree of delay in getting the results of your program. Moreover, the languages used on these machines were specific to each individual model. Thus, your abilities to program one type of computer were of little help to you on another.

1.9 All was not lost, however, for with the acceleration in development of the computers themselves (the HARDWARE), advances were being made in programming (the SOFTWARE). The concept arose of writing a program which would translate "English" of a sort into the code understood by the computer. This meant that programming became easier. More importantly, if the translator could be modified to translate the "English" into the different codes used by the more common computers it would mean that a person could program one type of machine in "English", move to a totally different computer and program it in the same language. Languages of this sort are known as High Level Languages (OPL is an example). The first of these was FORTRAN (FORmula TRANslation) developed by IBM in the mid-50s. As you can imagine from the name, it was geared up to mathematical and scientific applications but it wasn't long before the business world saw the light and COBOL (Common Business Orientated Language) was born. From then on, other languages began to sprout up.

1.10 Finally, the advent of the silicon chip meant that many transistors and other electronic components could be put onto a small wafer of silicon by a sort of micro-photography. This, in turn, lowered the cost of computers drastically and paved the way for micro-processors - computers on a single chip - and computers for all.

1.11 Before we go on to look at the internal structure of a computer, and the PSION Organiser in particular, I would like you to try out the questions contained in the post test below. The answers are given at Appendix A and show the paragraph/s you should consult if you give any wrong response/s. Ideally, you should take a look at any problem areas and re-attempt the questions before leaving this chapter.

POST TEST

1. Describe Pascal's invention.

2. Who improved it and how?

3. What were Automata?

4. What was Jacquard's claim to fame?

5. Who invented the "Analytical Engine"?

6. What occurrence gave computer development its impetus in the 20th century?

7. What were Colossus and ENIAC?

8. Which invention started the process of miniaturizing computers?

9. What is a high level language?

10. Name the first high level language.

11. Name the first business language.

Chapter 2

The Organiser and Computer Structure

2: The Organiser and Computer Structure

TRAINING OBJECTIVE:

At the end of this chapter, you will be able to describe the structure of a computer in general and the Organiser in particular.

ENABLING OBJECTIVES:

To enable you to do this, you must be able to:

a. State the functions of:

i) The CPU.

ii) ROM.

iii) RAM.

iv) I/O chips.

v) The Address and Data Buses.

vi) The Crystal Oscillator.

b. State the CPU used by the Organiser.

c. State the amount of memory held by the CPU internally.

d. Name the modes used by the CPU.

e. State the 3 modes of most interest to users of the Organiser and describe their meanings.

f. State the 2 main functions of the semi-custom chip.

INTRODUCTION

2.0 I am a biologist by trade and, understandably enough, see a computer in terms of "parts of the body". This analogy has helped me understand computer structure and, since most people have some degree of knowledge of what the various bits of their respective bodies do,I aim to use it here, too. Do remember , however, that it is only a loose analogy and not to be taken too literally. Moreover, it is based on that mythical entity, the "Typical Computer". Variations will occur from computer to computer, according to manufacture and application. The generalisation will hold true for most, however, and certainly for the Organiser. As we progress through the book, I will amplify some of the areas we are about to discuss in the light of the needs of the chapter being read.

THE CENTRAL PROCESSING UNIT (CPU)

2.1 Let's start at the top of our "Silicon Man". What controls your body? Your brain. Deep down, there is an area of the brain which does the thinking for you. You know the sort of thing - deals with logic and problems requiring powers of reasoning. It is this ability which raises us above Jellyfish. The equivalent component in our "Silicon Man" is the CPU. As the name suggests, it processes information. You'd be surprised at how little it can do in comparison with the human brain. Usually, it can only add and subtract with numbers less than 256, do a few of what we call logical operations and control the other chips connected to it. It scores over the brain in that it can do these things very quickly. Thus, multiplication is "faked" by repeated addition, division by repeated subtraction and so on. The great British mathematician Alan Turing showed in the late 30s that a computer can solve very complex problems by such simple means as long as the problem has a logical solution.

READ-ONLY MEMORY (ROM)

2.2 So, the mind we have described so far can process data for us but what tells it what to do? Let's think of a brand-new baby. It comes into the world complete with its own built-in programs. It knows how to feed, how to move, how to cling and how to do the 1001 other things babies do. We call this instinct. It's a set of survival strategies which nature has installed in each of us. Man is rather distant from instinct, in evolutionary terms, and has few obvious ones left such as self-preservation, the eye-blink reflex and keeping a beer glass level. It is better seen in other animals - a duckling, for example. As soon as it has hatched, it can paddle off after mother and feed itself. It has no need to be taught.

2.3 Your Organiser has a version of instinct in that it can respond to you as soon as it is switched on. It offers you a menu and provides a wealth of complicated routines, culminating in a complete language - OPL. All of these things are the result of programs because, as you have just seen, the native abilities of a CPU are normally rather modest. You did not have to type them in, so where did they come from? The answer is - PSION. They wrote the routines which give the Organiser its "identity" and placed them on a particular type of memory chip called "Read- Only Memory" or ROM for short. It's a bit like a textbook lying open under a locked glass case - you can read the words through the glass but you cannot write on the page or erase anything already there. This is a good thing, for if you were let loose on these routines, your Organiser would end up completely useless once you had altered the routines in any way. This type of program is known as FIRMWARE since it is written by the manufacturer.

RANDOM ACCESS MEMORY (RAM)

2.4 Of course, if all we had was unerasable instinct, we would be in a pretty bad way - we could never learn anything or change our behaviour since everything would be indelibly imprinted on our minds. That is why we have a portion of our memory which is given over to storing facts which we have picked up along the way. The interesting thing about this sort of memory is that the data in it can be erased or altered by learning/relearning. You would find it extremely difficult to survive without this type of memory. Indeed, there are some unfortunate people who have to. They cannot remember names, dates, faces or, indeed, who they are themselves despite constant re-inforcement.

2.5 Computers have a version of this sort of memory, too. We call it Random Access Memory or RAM. It is "random access" in that the CPU can put data into it, alter it, read it or delete it entirely - whatever you tell it to. This is an essential feature of the machine, for without it you could write no programs - there would be nowhere to store them. The great drawback of RAM is that when its power is switched off, the contents of the memory cells are erased - a bit like forgetting everything you ever learned each time you go to sleep! This is known as volatile memory and is the main reason why data is saved onto discs, datapacks and tape - these are relatively permanent media and their contents can be loaded back into the machine when it is powered up again.

INPUT/OUTPUT CHIPS AND THE BUSES

2.6 Let's recap, then. So far, in biological terms, we have described a person that can reason, possesses instinctive strategies built into his mind and can play about with data in his flexible memory. In other words, he still lacks all of the "five" senses and is totally paralysed - he has no communication with the outside world at all. So it is with the computer. If all we had was a CPU and some ROM and RAM chips, the machine would be rather useless - we could not program it and it could not tell us anything. For argument's sake, let's take hearing and speech and draw parallels in the silicon world. Sound strikes the ears and is converted into electrical impulses which the centre of hearing in the brain deciphers and passes on to our centre of reasoning for action. Similarly, the brain figures out what it wants to say and passes the data to the centre of speech which encodes it into a series of impulses directed at a whole range of muscles to produce the truly miraculous gift of speech. The point is that within the brain, the data of both speech and hearing (and all the other senses) exist as identical little peaks of electricity. To convert these from sound or into sound, we need 2 things - specialized organs outside the brain which do the business and discrete centres within it which deal with the conversion to/from the electrical blips which the brain understands.

2.7 The electronic equivalents in your Organiser could be the liquid crystal display (since it "talks" to you via the screen) and the keyboard (since it "hears" you through the keys). These are the external organs of your computer and, just like the biological versions, they must be connected to centres which will decode the information. These "centres" are collectively called Input/Output Chips (I/O).

2.8 But wait a minute. Go back to the biological system. How do the ears send the impulses to the brain? How does the brain send its data to the vocal cords? The answer is - through the nerves. The nerves are the body's lines of communication and, of course, the computer just has to have its "nerves", too. We call these "Buses". These are a related collection of "wires" like a highway, connecting the CPU with all its chips in exactly the same way that all parts of the body are connected to the brain via the nervous system. There are 2 main Buses in the computer - the Address Bus and the Data Bus.

2.9 Let's look at the Address Bus first. We could regard our memory chips each as a vast, isolated monastery, made up of thousands of little cells, each one capable of storing a single number in the range 0-255. We could send a message to one of these cells, telling it the number we wished to store in it. However, the question arises, "How do we specify the particular cell we want the number stored in?" The answer is simple - we put the address on the "envelope" - the cell number. This number is converted into its binary equivalent and put on the bus. (Binary is a form of arithmetic that is so simple, it uses only 2 digits - "0" and "1". We will look more closely at binary in the next chapter) A pulse of electricity on a lane means a "1" and its absence means a "0". Don"t worry about this too much at this stage. It is important to be able to specify a unique address, for without it, you would find it awfully difficult at a later date to find the data you had stored. Putting the address of the chip on the address bus "opens the door" of the cell ready to accept the data. There is a limit to the number of cells that can be addressed by the computer. Essentially, this is decided by the number of "lanes" in the Address Bus highway. The more lanes, the greater the number which can be coded up on it and therefore the more cells which can be uniquely identified.

2.10 When the door of a specified cell has been opened by the Address Bus, the data we want to store is passed to it from the CPU along a different highway - the Data Bus. Again, this is in its binary equivalent. As I said previously, the sort of numbers we can store lies in the range 0-255. This is because the Data Bus is 8 lanes wide and the maximum number which can be coded in binary along 8 lanes is 255. Note that traffic on the Data Bus is bi-directional. In other words, it can move from the CPU to the cell when the CPU wants to store/alter/erase a number and from the cell to the CPU when it wants to retrieve a number previously stored. Traffic on the Address bus, however, is uni- directional. It is always the CPU that does the addressing and the address selected always goes from the CPU outwards to the cell within the chip in question.

2.11 So, there you have it. The Address Bus opens the door and the Data Bus pops the data in or retrieves it. Note that while you can put data in and take it out of a RAM chip, you can only retrieve data from a ROM chip - never put things in. If the CPU wants to display a message on the Liquid Crystal Display (LCD), it will "open the doors" of the cell where the message is stored and the I/O chip which controls the LCD. It then removes the message from the cell (really, the message stays in there until you actually erase it - only a copy is removed) along the Data Bus to the CPU and back out along the Data Bus to the I/O chip. This chip then translates the data into signals which the LCD can understand, passes it to the display and your message appears. This is a very simplistic description, but correct in its essentials.

2.12 The same sort of system applies to the keyboard of a computer. The CPU is told, at regular intervals, to check the entire keyboard to see if a key is being depressed. This is known as "polling" the keyboard. It does this by addressing the keyboard controller chip. In the case of the Organiser, this is a semi-custom-programmed chip. Under software, it then scans the keyboard and if a key is being pressed, the identity of the key is coded up into a specific value and passed along the Data Bus to the CPU which then takes action as appropriate.

2.13. So, now we have our complete "Silicon Man" who can communicate with the outside world. Other "senses" and facilities can be added to the ones we have just described - sound, RS 232, light pens, joysticks, robotic limbs - the list is long but all work on the same basic lines as those we've examined. To round off the biological analogy, we could regard the power supply to the computer (normally around +5v) as its equivalent of a blood supply - but what about a heart? Well, "Silicon Man" has a version of that, too. It takes the form of a crystal. Attached to the CPU, it oscillates when connected to the electrical supply and, just in the same way that an orchestra plays to the beat of the conductor's baton, the CPU executes its instructions in step with the pulses. Thus, all actions within our silicon Frankenstein are perfectly synchronised.

THE INTERNAL ARCHITECTURE OF THE PSION ORGANISER

2.14 While all the above is fresh in your mind, let's turn to the Organiser and see how we can put it into context. Inside the outer casing, the

2.15 The System Board

Organiser is essentially made up of 2 printed circuit boards (PCB) - the main system board and the power supply board. The latter contains the circuitry necessary to ensure that all the chips in the computer receive just slots and buzzer. I do not propose to go any deeper into the workings of this particular board since it does not really come into the area of programming. Instead, we will concentrate more on the main system board.

2.15 Main System Board. The system board has all the digital electronics we discussed earlier and connects to the Liquid Crystal Display (LCD) and the keyboard. The space taken up by all this has been minimised by clever use of chips which can be mounted directly on to the surface of the PCB and by the design of a special chip which alone carries out functions which would normally require a complete circuit. In addition, the power consumption has been minimised by utilising CMOS chips, which require very little current, wherever possible and by taking advantage of the special "Sleep" modes of the CPU. All this, of course, is very important since the Organiser is basically a battery driven computer.

2.16 The board holds:

a. CPU - the HD6303X 8-bit processor manufactured by Hitachi.

b. ROM - 32 kilobytes (32*1024) on a Programmable Read Only Memory (PROM).

c. RAM - depending on the version, this can be 8,16 or 31 kilobytes.

d. LCD - this is a 16 character by 2 line display, also by Hitachi.

e. Clock - a real time clock runs from a 32767 Hz crystal.

f. Connectors - connectors link the PCB with the power supply board and the keyboard.

2.17 The CPU uses an 8-bit data bus and a 16-bit address bus. The processor can operate in 5 different modes - standby, reset, active, halt and sleep. Since the halt mode is not used by the Organiser and reset is used rarely, only the other 3 are of concern to us. In standby mode, the Organiser is under power but switched off. The contents of the RAM are retained and power consumption is at a minimum. In active mode, of course, everything is up and running. This continues until either you switch the machine off (and the CPU returns to standby mode) or the Organiser decides that it has been waiting around for long enough and it accesses a particular memory address to switch itself off. Sleep mode is used while the processor is active to reduce power consumption. Typically, this can be as little as 0.2 of that consumed in active mode. Using the crystal, the CPU runs at a frequency of .9216 MHz. In other words, the Organiser's "heart" beats 921,600 times per second! This may seem incredibly fast but, in computer terms, it is rather on the tardy side.

2.18 The LCD is controlled by 2 chips. One is the boss of the two and holds all the patterns for the characters which the Organiser can display burnt into a section of internal ROM. It also has a little RAM inside (as does the CPU) to hold the data currently being displayed on the screen. The other chip is a sort of slave, used to extend the normal capabilities of the main display driver.

2.19 The real workhorse of the board, with the sole exception of the CPU itself, is the Semi-Custom Programmed Chip. It carries out a number of essential operations:

a. Central Clearing House - as we discussed earlier on, the CPU puts the "telephone number" of the chip it wants to talk to on the Address Bus. That chip will then wake up. However, the Organiser's "telephone system" or Memory Map as it is called, is far more complicated than this and so, it acts as a sort of memory manager, making sense of the CPU's demands and calling up the appropriate chips. It also has dealings with the keyboard, the power supply board and the buzzer. In addition, it has an important part to play in the CPU's startup and shutdown procedures.

b. Time-keeper - using the XTAL as a reference, it keeps time for the computer. When you are actually using the Organiser, it receives a pulse once per second from the chip and stores the time in its own RAM. When you switch off the computer, it stores the time elapsed since switch-off. However, it can only keep track of the time difference up to 34 minutes and 8 seconds. At that point, it will wake up the Organiser, update its diary and clock and switch it off again. Having done so, it can then zero its timer and start the process again.

2.20 Memory Map. The ROM chips are of CMOS construction. They, like the RAM chips, are always powered up, irrespective of the operation mode of the CPU. There are also 2 other areas of RAM not immediately obvious to the user. The first is within the CPU itself. There are 192 bytes from $0040-$00FF located on board the chip. The contents are retained even when the machine is switched off. Secondly, there is the RAM store of the LCD driver but this is not within the Organiser's memory map.

2.21 Well, that's all I want to say on computer structure. Later, we will look more deeply into the internal architecture of the Organiser itself, prior to discovering how to program it in machine code. First, however, I would like you to try out the questions contained in the post test below. The answers are given at Annex A.

POST TEST

1. What is a micro-processor?

2. What does CPU stand for?

3. State 2 functions of a CPU.

4. What does ROM stand for ?

5. What is the name given to routines stored in ROM chips by manufacturers?

6. What does RAM stand for ?

7. How do I/O chips allow the CPU to communicate with the outside world?

8. What are the functions of the Address and Data Buses?

9. What is the maximum number which can normally be stored in a "cell"?

10. What is the function of a crystal oscillator?

11. Which CPU is used by the Organiser?

12. How much memory does it hold internally?

13. Name the operating modes used by the CPU.

14. State the modes of most interest to users of the Organiser and state their meanings.

15. Describe the 2 main functions of the semi-custom chip.

Chapter 3

Number Systems

3: Number Systems

TRAINING OBJECTIVE:

At the end of this chapter, you will be able to use numbers in decimal, binary and hexadecimal.

ENABLING OBJECTIVES:

To enable you to do this, you must be able to:

a. Use number boxes.

b. State the number base used by the computer.

c. Convert decimal numbers to and from binary.

d. Add two binary numbers together.

e. State the meaning of *Two's Complement*.

f. Subtract two binary numbers.

g. State the meaning of *Hexadecimal* .

h. Convert decimal and binary numbers to and from hexadecimal.

INTRODUCTION

3.0 Now that we have met "Silicon Man", our electronic cousin, and looked at how the various parts of his "body" equate to our biological world, let's look at how he handles numbers. In our organic framework, you and I use numbers in a particular way - in groups of ten. This, too, has a biological implication - we have ten fingers. Over the centuries and by courtesy of the Arabs, we have developed the unique digits 0-9 into the system we know and love as DECIMAL.

3.1 But what if we want a number bigger than ten? Well, we can look upon numbers as being made up of an infinite series of empty boxes, each of which is capable of holding a single digit in the range 0 to 9. For example, the number 156 would look like this :

Infinity ←						1	5	6

We know that the 6 is just 6 and that the 5 stands for 5x10 and the 1 is really 1x100 - but how? Through years of practice at school and in adult life, we get to be pretty good at looking at a number and subconsciously working out the value of the maximum occupied box - is it 100? 1000? 10000? - and then going back down the line giving scale to all the other digits until we can state the value of the whole number. Anything up to a million we can handle pretty quickly but once it goes beyond that number, things start to slow down. Take this number for example - 1001236745699 - figure it out and note just how long it took you to "decode" it and how you arrived at the answer. You had to say, "That one is Units, that one's Tens" and so on until you reached the leftmost (highest) digit. Once you had done that, you could move back down the line again. This dependence on calculating the highest digit in a number has led to the convention of calling the leftmost digit the MOST SIGNIFICANT and the rightmost the LEAST SIGNIFICANT.

3.2 Let's look at our first number again:

						10^2	10^1	10^0
Infinity ←						1	5	6

The powers of 10 shown above the boxes represents the "value" by which the contents of the box must be multiplied to give the correct number. So, the 1 is multiplied by 10x10 (2 tens multiplied together), the 5 is multiplied by 10 (1 ten) and the 6 is multiplied by no tens at all. This will give us 1x100 + 5x10 + 6 = 156. Easy! Let's try something more difficult, say 15134. Put into our number boxes, it would look like this:

					10^4	10^3	10^2	10^1	10^0
Infinity ←	[ ]	[ ]	[ ]	1	5	1	3	4	

This would give us 1x10000 (4 tens multiplied together) + 5x1000 (3 tens multiplied together) + 1x100 (2 tens multiplied together) + 1x10 (1 ten on its own) + 4 (no tens at all) =15134. We say that 10 is the NUMBER BASE and the digit in each box is multiplied by the base raised to the power of n (n being the box's position in the number line, starting from 0 and going to infinity).

OTHER NUMBER BASES
BINARY

3.3 "Silicon Man", sad to say, does not work in decimal. Think back to paragraph 2.9. Do you remember how I said that the addresses and numbers to be stored in cells are passed along the Buses as blips or no blips of electricity? Silicon Man uses this approach because it is simple - either there is a pulse of energy there or there isn't - and it resists spurious interference from other electrical sources. So, the system is "Pulse or No Pulse" - in other words 1 or 0. This is known as BINARY. Silicon Man, in other words, has only 1 finger on each hand. This means that the numbers we know as 2 to 9 simply do not exist in his world. If we are counting and have reached 9, the next number is 10 - we have put 1 in the next number box and zeroed the Units box. Silicon Man has to do this once he has gone beyond 1!

3.4 Binary to Decimal. Let's try an example. Suppose we wanted to translate the binary number 10011 into decimal - how would we do it? The first thing is to imagine our number boxes but this time instead of 10, the number base will be 2. Like so :

				2^4	2^3	2^2	2^1	2^0
Infinity ←	[ ]	[ ]	[ ]	1	0	0	1	1

This will give us 1x16 (4 twos multiplied together) + 0x8 (3 twos multiplied together) + 0x4 (2 twos multiplied together) + 1x2 (1 two) + 1 (no twos at all) = 19 (in decimal). Do you remember I said in paragraph

2.10 that the maximum number you could store on 8 lines of a Data Bus was 255? Let's prove it! To get the maximum number, all 8 lines must be carrying a pulse. That would give us the binary number 11111111. Our number boxes would look like this:

	2^7	2^6	2^5	2^4	2^3	2^2	2^1	2^0
Infinity ←	1	1	1	1	1	1	1	1

To turn it into decimal, we do everything as before:

1x128	(7 twos multiplied together)	=	128
1x64	(6 twos multiplied together)	=	64
1x32	(5 twos multiplied together)	=	32
1x16	(4 twos multiplied together)	=	16
1x8	(3 twos multiplied together)	=	8
1x4	(2 twos multiplied together)	=	4
1x2	(1 two on its own	=	2
1	(1 times no twos at all)	=	1
			255

So you see, there are 8 lines into each cell of the memory chips. Each line can hold a 0 or a 1. The combination of these two digits makes up the complete number just in the same way that we can make up complex numbers according to how we combine our decimal digits 0 to 9. I also said in paragraph 2.9 that there was a limit to the number of cells which the computer could address and that this limitation was due to the fact that the system used for writing numbers on the Data Bus was the same as that used for writing addresses on the Address Bus. In other words, there was a maximum number possible. In most home computers these days, the Address Bus is 16 lines wide, so here's a little test for you - what is the maximum number addressable on a 16 line bus? Use the same techniques we have discussed so far. The answer should be 65535! Surprised? It is a large number when you consider that the Data Bus with half the number of lines can still only manage 255 as its maximum number but remember that each line is worth TWICE THE VALUE OF THE PREVIOUS LINE. This can give rise to some surprising numbers.

3.5 Decimal to Binary

3.5 Decimal to Binary. So far, I've shown you how to take a binary number and to translate it into decimal. What if we have a decimal number and we want to discover its binary equivalent? We use the process of repeated division. Think back to paragraph 3.1. We used the number 156 to illustrate the number box system. Let's suppose we now want to convert this number to its binary equivalent. Since we want binary, we must divide by 2. Each time we divide by 2, we take note of the remainders - like so:

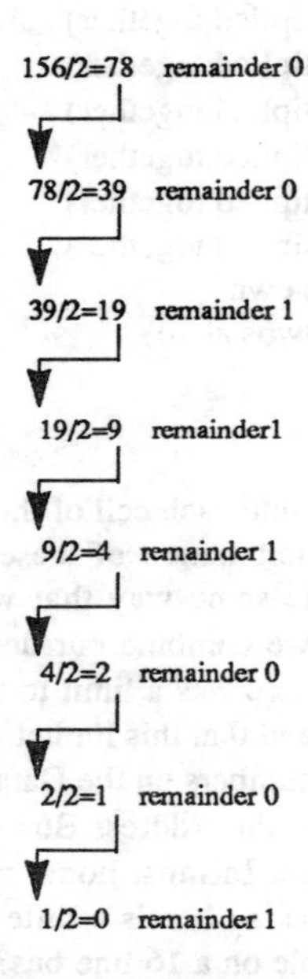
Decimal Binary
156/2=78 remainder 0
78/2=39 remainder 0
39/2=19 remainder 1
19/2=9 remainderl
9/2=4 remainder 1
4/2=2 remainder 0
2/2=1 remainder 0
1/2=0 remainder 1

The topmost binary digit is in box zero of our number line, the next one down in box one and so on, giving us the binary number of 10010100. So 156 in decimal is equivalent to 10010100 in binary. Convert 255 in decimal to binary. (You should already know the answer.)

3.6 Adding and Subtracting Binary Numbers. Addition and subtraction of binary numbers couldn't be easier. Let's look at addition first by considering the table below:

0 + 0 = 0
0 + 1 = 1
1 + 0 = 1
1 + 1 = 10

That's all there is to it! You can see in the last line of the table that 1 + 1 in binary is equal to 10 - NO, NOT TEN !!!!!!! One-zero in binary is equal to 2 in decimal - think about it. While you're doing that, I'll give you a little binary addition sum. Try this:

10100100
+00110011

The binary numbers 10100100 and 00110011 are 164 and 51, respectively, in decimal. You could work this out using the method I outlined in paragraph 3.4 but really, it is not necessary - if you want to do the conversion, do it more as a check of the answer rather than as a means to it. Think of the little table above and remember to carry one over into the next column if you add 2 ones together. The answer is 11010111. If you convert this back into decimal, you can see that it is equal to 215, which is the result you would expect on adding 164 and 51.

3.7 Well, what about subtraction? The process is just the same. Look at the table below:

0 - 0 = 0
0 - 1 =-1
1 - 0 = 1
1 - 1 = 10

Armed with this info, try the following test:

10100100 -00110011
76543210

Notice that I am using the same 2 numbers - 164 and 51 (decimal). At first, you may find binary subtraction slightly more difficult than addition, but keep with it. To make things easier for you to understand my explanation of the process, I've labelled the "boxes" underneath with their powers of 2. Starting with box 0, we can see that we must subtract 1 from 0. Since we cannot do this, we must borrow. If this were a decimal subtraction, we would borrow 10 from box 1. We are dealing with a binary sum and so we borrow 2 from box 1. This means we now subtract the 1 from 2 to give us a remainder of 1. Moving on to box 1, we see that it contains 1 AND the carry to make 2. This is to be subtracted from 0. Borrowing again from box 2, makes the problem 2-2 = 0. We therefore put 0 in the space at box 1. Box 2 contains a 0 plus the carry, which makes 1. This is to be subtracted from 1, which means we put 0 into the box 2 space. Box 3 is simple - 0 minus 0, giving 0 in box 3. In box 4, we are back to the same problem of subtracting 1 from 0. Borrowing 2 from the next box makes it 2-1, giving 1 in box 4. Box 5 now has its own 1 plus the carry to make 2. This is to be subtracted from 1, forcing us to borrow yet again. The 2 we borrow plus the 1 already there makes the subtraction 3-2 = 1. Box 6 has only the carry but this is to be subtracted from 0, so we have to borrow from the last box. This subtraction then becomes 2-1 = 1 in box 6. The final box, box 7, has 0 plus the carry to be subtracted from 1. This makes 1-1 and results in 0 in box 7. So, then, the final answer is 01110001. This is equal to 113 in decimal and, indeed, is the result when you subtract 51 from 164.

3.8 You'll be glad to know, however, that there is an easier way of doing it but first of all, let me talk about that magical word - the BYTE. Remember the 8 lanes in the Data Bus? - well, that determines the maximum number we can store in one memory cell. We call this a BYTE of information and we can say that this byte is made up of 8 bits of discrete data. In other words, it is an 8- bit byte. Most home computers use 8-bit bytes, although 16-bit computers are becoming increasingly popular. What's the maximum number we could store in a cell if the Organiser used 16-bit bytes? (You should already know the answer.) Back to the 8-bit job. The leftmost bit (see paragraph 3.1) is known as "The most significant bit" and the rightmost, "The least significant". This is because the most significant bit is in the 2 to the power of 7 column i.e. 128 and is the biggest single bit in the byte. The converse applies to the least significant. So, even if you have a small binary number, it is convention to pad it out ON THE LEFT HAND SIDE with leading zeros to give 8 digits. For example, the binary number 101 (5 in decimal) would normally be written as 00000101. The leading zeros do not affect the number. Now then, switch over to decimal. If we wanted to subtract, say, 4 from 10, we would say 10-4 = 6. But we could equally have said, "Let's turn the 4 into a negative number and ADD it to the 10. This would give us 10+ -4 = 6. Exactly the same result. Why bother? Well, it may seem pointless in decimal to do that little piece of legerdemain, but it helps us a lot in binary.

3.9 Two's Complement. Whereas in decimal, we can simply stick a minus sign in front of a number to turn it into a negative number, in binary we have to do just a little more. Remember that the little blips of electricity on the Data or Address Bus lanes cannot carry a sign saying minus or positive, so we have to do something else to convey this. We use the convention of making the most significant bit stand for the sign of the byte. So, a 0 in bit 7 means that the whole byte is positive, while a 1 means that it is negative. Of course, using bit 7 to indicate the sign of the numbers means that instead of 8 bits to store your number, you now only have 7. For this reason, SIGNED numbers in an 8-bit system lie in the range -128 to +127. The process of negating a binary number goes like this. Let's take the number 34 (decimal) and express it as a binary number. This will give us 00100010. To turn it into -34 we do the following:

1. Change all the ones to zeros and all the zeros to ones.

2. Add 1.

In the first stage, this would change our 00100010 to 11011101. Adding 1 to this number would result in the negative binary number 11011110 which is equal to -34. To prove that this is so, we could add it to the binary equivalent of PLUS 34. That should give us 00000000 since 34+ -34 = 0. Let's try it:

```
 00100010
+11011110
---------
100000000
```

Notice that we seem to have a ninth bit. This is the carry over but since there are only 8 bits in our byte, this is simply thrown away (although the computer "sticks its hand up" to let you know that a carry has been generated - more on that later) and the result is 00000000 - in other words, zero. The proof of the pudding. Why this works is beyond the scope of this book. Just believe in it - it works.

HEXADECIMAL

3.10 I can just see you now, tearing your hair out at the thought of having to type in all these little 1's and 0's, but don't worry - there is a way round it. We humans, unlike our silicon cousins, are very prone to error. So, when confronted by a long series of binary bytes to input into a computer, we would naturally make the odd error. This might take the form of inputting a "0" when you meant a "1" and vice versa. While this may not seem too drastic to you, it can be catastrophic to the program. Try the following little test. On the left is the correct version of a binary coded program and on the right is one which was typed in by an amateur. It contains a single error. Time yourself to see just how long it takes you to spot it.

CORRECT	WRONG
01001010	01001010
11010010	11010010
00100101	00100101
10101101	10101101
01011111	01011111
11111000	11111000
11001100	11001100
11010100	11010110
11111100	11111100
11010100	11010100
00000001	00000001
11111110	11111110
11011111	11011111

How long did that take you? You can imagine, therefore, the immense problem that would arise if an error had to be found among 65535 bytes instead of 13. To help prevent this sort of difficulty, we use a different number system - HEXADECIMAL - or base 16. Naturally, if we work to base 16, we will need 16 individual digits and we humans really only have 10. For this reason, hexadecimal (or "hex" for short) uses the digits 0 to 9 and then continues on to employ the letters A to F where we, in decimal, would go into double figures. So then, the hex number line looks like this:

Base 16   0 1 2 3 4 5 6 7 8 9 A B C D E F

Base 10: 0 1 2 3 4 5 6 7 8 9 10 11 12 13 14 15

3.11 Coding a Byte. Note that the maximum number which can be coded on 4 bits is 15. This means that we can conveniently split the byte into 2 parts (called "nibbles" - honestly!) and code them separately. So, each byte is represented by 2 hex digits. Try it out by converting the binary number 01101101 into base 16.

Stage 1	Split the byte into 2 nybbles	0110	1101
Stage 2	Convert to decimal equivalent	6	13
Stage 3	Express as 2 hex digits	6	C
Stage 4	Join them together	6C	

So then, the binary number 01101101 is 6C in hexadecimal. Converting back to binary is a simple reversal of the above procedure.

CONCLUSION

3.12 That is all we need to know at this point about number systems. We have seen how Silicon Man uses binary to handle numbers. However, while we humans CAN deal with numbers to base 2, our susceptibility to Murphy's Law forces us to use a more compact number system. We use hexadecimal for this reason and because it has such a nice equivalence to the half byte range.

3.13 You should now attempt the post test below. As before, the answers are contained in Appendix A. Note however, that to enable you to try out your own conversions, additions and subtractions, I have written a short program. This is listed at Appendix B and should be used only to check the answers of problems you have set yourself

POST TEST

1. What number base do we use in every day life?

2. What number base does Binary use?

3. Convert the following Decimal numbers to binary:

a. 128 b. 224 c. 34 d. 50 e. 65 f. 101
g. 202 h. 195 i. 77 j. 132 k. 200 l. 240

4. Convert the following binary numbers to decimal:

a. 01001100 b. 11010011 c. 00101101 d. 11110001
e. 10101010 f. 01010101 g. 11100011 h. 01111110
i. 10000001 j. 01011110 k. 11111110 l. 01111111

5. Complete the following binary additions:

a. 11000000 b. 11001010 c. 11111011 d. 10000011
+00010111 +01100001 +00000011 +01111000

6. What is Two's Complement?

7. Repeat Question 5, this time subtracting the numbers.

8. Why don't we use binary to enter our programs?

9. What base do we use instead of binary?

10. What number base does hexadecimal use?

11. Convert the numbers in questions 3 and 4 into Hexadecimal.

Chapter 4

Byteing the Bullet

4: Byteing the Bullet

TRAINING OBJECTIVE:

At the end of this chapter, you will be able to describe the meaning of machine code in the context of the PSION Organiser.

ENABLING OBJECTIVES:

To do this, you must be able to:

a. State two advantages of machine code over a high level language.

b. State one major disadvantage of machine code and how, in the context of the Organiser, it can be circumvented.

c. Describe one strategy for storing machine code.

d. State the meaning of the word *operator* in the context of machine code.

e. State the meaning of the word *operand* in the context of machine code.

f. State the meaning of the term *assembly language*.

g. State the number of registers in the Organiser's CPU, their bit-size, names and functions.

INTRODUCTION

4.0 Now we're ready to start on machine code itself. But first, it'll be necessary to look at the language in context - what exactly is machine code, where can we store it, what are its KEYWORDS and how does it affect the CPU? We need to know all of these things in order to use machine code, unlike OPL where the inbuilt routines do all of that for you.

WHAT IS MACHINE CODE?

4.1 Let's suppose you have decided to build yourself a house. You do not actually intend to put mortar to brick yourself but are looking about for suitable contractors. Sadly, it is the time of the World Cup. England is in the final, to be played, funnily enough, at Wembley. Naturally you cannot find workmen for love nor money but, what with the Common Market and 1992 and all that, you can lay you hands on a German workforce with no trouble at all.

4.2 So, they start work, laying the foundations of your house. But wait a minute - you can speak not a word of German except "Guten Tag". How on earth are you going to communicate with them? More to the point, what will your house end up like if you can't? Fortunately for you, you have a friend who can speak the language and you hire him for the duration. Now all you have to do to get something done is to tell your friend, who will translate it into German, tell the appropriate person, and the thing will be done.

4.3 What a rigmarole! Especially if you need something done very urgently. This sort of translation builds in a delay and causes everything to be done more slowly. OPL is a bit like that. As I mentioned in Chapter 1, OPL is a High Level Language, where the routines built into the Organiser translates your "English" into machine code which the Computer can understand. Just like your linguistic, friend, however, it has a limited vocabulary. If you had been able to speak German, you could more easily have expressed exactly what you wanted, and quicker, too.

4.4 So, then, the benefits of learning machine code for the Organiser are:

a. Speed. Your instructions will be executed MUCH faster, since they do not have to be translated from another language.

b. Flexibility. You will be able to make the Organiser do things which are impossible to achieve using OPL.

4.5 But I can hear you thinking, "This sounds terrific, so where's the catch?" The catch is that the language which you will acquire will be usable only on the Organiser or a computer using the HD6303X chip. Moreover, you will be working without the aid of a safety net. When you use OPL, there are routines which detect errors, either at translation time or at run time. These facilities will politely inform you of your gaff and even assist by pointing out the likely error. Machine code has none of this. When you make a mistake at run time, disaster could strike. At the best, you will produce garbage. At the worst, the computer will irretrievably freeze, leaving you the sole option of "pulling the plug". Normally, with a home computer, this is no great problem. You will have saved your program to disc. When the big freeze comes, you simply press the RESET button or BREAK and load the program back in, debug it and run it again. The Organiser, however, may hold important data such as telephone numbers and diary files.

4.6 For this reason, you are STRONGLY advised to save all valuable information on to a datapack before running a machine code routine. YOU HAVE BEEN WARNED. MACHINE CODE CAN SERIOUSLY DAMAGE YOUR DIARY. You will have many frustrations and setbacks but I promise you that if you follow my instructions, these will be minimized.

WHERE CAN WE STORE MACHINE CODE?

4.7 Unlike OPL, which does all the housekeeping for you, machine code has to be stored at an address specified by the user. This then means that he must be familiar with the way in which his computer uses its available RAM and ROM. This is known as a Memory Map and the map for the Organiser is at Annex C. The letter/number combinations preceded by the "$" sign are the hexadecimal addresses. Note that the addresses run from $0000 to $FFFF. The system ROM, which contains all the routines created by PSION, starts from $8000. The address of the very top of RAM depends on which type of Organiser you are using, but it is listed in the first diagram. Also note that addresses $0000-$0020 are actually INSIDE the HD6303X chip. Normally these are hidden from the OPL user but we in the machine code world will be able to access them with relative ease. Following the main column drawing which gives an overview of the Organiser's memory, the data storage locations, or Registers as they are more properly known, are listed. These addresses are actually inside the CPU. Don't worry too much about them at this time but when you come to use them in your own programs, you will find this Annex invaluable. In particular, look carefully at the memory location $2065. This is the address of the language stack. We will move it down by the amount we need. This can be done using OPL and is the strategy we will adopt, although there are other methods.

MNEMONICS

4.8 Machine code itself is composed of a series of numbers in the range 0-255. Usually, but not always, more than one byte is required to completely describe an instruction. For instance, if we wanted to tell the computer to load one of its registers with a specific number, we would input the code for the load instruction, followed by the actual number to be stored. We call the instruction code the OPERATOR and the number to be stored the OPERAND. Note that the operand does not have to be a physical number to be stored. If we wanted to copy the contents of the register we used in the last example into a location in memory, we would use a byte for the copy operator and this time the operand would be the address of the memory location we want to use. Moreover, if the address of this location was more than 255, it would take 2 bytes to describe it. Thus, the complete instruction would have taken 3 bytes.

4.9 Normally, we use hexadecimal numbers to describe the codes. However, please note at this point that there is no fundamental difference in a number stored in memory which is an operator and one which is an operand. It all depends on the context. But cast your mind back to the last chapter. Do you remember how I said that humans were not really very good at entering long lists of binary numbers? Well, it is pretty much the same in hexadecimal if the program is very long or intricate. For this reason, we sometimes use mnemonics to describe the codes. Thus, "STA A" is the mnemonic for the hex code $97. Since that particular operator STores the Accumulator A in the memory location which follows the operator, it is quite a good mnemonic and much better than remembering $97.

4.10 We call these mnemonics "Assembly Language". But do not think that this means it is a high level language like OPL. Keywords in a high level language cause lots of machine code to be executed in order to bring about the result expected. Assembly language, on the other hand, is a one-to-one relationship with the respective codes. The problem is, of course, that you cannot directly enter the mnemonics unless you have a special program to do this for you. Not surprisingly, this is called an Assembler. At the present moment, sadly, no assembler for the Organiser itself exists, although there is a PC version which allows the user to develop an assembly language program on an IBM-compatible machine with its excellent keyboard, debug it and download it to the Organiser, courtesy of the RS232 port. This kind of assembler is known as a cross-assembler since the code it develops is not intended for, indeed cannot be run on, the host machine. It is destined to be transferred onto the target machine on completion.

4.11 Although we do not have an assembler (we will use another program which I have written, known as a Hex Loader) I will refer to the operators by their assembly language names. This is far easier than using the code numbers. However, an instruction like STA A can exist in no less than 3 different flavours, according to how it is actually being used in context. This is known as the Addressing Mode. Some operators have far more variety even than this.

THE HD6303X MCU

4.12 The HD6303X was introduced in Chapter 2 as the "Brain" of the Organiser. It is a fact of life that to exploit the capabilities of this chip fully, you have to use machine code and you must be completely familiar with its internal organization.

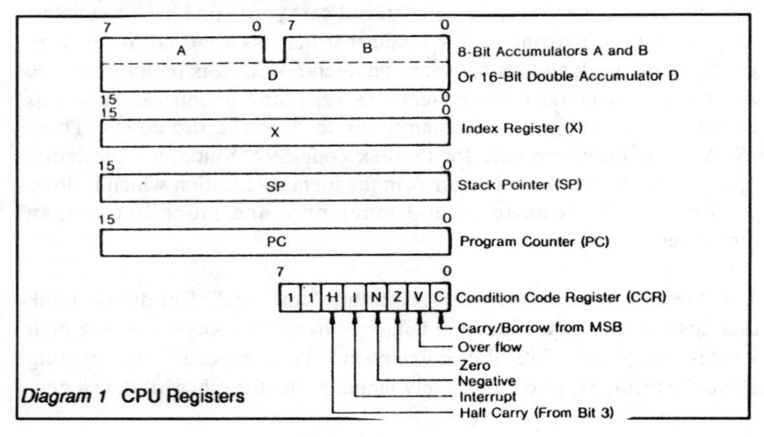

Diagram 1 CPU Registers

4.13 Inside the CPU of the Organiser, there are 3 8-bit and 3 16- bit data storage areas known as REGISTERS. These registers have very particular functions to perform and it is largely due to their good offices that we can keep track of what is going on. The registers are arranged as follows:

a. Accumulators A and B (ACCA and ACCB). An accumulator is a data storage area which holds the results of arithmetic or logical operations. Both accumulators are 8-bit.

b. Accumulator D (ACCD). Accumulator D is a 16-bit register
made up by combining Accumulators A and B together. No special processes are needed to reconfigure the 8-bit registers into a 16-bit one. All that is needed is for the user to employ a double-byte instruction. This will be covered later but it is important to note that the original contents of A and B are trashed when they are combined in this fashion.

c. Index Register (IX). The 16-bit IX register stores information which is important in identifying memory locations. Alternatively, it can be used for general purposes.

d. Stack Pointer (SP). The 16-bit SP holds the address of a stack. Stacks will be covered in a later chapter. As with the IX, the SP can also be used as a general-purpose register.

e. Program Counter (PC). This 16-bit register, which you the user cannot access by software, holds the address in memory of the instruction which is currently being executed.

f. Condition Code Register (CCR). This 8-bit register holds 6 bits of information, or FLAGS, which are extremely important to the programmer:

1) Carry Flag (C). Bit 0 of the CCR holds the C flag. This will be set to 1 whenever a carry or borrow is generated. Otherwise, it is cleared.

2) Overflow Flag (V). Bit 1 of the CCR holds the V

flag. This is set to 1 whenever the Two's Complement overflows. Otherwise, it is cleared.

3) Zero Flag (Z). Bit 2 of the CCR holds the Z flag, which is set to 1 whenever the result of an operation is zero. Otherwise, it is set.

4) Negative Flag (N). Bit 3 of the CCR holds the N flag. This is set to 1 when the MSB of a result equals 1. It is cleared otherwise.

5) Interrupt Mask (I). Bit 4 of the CCR holds the Interrupt Mask. If this is set to 1, no maskable interrupts will be accepted. This means that any task you have set the CPU will be carried out irrespective of the needs of the rest of the computer. The only exception to this is the Non-Maskable Interrupt which, as the name implies, cannot be disabled. This is because it is responsible for the highest priority matters such as time keeping and cannot therefore be ignored.

6) Half-Carry Flag (H). Bit 5 of the CCR contains the H flag which is set to 1 whenever there is a carry at bit 3 or 4 during an arithmetic operation. It is cleared otherwise.

4.14 You must be fully conversant with the above registers and flags if you are to use machine code since most operations will involve them to some degree. A deeper description of the HD6303X MCU for more advanced readers is contained in Annex D.

CONCLUSION

4.15 Just to recap, we have considered the nature of machine code and where we can store it. In addition, I pointed out that the use of machine code forces the programmer to be far more careful about his coding practices because of the potentially catastrophic consequences of getting it wrong. A good practice is to save all valuable data to datapack before carrying out machine code programming.

4.16 If you remember, we then went on to see how we fallible humans can use a one-for-one mnemonic code which enables us to more easily compose machine code programs. This is called Assembly Language. It needs, however, a special program known as an Assembler to decode the mnemonics. We will have to enter our code in the original hexadecimal. Nevertheless, all programs will be written in both assembly language and hexadecimal. Moreover, the instruction set is presented in both forms and its use should present no problems.

POST TEST

1. What are the 2 advantages of machine code over a high level language?

2. State one major disadvantage of machine code and how, in the context of the Organiser, it can be circumvented.

3. Describe one strategy for storing machine code.

4. State the meaning of the word *operator* in the context of machine code.

5. State the meaning of the word *operand* in the context of machine code.

6. State the meaning of the term *assembly language*.

7. State the number of registers, their bit-size, names and functions.

Chapter 5

Machine Code - At Last!

5: Machine Code - At Last!

TRAINING OBJECTIVE:

At the end of this Chapter, you will be able to store and retrieve numbers using machine code.

ENABLING OBJECTIVES:

To do this, you must be able to:

a. Describe the machine code equivalent of OPL variables.

b. Describe the use of the LDA A mnemonic.

c. Describe the use of the STA A mnemonic.

d. State the machine code equivalent of the OPL statement "INTEGER%=25".

e. State the machine code equivalent of the OPL statement "NUMBER%=INTEGER%".

e. Describe the use of the D Accumulator.

f. State the mnemonic needed to load a number into the D Accumulator.

g. State the mnemonic needed to store the contents of the D Accumulator in a given memory location(s).

INTRODUCTION

5.0 At last, we can get down to actually programming the Organiser in machine code! If all of the foregoing text has done nothing else but to impress upon you how different machine code programming is from a high level language, then it has been worthwhile. In this chapter, we will look at how we deal with numeric variables and methods of assigning values to them. This will then form the foundation for simple arithmetic, examined in Chapter 6.

VARIABLES

5.1 In OPL, it is a simple matter to make up variables - you just declare them at the beginning of your procedure and assign values to them as need dictates throughout the remainder of your code. But have you REALLY thought how the Organiser does this? OPL must store the name of your variable and, according to the type of variable (string, integer, real or array) reserve some space for it. The question is - WHERE? The machine takes care of that and decides a suitable location. Thus, whenever you want to "PRINT INTEGER%", OPL finds the name of the variable, remembers where it stored the associated value, locates it, retrieves it and passes it to the PRINT routine to magically appear on the display. The point is, however, that in machine code YOU have to do all of these things yourself!!

5.2 To set up a variable in memory, we must look around for some suitable area in which to store its data. Remember that data and machine code are indistinguishable from each other and that a location can only store a number in the range 0-255. I suggest that you reserve the topmost 50 bytes of the space you have grabbed to store your data. Moreover, it is not possible to use meaningful names as you would in OPL. Simply say to yourself "I am going to use location $7EF0 to store the first number". You, however, must keep track of where everything is - so write it all down.

THE ACCUMULATORS

5.3 Everything in machine code is channeled through the Accumulators. The 2 we are most interested in are the 8-bit A and B Accumulators (which can be combined to give a 16-bit version called the D Accumulator). All arithmetic is done in the Accumulators and the act of moving the contents of one memory location into another has to go via this route, too. They are, therefore, extremely important and you must learn how to use them straight away.

ASSIGNING A VALUE TO A "VARIABLE"

5.4 Let's suppose you want to write the equivalent of the OPL statement "INTEGER%=25". We go about this in 3 stages -

a. If we haven't already used the variable, we must decide on a suitable, SAFE location for the data and write down this address and the nature of the information stored there (Use the "variable name" if it is meaningful). If we HAVE used the variable before, we must look on our piece of paper for the address we assigned to it.

b. Place the number 25 in one of the Accumulators (let's say the A Accumulator, although the B one would apply equally).

c. Tell the CPU to store the contents of the Accumulator in the memory location arrived at in sub-paragraph a.

5.5 I suggest that you reserve 500 bytes or so for your machine code programs - set the base address to $7D0B. Check this using the INFO option in the Hexloader. Let's decide, for example, that we are going to assign location $7EF0 to be our machine code equivalent of INTEGER%. Start with a sheet of paper on which you are going to create your program and write:

LOCATION $7EF0 - INTEGER%

This will allow you to refer to the location whenever you need to code a subsequent access to the location (not actually necessary in this particular example).

5.6 Now we need to ascertain the machine code instruction needed to load Accumulator A with the number 25. Turn to Annex E and look up the mnemonic LDA A. This stands for LoaD Accumulator A. It comes in 4 flavours - Addressing Modes - but don't worry too much about that at the moment. The one we are most interested in is the first of these -

the Immediate Mode. This is where we want to load an actual number, as opposed to the contents of a memory location, into the Accumulator. The mnemonic format of this instruction would then be:

LDA A #25

This is how we would have typed it in if we had been using an assembler. Of course, we are limited strictly to machine code (which follows a one-to-one relationship with the mnemonic codes - it's just easier to remember the mnemonics than the hexadecimal versions). In the "BYTES" column, we see that the instruction takes 2 bytes - one for the instruction code itself and one for the number you want to load into the Accumulator. The code, as you can see under the appropriate column, is $86. Thus, the instruction to load Accumulator A with the number 25 seems to be:

$86 25

5.7 Now we need to store the contents of the Accumulator into the memory location we decided upon in 5.5. We do this using the Store Accumulator A (STA A) command. Look it up in Annex E. This command has 3 different Addressing Modes. The first (Direct) allows you to store the Accumulator's contents in a memory location whose address consists of a single byte - i.e. it is in Zero Page (See Annex C for further details). Since we are using location &7EF0, a double-byte address, this is obviously not appropriate. The next one - Extended - uses a double byte address - bingo. The code for the mnemonic is $B7 and must be followed, as indicated by the format column, by an address made up of 2 bytes. Our code now becomes:

$86 25 $B7 $7EF0

RETURNING TO OPL

5.8 But we are not quite there, yet. If we were to RUN the machine code program in the above paragraph, the machine would certainly load the accumulator with the number but would then become totally lost. It would try to execute the number in the memory location after the "25" as if it were an instruction. Chaos would ensue in a nanosecond. So, we have to have some way of re-directing the Organiser back into OPL once the machine code routine has been executed. We do this with the Return To System command or RTS. Look it up in Annex E. There is only one version of this command and its machine code is $39. BURN THIS CODE INTO YOUR MEMORY, for you HAVE to end your machine code programs with this code if you want it to do anything sensible afterwards. Thus our machine code becomes:

$86 25 $B7 $7EF0 $39

These numbers are entered individually, pressing the EXE key after each.

PROGRAM LAYOUT

5.9 Before we actually use the Hexloader, let's look at program layout. It is important that you document your efforts - far more so than in the case of OPL, for while you could decipher an OPL after leaving it for a few months, it would be EXTREMELY difficult to do the same for a machine code routine. This is because OPL is in a sort of English. Machine code is gobbledegook. You must therefore write your programs down. The following is a suggested format for your efforts:

PROGRAM NAME: "ASSIGNMENT"

PURPOSE: Loads Accumulator A with the number 25 (decimal) and stores it in the memory location $7EF0.

VARIABLES: $7EF0 "INTEGER%"

PROGRAM START:

$7D0B	LDA A #25	$86 25
$7D0D	STA A $7EF0	$B7 $7EF0
$7D10	RTS	$39

USING THE HEXLOADER

5.10 Enter the routines described at Annex F, translate and save them. Put "MC" in the top level menu and call it. Select the "SPACE" and set the memory base to, say $7D0B. Use the "INFO" option to check that it has been set. The Hexloader is now in a position to accept your code.

5.11 Enter the first number -$86, remembering not to use the "$". Press <EXE> to enter it. Now repeat the process with the other bytes until you have finished. Press the <ON/CLEAR> key to exit back to the main menu of the Hexloader.

CHECKING THE PROGRAM

5.12 You should now check your program. Examine the screen carefully to ensure that you have entered the correct codes, i.e. the codes you intended to enter. This will ensure that there was no "finger trouble" invoking Murphy's Law and that you did things right. However it does not tell you if you did the right things. In other words, did you correctly identify the codes for the mnemonics?

You can now check this using the DECODE option. Again, it will ask you for a start address. Enter this as before. This time, instead of printing the hexadecimal numbers it will print the Assembly Language equivalent of your program. Check this against your program. If this is OK, you've done as much as you can to ensure that the program will run. Note that if you have made a bad program, there is nothing the system can do to help you. This is called EXPERIENCE!

5.13 Now you can RUN the program from the main menu. You will be asked for a start address. Type in the base address you stored the program at and press the EXE key. If all goes well, there will be a short pause and the display will change to ask you if you want to RUN another. Press "N" to this and you will return to the main menu where you should select the VIEW option. Enter the INTEGER% address as the area you want to dump and there, in all its glory, should be the magical $19, telling you that you have just completed your first machine code program - well done.

COPYING A VALUE FROM ONE VARIABLE TO ANOTHER

5.14 So far, then we can assign an actual number to a variable whose address we have decided upon. At the moment, location $7EF0 holds the value 25 decimal ($19 hexadecimal). What if we wanted to express the OPL statement "NUMBER%=INTEGER%" in machine code? Well, we're half way there, aren't we? we already HAVE a variable INTEGER% - it"s at location $7EF0. All we have to do is to decide on an address for the NUMBER% variable. Let's use location $7EF1. So, we will need to Load the Accumulator with the contents of location $7EF0 and then STore the contents of the Accumulator in location $7EF1 - but don't rush ahead just yet. Look up the LDA A mnemonic in Annex E. Last time we loaded an actual (called IMMEDIATE) number into the Accumulator. THIS time, we are loading the contents of a memory address. As with the STA A mnemonic, the DIRECT mode is not appropriate since it uses Zero Page. The Extended Mode, on the other hand, is just what we need. This is how your program should look:

PROGRAM NAME: "DUPLICATE"

PURPOSE: Loads Accumulator A with the contents of the memory location $7EF0 - the "INTEGER%" variable - and stores it at location $7EF1 - a new variable called "NUMBER%".

VARIABLES: $7EF0 "INTEGER%"
$7EF1 "NUMBER%"

PROGRAM START:

$7D0B	LDA A	$7EF0	$B6 $7EF0
$7D0E	STA A	$7EF1	$B7 $7EF1
$7D11	RTS		$39

5.15 DO remember the RTS at the end of the program!!! Load the program into the Hexloader (starting at the same address as the previous program - it will be over-written) as described earlier in the Chapter, and VIEW the contents of $7EF0 to assure yourself that the $19 is still there and that the next location has something totally different in it (if you like, you can alter the contents of $7EF1 to 0). Check the program with DUMP and DECODE and, when you are 100% happy, RUN it.

5.16 You should now politely decline the chance to RUN another program and instead select the DUMP option with $7EF0 as the start point. If everything has gone according to plan, you should see not one but two versions of $19, indicating that you have completed another successful machine code routine.

USING BIGGER NUMBERS

5.17 The problem with all of the above is that it can only handle numbers in the range 0-255. The chances are that you will need to go beyond that limit. This being the case, we could express a number in 2 bytes - in fact, this is exactly what OPL does. Integers are stored in 2 bytes. See if you can work out what the range SHOULD be .... yes, it ought to be 0- 65535 but you, as an expert in OPL, are very well aware of the fact it is in reality -32768 to +32767. The reason for this is that the most significant bit of the 16 bits which make up the number is used to indicate the sign. We still have the same range but, instead of starting at 0 it starts at -32768.

5.18 The problem is that both Accumulator A and Accumulator B are 8-bits wide. They are therefore of little use to us - or so it seems at first glance. There is, however, a way to combine the two Accumulators into one 16-bit version called Accumulator D (no, I don't know why it's not called "C"). But beware!! The original contents of the two 8-bit Accumulators is lost when they are combined. If you have anything important in them, store it away in memory somewhere, first. Look at the mnemonic LDD in Annex E. This is the operation LoaD accumulator D. As with the other Load instructions, it comes in 4 flavours. If you want to load an actual number, use the Immediate Mode, presenting the most significant byte first and the less significant second. If you want to Load from Zero Page, use the Direct Mode. Here, the system will load the first byte from the location specified and the second from the next location. Extended Mode fulfils the same function, but beyond Zero Page. Don't worry about Indexed Mode just yet (although, if you are REALLY impatient, you can read a short explanation of the different Addressing Modes at Annex D.45).

5.19 Double-Byte Assignment

5.19 Let's look back at our program "INTEGER%=25". Suppose we wanted to store the number $FFEE instead of 25 decimal - how are we going to deal with this? The answer is "pretty much in the same way as we did with the first one". The differences are that we will need a 2-byte storage location and a 2-byte Accumulator. We have already used location $7EF0 and $7EF1 for INTEGER% and NUMBER%, respectively. They are both currently holding the number $19. Let's combine them into one variable called SUM%. As before, we will need to load the Accumulator with an immediate number and then store it in the appropriate address, remembering to finish with an RTS. How would that look on paper?

PROGRAM NAME: "DOUBLE-BYTE ASSIGNMENT"

PURPOSE: Loads Accumulator D with the number $FFEE and stores it in the memory locations $7EF0-$7EF1.

VARIABLES: $7EF0/1 "SUM%"

PROGRAM START:

$7D0B	LDD	#$FFEE	$CC $FFEE
$7D0E	STD	$7EF0	$FD $7EF0
$7D11	RTS		$39

5.20 If you now use the VIEW facility to examine locations $7EF0 onwards, you'll see that addresses $7EF0/1 hold the value $FFEE.

Success, once again! Note that I have asked you to enter your programs, starting each time at the base address of the reserved space. However, if you had wanted to keep each of the above programs, all you would have had to do was to see where one finishes and enter the next one at the next address. The thing is that you MUST use the address of the FIRST BYTE OF THE PROGRAM YOU WANT TO CALL when you RUN it. In this way, you can have as many programs in memory simultaneously as you want, capacity permitting.

CONCLUSION

5.21 We have looked at how you, the user, can imitate the concept of variables in machine code by reserving areas of memory. The drawback of this system, in that YOU must keep track of which variable is stored where, was highlighted and a suggested way of documenting this outlined. The machine code equivalents of the OPL expressions "INTEGER%=25" and "NUMBER%=INTEGER%" were discussed and tried out. Finally we saw that our machine code programs could only handle numbers in the range 0-255 and examined a way in which we could use the range 0-65535. In the next Chapter, we will look at how we add and subtract in machine code.

POST TEST

1. How do we store integers in machine code?

2. Which Mnemonic should we use to load Accumulator A with a number?

3. What does the Mnemonic STA A do?

4. What does Accumulator D do that Accumulators A and B cannot?

5. What is the hexadecimal code for loading Accumulator D with the contents of a 2-byte memory location?

6. What is the code for storing the contents of Accumulator D in a Zero Page location?

Chapter 6

Simple Arithmetic

6: Simple Arithmetic

TRAINING OBJECTIVE:

At the end of this Chapter, you will be able to add and subtract numbers up to 32 bits in length using machine code routines.

ENABLING OBJECTIVES:

To do this, you must be able to:

a. Name the mnemonics used in the add operation.

b. Name the mnemonics used in the subtraction operation.

c. State the importance of the Carry Flag.

INTRODUCTION

6.0 In this Chapter, we will look at how we go about adding and subtracting in machine code. Just as in Assignments, we have to take different approaches to handling single and double-byte numbers.

A SIMPLE ADDITION

6.1 Suppose we want to code the following operation - "INTEGER%=NUMBER1%+30". You already know how to create variables in machine code and assign values to them, so let's take a look at this aspect, first. We will need to provide for 2 different variables. I suggest we use $7EF0 for INTEGER% and $7EF2 for NUMBER1%. So, our declaration will look like this:

PROGRAM NAME: "SIMPLE ADDITION"

PURPOSE: This program takes the contents of the single-byte variable NUMBER1%, adds 30 to it and stores it in a second variable, INTEGER%.

VARIABLES:

$7EF0	INTEGER%
$7EF2	NUMBER1%

6.2 The next thing we have to do is to put a number in NUMBER% to begin with. This is the sort of thing we did in the last Chapter. We LoaD Accumulator A with whatever value we want (in the range 0-255) and store it at location $7EF2. Use the value 90, for argument's sake. The code should look like this:

$86 90 $B7 $7EF2

6.3 We now have to load this value into an Accumulator, add 90 to it and store in location $7EF0. It may seem that we all the trouble we went to in storing the value in NUMBER% was pointless, but remember that we are pretending that we are taking its contents WHATEVER IT MAY BE and using it in the addition. It is something of an artificiality forced upon us by teaching constraints. So, forget temporarily about the first part of our program but check that the code you created to put NUMBER% into the Accumulator looks something like this - $B6 $7EF2. Let's recap so far:

PROGRAM NAME: "SIMPLE ADDITION"

PURPOSE: This program takes the contents of the single-byte variable NUMBER1%, adds 30 to it and stores it in a second variable, INTEGER%.

VARIABLES:

$7EF0	INTEGER%
$7EF2	NUMBER1%

PROGRAM START:

```
LDA A #30     $86 30
STA A $7EF2   $B7 $7EF2
LDA A $7EF2   $B6 $7EF2
```

6.4 To add 30 to Accumulator A, we should use the ADD A operation in preference to the ADC A version. This is because the former ignores the Carry Flag while the second adds it in to the sum. Since we are using single-byte numbers, the Carry is immaterial. We are going to add an immediate number to the Accumulator. A swift reference to Annex E will reveal that the code for this operation is $8B. This gives us the sequence:

$8B 30

6.5 Now we must store the result in the INTEGER% location. This is something we already know how to do. To wrap it all up, then, our finished product looks like this:

PROGRAM NAME: "SIMPLE ADDITION"

PURPOSE: This program takes the contents of the single-byte variable NUMBER1%, adds 30 to it and stores it in a second variable, INTEGER%.

```
VARIABLES:       $7EF0         INTEGER%
                 $7EF2         NUMBER1%

PROGRAM START:   LDA A #90     $86 90
                 STA A $7EF2   $B7           $7EF2
                 LDA A $7EF2   $B6           $7EF2
                 ADD A #30     $8B30
                 STA A $7EF0   $B7           $7EF0
                 RTS                         $39
```

6.6 Enter the code into the Hexloader and check it out using the DUMP and DECODE options. When you are happy that all is well, RUN it and use the DUMP option to check the contents of $7EF0 which should be $78 (120 decimal). And that's all there is to single-byte addition.

A SIMPLE SUBTRACTION

6.7 Subtraction is carried out in the same way. In fact to SUBTRACT 30 from 90, we only have to change a single byte - ADD A becomes SUB A. Again, there is a version which takes into account the Carry Flag but it is not appropriate in the single-byte context. The code for the statement "INTEGER%=NUMBER1%-30" is as follows:

PROGRAM NAME: "SIMPLE SUBTRACTION"

PURPOSE: This program takes the contents of the single-byte variable NUMBER1%, subtracts 30 from it and stores it in a second variable, INTEGER%.

VARIABLES:

```
$7EF0         INTEGER%
$7EF2         NUMBER1%
```

PROGRAM START:

```
LDA A #90      $86 90
STAA $7EF2     $B7 $7EF2
LDA A $7EF2    $B6 $7EF2
SUB A #30      $80 30
STA A $7EF0    $B7 $7EF0
1RTS           $39
```

6.8 All you have to do in this particular case is to use the DUMP facility and alter the relevant byte. Check the code using the DECODE facility, RUN it if you are happy and then DUMP the contents of $7EF0. It should be $3C (60 decimal).

SO, WHAT ABOUT NUMBERS GREATER THAN 255?

6.9 Of course, Mother Nature (and the user) frequently deals in numbers greater than 255. We will therefore need to look at this aspect of machine code arithmetic. Try out the following program. What do you think INTEGER% should hold after you RUN the program? Check it out.

PROGRAM NAME: "FUNNY ADDITION"

PURPOSE: This program takes the contents of the single-byte variable NUMBER1%, adds 100 to it and stores it in a second variable, INTEGER%.

VARIABLES:

```
$7EF0         INTEGER%
$7EF2         NUMBER1%
```

PROGRAM START:

```
LDA A #190     $86 190
STA A $7EF2    $B7 $7EF2
LDA A $7EF2    $B6 $7EF2
ADD A #100     $8B 10
STA A $7EF0    $B7 $7EF0
RTS            $39
```

6.10 You were probably expecting to find decimal 290 but of course this number cannot fit within a byte which has a width of 256. If all went well, you should have found hexadecimal 22 (decimal 34). What do you get when you add this number to 256? So, then, it is apparent that when you get a result which exceeds the "holding limit" of the byte, it wraps round again and you are left with the "remainder" in the byte. It doesn't matter if the sum exceeds 256 many times, you will simply get what's left after 256 is successively subtracted from it. Try this out using the program above, substituting your own numbers. In each case, see if you can work out what SHOULD be there and what will ACTUALLY be there.

6.11 "Surely there should be some way of indicating that the 34 we ended up with was really 290?", I hear you saying. Quite right, there is indeed. It is called the CARRY FLAG and is essential in double byte arithmetic. If you have another look at Diagram 4-1, you will see the Condition Code Register. This holds a number of flags which can be toggled on or off according to certain conditions within the CPU. The Carry Flag is one of these and is set when an overflow occurs in an addition. Let's suppose we needed to add one double-byte number to another. We would add the first byte of the first number to the first byte of the second. Should this number exceed 255, we will be left with the residue in store. However, THE CARRY FLAG WILL BE SET TO INDICATE THE OVERFLOW. If we now add the second bytes to each other, TOGETHER WITH THE CONTENTS OF THE CARRY FLAG, the result will be arithmetically correct. Note that any overflow from the second addition will be thrown away but the Carry Flag will again be set and, if we were involved in triple byte additions, we could take it into consideration. The Organiser's CPU takes care of double- byte arithmetic by using the D Register. To illustrate its use, we will try out the addition in 6.9. Note that we use the "LDD" instruction to load the D register with the 2-byte number (which STARTS at the address indicated) and STD to store it. Moreover "ADD D" is used instead of the "ADD A" version.

PROGRAM NAME: "16-BIT ADDITION"

PURPOSE: This program takes the contents of the double-byte variable NUMBER1%, adds 100 to it and stores it in a second double-byte variable, INTEGER%.

VARIABLES:

$7EF0/1	INTEGER% (High/Low)
$7EF2/3	NUMBER1% (High/Low)

PROGRAM START:

```
LDD#$00BE    $CC        $00BE
STD $7EF2    $FD        $7EF2
LDD $7EF2               $FC $7EF2
ADD D        #$0064     $C3 $0064
STD $7EF0    $FD        $7EF0
RTS                     $39
```

6.13 RUN the program and take a look at locations $7EF0/1. You should see the double-byte answer $01 $22. The $22 stands for 34 decimal and the $01 means ONE TIMES 256. Added together, they come to 290 = 190+100. Try the program our using your own sums.

6.14 Subtraction follows pretty much the same process. Let's try out a double-byte subtraction using the previous variables. Try taking $135E from $3020. The answer should be $1CC2.

PROGRAM NAME: "16-BIT SUBTRACTION"

PURPOSE: This program takes the contents of the double-byte variable NUMBER1%, subtracts $135E from it and stores it in a second double-byte variable, INTEGER%.

VARIABLES:

$7EF0/1	INTEGER% (High/Low)
$7EF2/3	NUMBER1% (High/Low)

PROGRAM START:

```
LDD #$3020   $CC $3020
STD $7EF2    $FD $7EF2
LDD$7EF2     $FC $7EF2
SUB D#$135E  $83 $135E
STD $7EF0    $FD $7EF0
RTS          $39
```

GOING ONE STAGE FURTHER

6.15 So, the difference between 8-bit and 16-bit addition or subtraction seems only to be one of selecting the correct Register (and, thereby, the correct instruction codes) for the job.What if we want to deal in 32-bit integers? It may interest you to work out the maximum possible number using a 32-bit code. The 8-bit byte gives 256, while the 16-bit version can code 65535. The 32-bit byte, however, holds the staggering maximum number of 4,294,967,296!! You can see, then, that any procedure to add or subtract numbers of this order could be very powerful indeed. Moreover, the strategy I am about to outline can be used for even higher byte combinations. This is one of those things you can do in machine code which are not possible in OPL. It will also do it much faster.

6.16 As an example, we will add the numbers $11112222 and $33334444 together. We do not have a 32-bit register, so we will have to use two 16-bit ones - the D and IX Registers (have another look at Diagram 4-1) to hold one of our 32-bit numbers. We'll store the other number in INTEGER1% at $7EF0/1/2/3. The routine starts by storing the SECOND number in INTEGER%. Then, we put the upper 16-bits of the first number into the IX Register and the lower 16-bits into the D Register. At this point we have all the data in the system. We add the numbers in 2 stages - the lower 16-bits followed by the upper 16. Since we cannot do arithmetic IN the IX Register, we must get its contents into the D Register when we need to add the upper 16-bits. We can't just plonk it in there, however, or we would lose the sum of the lower 16-bits we have just calculated. Fortunately, there is an instruction which will simply EXCHANGE the contents of the 2 Registers. We can then add the upper 16-bits of INTEGER% to the D Register, which now holds the upper 16-bits of the first number.

6.17 Of course, there may be an overflow resulting from the addition of the first 16-bits. This will be stored in the Carry Flag of the Condition Code Register. Sadly, however, the ADD D instruction itself does not take the Carry Flag into account when it does an addition. This means that we cannot use it in the second part of the 32-bit addition if we want accuracy. Instead, we will have to do two consecutive 8-bit additions of the 16-bits remaining. Moreover, we cannot use the ADD instruction we know and love because this also takes no account of the Carry Flag, although like the ADD D instruction, it can GENERATE a carry. So, we will use the

ADd with Carry (ADC) instruction which will add the contents of the Carry Flag into the calculation. Naturally, we will employ the A and B Registers to do the 8-bit work in the second part. At the end of the routine, the upper 16-bits of the sum will be in the D Register, while the lower 16-bits will be in the IX Register. If we do another exchange of the 2 Registers, we will get them in the correct order. The result will then be stored in the 32-bit variable SUM% at $7EF4/5/6/7. The code looks something like this:

PROGRAM NAME: "32-BIT ADDITION"

PURPOSE: This program takes the contents of the 32-bit variable INTEGER% (which holds $11112222) and adds it to the 32-bit number held in the D Register (lower 16-bits) and the IX Register (upper 16- bits). On conclusion of the routine, the result is stored in the 32-bit variable SUM%.

VARIABLES: $7EF0/1/2/3 INTEGER% (High 16-bits/Low 16-bits)
$7EF4/5/6/7 SUM% (High 16-bits/Low 16-bits)

PROGRAM START:

```
LDD #$1111     $CC $1111
STD $7EF0      $FD $7EF0
LDD #$2222     $CC $2222
STD $7EF2      $FD $7EF2
LDX #$3333     $CE $3333
LDD #$4444     $CC $4444
ADD D $7EF2    $F3 $7EF2
XGDX           $18
ADC B $7EF1    $F9 $7EF1
ADC A $7EF0    $B9 $7EF0
XGDX           $18
STX $7EF4      $FF $7EF4
STD $7EF6      $FD $7EF6
RTS            $39
```

6.18 I'm sure you can work out what the answer will be. Note that it is spread over 4 bytes starting at $7EF4. Try the routine out, using your own numbers. Note that if you add two, large 32-bit numbers together, an overflow condition could result. This would mean that the program would terminate with the Carry Flag set. If necessary, the state of this flag can be tested or used if more than 32-bits accuracy is needed.

6.19 Again, subtraction works in pretty much the same way as addition. The instruction "SUB D" is used instead of "ADD D" and "SBC A" or "SBC B" instead of their addition counterparts. An underflow (indicating a negative result) would set the Carry Flag. Try out the following subtraction:

PROGRAM NAME: "32-BIT SUBTRACTION"

PURPOSE: This program takes the contents of the 32-bit variable INTEGER% (which holds $55556666) and subtracts it from the 32-bit number held in the D Register (lower 16-bits) and the IX Register (upper 16-bits). On conclusion of the routine, the result is stored in the 32-bit variable DIFFERENCE%.

VARIABLES:
$7EF0/1/2/3 INTEGER% (High 16-bits/Low 16-bits)
$7EF4/5/6/7 DIFFERENCE% (High 16-bits/Low 16-bits)

PROGRAM START:

```
LDD #$5555    $CC $5555
STD $7EF0     $FD $7EF0
LDD #$6666    $CC $6666
STD $7EF2     $FD $7EF2
LDX #$7777    $CE $7777
LDD #$8888    $CC $8888
SUB D $7EF2   $B3 $7EF2
XGDX          $18
SBC B $7EF1   $F2 $7EF1
SBC A $7EF0   $B2 $7EF0
XGDX          $18
STX $7EF4     $FF $7EF4
STD $7EF6     $FD $7EF6
RTS           $39
```

CONCLUSION

6.20 Now you know how to add and subtract 8-, 16- and 32-bit numbers, giving integer ranges of 256, 65536 and 4294967296, respectively. The last of these is considerably beyond the Organiser's OPL abilities and therefore indicates one of the advantages of machine code in that you can accomplish things denied to you using a higher level language. To reinforce material learnt in this chapter, try the post test before starting on the next subject.

POST TEST

1. Which mnemonic would you use to add an 8-bit number to Accumulator A?

2. Which Accumulator do we use for 16-bit additions?

3. Which instruction adds numbers to this Accumulator?

4. What does the Carry Flag do in addition?

5. What does it do in subtraction?

6. In carrying out the second half of a 32-bit addition, why must we employ two 8-bit additions instead of a single 6-bit one?

7. What is the difference between "ADC A" and "ADD A"?

Chapter 7

Decisions, Decisions

7:Decisions, Decisions

TRAINING OBJECTIVE:
At the end of this chapter you will be able to write a program which uses loop structures and decisions.

ENABLING OBJECTIVES:

To enable you to do this, you must be able to:

a. State how decision-making is implemented in machine code.

b. List the tests used to assess the state of the flags in the Condition Code Register.

c. Describe how to compare two numbers.

d. Describe the use of Relative Addressing.

e. State the machine code equivalent of IF .. THEN .. GOTO.

f. Write a program employing a DO .. UNTIL loop.

g. Write a program employing a WHILE .. ENDWH loop.

h. Write a program employing a FOR .. STEP .. NEXT loop.

INTRODUCTION

7.0 Of course, programs do not flow in nice straight lines, as you have already discovered in OPL. We now need to examine the use of loop structures and decision making at the machine code level. The reader should note at this point that machine code loops run VERY FAST in comparison with their OPL equivalents, a fact which I hope to demonstrate to you very soon. To begin with, then, let's start with the Carry Flag.

DO .. UNTIL LOOP%=101

7.1 In OPL, we have a loop structure known as DO .. UNTIL. This will cause a section of code to be executed until a specific circumstance, or set of circumstances, is satisfied. To take the simplest expression of this structure, imagine that we had to repeat some code 100 times. We would set up a variable to hold the count, give it an initial value ("1" for example) and enter the loop. After executing the section of code we are interested in, we would increment the count and test it with the "UNTIL" part to see if it meets the condition for exit (i.e. it is greater than 100). If it doesn't, we would repeat the section below the "DO" until it does. Such a program would look like this:

```
LOOP%=1
DO

        ___
        ___
        ___
        LOOP%=LOOP%+1
        UNTIL LOOP%=101
```

7.2 We can simulate this structure in machine code by using an Accumulator to store the loop counter. We could initialise it using an approach like this:

```
LDA A #1        $86 $01
```

We now need to somehow mark the code so that we can loop to it. OPL does this by delimiting the loop code with a DO and an UNTIL. If we had an Assembler, we could use a label, just as we can do in OPL. In machine code, however, we need to remember the ADDRESS of the first instruction of the code we wish to repeat. For this reason, all future listings will be shown with associated memory locations down the left hand side and labels inserted in the Assembly Language part. In this way, we can code it up in machine code but use Assembly Language when a ROM-based Assembler comes on the market. If we set it out as I have suggested, we would produce the following listing:

PROGRAM NAME: "LOOP STRUCTURE"

PURPOSE: This program loops round 100 times. No code is executed in between. It therefore acts as a sort of delay loop. The loop counter is held in the A Accumulator.

VARIABLES: Nil.

```
ORG:        $7D0B
            7DOB        LDA A #1     $86 $01
            7D0D         .loop
```

7.3 The ORG statement is an Assembler command which simply causes the machine code to be placed at that address. Since we have no code to actually execute, we can go straight to incrementing the loop counter. In OPL, we would have to say "LOOP%=LOOP%+1" but in machine code, things are actually simpler (for a change!). All we have to do is to use the INCrement instruction. This will simply add 1 to the indicated target. If you look at this instruction in Annex E, you will see that it has a number of Addressing Modes. Obviously, we need to use the "INC A" command.

THE CONDITION CODE REGISTER (CCR)

7.4 Now we need to compare the contents of this Accumulator with 100 to see if we need to loop back or not. Comparisons are made using the following instructions:

a. CBA - where the contents of Accumulators A and B are compared with each other.

b. CMP A - where the contents of Accumulator A are compared with:

1) An immediate number or value.
2) The contents of a zero page location (ie a single-byte address).
3) The contents of a specified double-byte address.
4) The contents of a memory address described as the address indicated by the Index Register (X) plus the specified offset.

c. CMP B - as for CMP A.

d. CPX - where the contents of the double-byte Index Register are compared with the range of values indicated in sub-paragraphs b and c above. Note that because the Index Register holds a double byte value, the comparison value is also assumed to be double-byte. This means that the value stored at a memory location is taken as the high byte and the NEXT LOCATION automatically taken as the low byte.

These comparisons will result in one or more of the flags in the CCR being set or cleared. It is important to note, however, that the actual numbers involved in the comparison are left unchanged. The question then arises, "What can we do with this information?" and the answer swiftly returns, "Branch to a different part of the program according to the result of the test you have just made!".

BRANCH INSTRUCTIONS

7.5 Just as there are a number of comparison commands, there are a few branch instructions. They differ in the flag tested and the actions to be taken on a result being returned but all jump to a point RELATIVE TO THE START OF THE BRANCH INSTRUCTION. This point is calculated by the CPU by taking the current value of the Program Counter (PC) - which at that point would be indicating the beginning of the branch instruction - adds the jump value indicated as the operand of the instruction and then, for some mysterious reason, adds another 2. The resulting figure is then placed in the PC, the CPU turns its attention to that address and everything carries on (if you have done it right). This form of adressing is known as Relative Addressing, since the actual jump address is indicated by a number of bytes RELATIVE TO THE JUMP INSTRUCTION. We will look at the jump calculation shortly but first, here are the branch instructions available to you:

a. BCC - Branch if Carry Clear - will branch to the relative location if the Carry Flag of the CCR is clear (ie = 0).
b. BCS - Branch if Carry Set - this is the opposite of BCC and will branch if the value of the Carry Flag = 1 (ie if a carry has been generated by the instruction preceding the branch command).
c. BEQ - Branch if EQual - this instruction tests the Z Flag of

the CCR to determine whether the 2 numbers compared in the preceding instruction were equal. Z=1 if they were equal and Z=0 if not. Thus, the branch will be made when Z=1.

d. BGE - Branch if Greater than or Equal to zero - this instruction tests the N and V Flags of the CCR. A branch is made if the result of the preceding comparison was greater than or equal to zero.

e. BGT - Branch if Greater Than zero - this instruction tests the Z, N and V Flags of the CCR. A branch is made if the result of the preceding instruction was greater than zero.

f. BHI - Branch if HIgher - this instruction tests the C and Z Flags of the CCR. A branche is made if the preceding instruction shows the accumulator contents to be higher than the other value.

g. BLE - Branch if Less than or Equal to zero - this instruction tests the Z, N and V Flags of the CCR. A branch is made if the result of the preceding instruction was less than or equal to zero. This is used in the case of two's complement values.

h. BLS - Branch if Lower or Same - this instruction tests the C and Z Flags of the CCR. A branch is made if the result of the preceding instruction show the contents of the accumulator to be less than or equal to the other value. This is used where unsigned binary values are being used.

i. BLT - Branch if Less Than zero - this instruction tests the N and V Flags of the CCR. A branch is made if the result of the preceding instruction is less than zero.

j. BMI - Branch if MInus - this instruction tests the N Flag of the CCR. A branch is made if the N Flag is set to 1.

k. BNE - Branch if Not Equal - this instruction tests the Z flag of the CCR. A branch is made if the Z Flag is set to 0.

l. BPL - Branch if PLus - this instruction tests the N Flag of the CCR. A branch is made if the N Flag is set to 0.

m. BRA - BRanch Always - this instruction tests NO flags of the CCR and acts like an unconditional GOTO statement.

n. BRN - BRanch Never - the opposite of BRA!!!

o. BSR - Branch to SubRoutine - this instruction also tests no flags of the CCR. It acts like BRA except that it branches to a subroutine. A subroutine, of course, acts like a procedure in OPL. It must therefore be terminated by some form of RETURN statement which will return it to the point immediately after the calling instruction. I advise you to avoid BSR for the moment - there is a better way of doing this.

p. BVC - Branch if oVerflow Clear - this instruction tests the V Flag of the CCR. A branch is made if V=0.

q. BVS - Branch if oVerflow Set - this instruction is identical to BVC except that the branc is made if the V=1.

You can see from the above that there are many instructions which can cause this sort of branch. It is also interesting to note that the branch instructions function very much like the IF .. THEN .. GOTO construct in that you are comparing 2 things to assess some sort of relationship and jumping to another part of the program on the result. All comparisons which can be written in OPL can be supported in machine code - if you just know how.

7.6 Let's get back to our program. We know that we need to compare the value held in the A Accumulator to see if it is equal to the immediate number 101. This is done using the "CMP A" instruction in Immediate Mode. This will compare the Accumulator with any number we choose to complete the loop and set the CCR Flags accordingly. We can then test the most appropriate Flag and jump backwards or forwards to any specific loop point using one of the conditional branch instructions. We want to check the counter against the value 101. If the counter is NOT EQUAL to 101, we want to loop back and execute the sequence again, otherwise, we proceed to the next instruction which will be the RTS command. When we ask the CPU to compare 2 values, it "notionally" subtracts the second value from the first. I say "notionally" because the 2 values are actually left unchanged. The result of this subtraction affects a number of flags such as the Carry Flag and the Z Flag. Obviously, if the 2 numbers are the same, the result will be zero and the Z Flag will be clear. The branch instruction we need, therefore, is "BNE" followed by the number of bytes to jump. However, things begin to go a little pear-shaped at this point. As I said earlier, Hitachi, in their wisdom, have decided that the Program Counter (PC) will calculate the address to jump to by taking its current value, adding the jump specified in the branch instruction AND ADDING 2. To work this out, write down your program, leaving the branch values until last and then work out the number of bytes you need to skip to get to the beginning of the loop. We would need a jump of -3 (since the jump is calculated from the BEGINNING OF THE "BNE") to get to the start of the loop. The CPU will then take the current value of the PC and subtract the 3 bytes. BUT, because it then adds 2 to the PC, the net jump will be -1 and, believe me, the famous "TRAP" display and the frozen keyboard is but a millisecond away! To avoid this, you must SUBTRACT 2 from the actual jump. Thus, we need to branch -5. This also works for forward branches. If you need to jump forward by 15 bytes, you should actually specify 13, since 2 will be added by the CPU. Remember to reference the jump from the BEGINNING of the branch instruction and not the branch value itself.

7.7 I can probably hear you saying, "Alright, but how do I specify a negative number?" Think back to paragraph 3.9 where we talked about Two's Complement. Take your branch (5 in this case) and turn it into a binary number. The result should be 00000101 (padding it out to the left to make 8 bits). The first stage in Two's Complement was to turn all the ones to zeros and vice versa. This gives us 11111010. We then add 1 to this number and the result is 11111011 in binary or 251 in decimal. This is the value that we use as the jump value. You can probably see a shortcut here - simply subtract the jump from 256. Note, however, that this will only work for a certain range, since the branch instruction is limited in how far it can go. Work this range out for yourself by looking at the numbers generated by a single byte when the 8th bit is used to indicate the sign of the number. (You should arrive at -126 to 0 to +129). I should point out at this point that if you are using the decode function in the hexloader, be aware that it automatically takes into account the extra two bytes which the CPU adds on. It will therefore show you the ACTUAL NUMBER OF BYTES BETWEEN THE BEGINNING OF THE INSTRUCTION AND THE LOOP. In our case it shows "BNE -3", even although you have actually used -5 to comply with the CPU's requirements. Anyway, here is the complete program - have a go at typing it in - BE CAREFUL!!

PROGRAM NAME: "LOOP STRUCTURE 1"

PURPOSE: This program loops round 100 times. No code is executed in between. It therefore acts as a sort of delay loop. The loop counter is held in the A Accumulator.

VARIABLES: Nil.

```
ORG:    $7D0B
        7DOB    LDA A #1      $86 $01
        7D0D    .loop         INC A       $4C
        7D0E    CMP A #101    $81 $65
        7D10    BNE loop      $26 251
        7D12    RTS           $39
```

7.8 For your first loop in machine code, the program above must have been somewhat disappointing, in that there was no outward expression of the act taken place (unless it was "TRAP" !). We can get round this by setting up a variable, clearing it using the hexloader and extending the machine code program to place the final value of Accumulator A in this variable. You should know how to do this already. Just be careful that your STA A instruction takes place AFTER the BNE command. Your answer should look something like this:

PROGRAM NAME: "LOOP STRUCTURE 2"

PURPOSE: This program loops round 100 times. The count is held in Accumulator A and the final value is placed in RESULT%

VARIABLES: $7D16 RESULT%

```
ORG:        $7D0B
            7D0B          LDA A #1          $86 $01
            7D0D .loop    INC A             $4C
            7D0E          CMP A #101        $81 $65
            7D10          BNE loop          $26 251
            7D12          STA A  RESULT%$B7 $7D16
            7D15          RTS               $39
            7D16          << RESULT% >>     ———
```

If you amend your program (no need to type it all in again) and use the VIEW facility, you will be able to place 00 in whatever location you have chosen. Then use the RUN option. When the program has finished, call the VIEW facility again - it should hold $65 (101 decimal). Note that the addresses I have used are convenient for *my* machine and with the amount of memory reserved by the hexloader. You may wish to use different locations - fine - just check out the memory map first.

7.9 What if you had wanted to implement the loop as "DO .. UNTIL LOOP%>100" ? - easy - you know that while the value in Accumulator A is less than or equal to 100, you want to continue the loop. The branch instruction for this is BLS. Note, however, that instead of comparing BLS with 101, you will want to compare it with 100. Make those 2 changes and try the program out. What are you expecting to find in RESULT%? It HAS to be 101 since the loop will fall through when the accumulator has BECOME 101 and no longer fulfills the conditions for loop. You could look upon this sort of loop as being a sort of "WHILE LOOP%<=100 .. ENDWH" construct.

FOR LOOP% = 0 TO LIMIT% STEP 3...NEXT LOOP%

7.10 What is this strange statement? It really belongs to BASIC and I feel it is a GREAT shame that it is not implemented in OPL for it is a very simple and elegant way of setting up and running a loop. If you are not familiar with BASIC, let me show you how we would have to write this structure in OPL:

OPL	*BASIC*
LOOP%=0	FOR LOOP%=0 TO LIMIT%
STEP 3	
DO	—
—	—
—	—
—	—
LOOP%=LOOP%+3	—
UNTIL LOOP%>=LIMIT%	NEXT LOOP%

A much simpler structure, I'm sure you'll agree. For loops which operate on simple counts, rather than complex conditions, this is the statement I would recommend you to use. Note that the BASIC count does not have to exactly match the value of LIMIT%. The loop would terminate on observing that the value of LOOP% had equalled or exceeded LIMIT%. Let's try it out. Write a program, using the FOR .. NEXT structure which will loop round by the number of times held in a variable called LIMIT%, incrementing the count by 3 each time. BE VERY CAREFUL TO TEST FOR GREATER THAN OR EQUAL TO THE LIMIT RATHER THAN SIMPLY EQUAL TO - UNLESS YOUR ARITHMETIC IS VERY GOOD AND YOU ARE ABSOLUTELY SURE THAT A CERTAIN NUMBER OF ITERATIONS WILL GIVE YOU EXACTLY THE VALUE OF LIMIT, YOU MAY END UP IN AN INFINITE LOOP. Store the end value of the count in RESULT%.

PROGRAM NAME: "FOR .. NEXT STRUCTURE 1"

PURPOSE: This program consists of a loops whose count starts at zero and is incremented by 3 until its value equals or exceeds the contents of the variable LIMIT%. The final value of the count is then stored in the variable RESULT%

VARIABLES: $7D19 RESULT%
$7D1A LIMIT%

ORG: $7D0B

```
7DOB        LDA A #0    $86 $00
7D0D .loop  CLC         $0C
```

```
7D0E    ADC A #3          $89 $03
7D10    CMP A LIMIT%      $B1 $7D1A
7D13    BLS loop          $23 248
7D15    STA A  RESULT%    $B7 $7D19
7D18    RTS               $39
7D19    << RESULT% >>     ---------
7D1A    << LIMIT% >>      ---------
```

7.11 There are a couple of points to note here. First, ensure that you clear the Carry Flag before adding 3 to the count. Next, observe that you are not comparing the A Accumulator with an immediate number but rather an extended address. You must also be aware of the fact that, since you are using an unsigned binary value for the loop, you must employ the BLS instruction in preference to the BLE one which concerns itself with two's complement numbers. Finally, you must ensure that you calculate the correct branch distance (-8). Before you run the program, set the RESULT% to zero and the LIMIT% to, say, 16 decimal. Note that this does not mean that you will repeat the loop 16 times. It means that the program will loop from zero to the number which equals or exceeds 16. When you have run it, VIEW the program to discover the final value of RESULT%. It will be 18 ($12). Why is this? Well, if you subtract 3 from 18 to find out what the last iteration was worth, you arrive at the figure 15. This is obviously less than 16 and so the loop will repeat to give the loop counter the value 18. At this point, the comparison discovers that the counter exceeds the LIMIT value and the loop terminates. Try the program out using other LIMITs, each time trying to work out what the terminal value will be.

FOR LOOP% = LIMIT1% TO LIMIT2% STEP INCREMENT%

7.12 This is a much more interesting problem - not only are we unsure of the value of the start point this time, but we also do not know the increment. In BASIC, it matters little whether the increment is positive or minus but it makes a great deal of difference in machine code. In one case, we would add the increment and in the other, we would subtract. There are ways round this but let's keep things simple. We will assume that our increments are POSITIVE. See if you can code the program in the previous paragraph, using the variable-based system. Remember the points arising from the last one.

PROGRAM NAME: "FOR .. NEXT STRUCTURE 2"

PURPOSE: This program consists of a loop which has the start value equal to the contents of the variable LIMIT1%. The count is increased by the positive value held in the variable INCREMENT% and continues until the count equals or exceeds the value held in the variable LIMIT2%. The final value of the count is then stored in the variable RESULT%.

VARIABLES:

$7D1B	RESULT%
$7D1C	LIMIT1%
$7D1D	LIMIT2%
$7D1E	INCREMENT%

ORG:

```
$7D0B
7DOB   LDA A LIMIT1%        $B6 $7D1C
7D0E   .loop                CLC      $0C
7DOF   ADC A INCREMENT%     $B9 $7D1E
7D12   CMP A LIMIT2%        $B1 $7D1D
7D15   BLS loop             $23 247
7D17   STA A  RESULT%       $B7 $7D1B
7D1A   RTS                  $39
7D1B   << RESULT% >>        --------
7D1C   << LIMIT1% >>        --------
7D1D   << LIMIT2% >>        --------
7D1E   << INCREMENT% >>     --------
```

If you try the routine using the values LIMIT1%=$10, LIMIT2%=$20 and INCREMENT%=$01 you will see that RESULT% will end up as $21. Try it out with other values. See if you can predict the results.

FOR LOOP% = 0 TO 1000 STEP 1

7.13 Here is the final wrinkle I want to touch upon in describing machine code loop structures - a loop greater than 256, the maximum number which can be held in a single byte. Although there IS a double-byte Accumulator facility in the PSION CPU, I will describe a more flexible approach using two single-byte numbers. The first stage in this method is to discover the largest number less than 257 which can divide EXACTLY into the upper range of the loop. In our case, it will be 250, which goes into 1000 four times. Thus, to execute our loop, we use 2 counters - one to repeatedly count an inner loop from 1 to 250 and one to run the inner loop 4 times. We will use the A Accumulator for the inner loop and the B accumulator for the outer. Let's try to code this new form of nested loop - store Accumulator A as RESULT1% and Accumulator B as RESULT2%.

PROGRAM NAME: "FOR .. NEXT STRUCTURE 3"

PURPOSE: This program consists of a loop starting at 0 and incrementing by 1 until the count exceeds 1000. Two Accumulators are used - A to hold the inner count and B to hold the outer. On termination, the A Accumulator is stored as RESULT1% and Accumulator B is stored as RESULT2%.

VARIABLES:

$7D20	RESULT1%
$7D21	RESULT2%

ORG: $7D0B

```
7DOB   LDA B #01          $C6 01
7D0D   .loopl   LDA A #01             $86 01
7D0F   .loop2   INC A   $4C
7D10   CMP A #250         $81 250
7D12   BLS loop2          $23 251
7D14   INC B              $5C
7D15   CMP B #04          $C1 04
7D17   BLS loop1          $23 244
7D19   STA A  RESULT1%                $B7 $7D20
7D1C   STA B  RESULT2%                $F7 $7D21
7D1F   RTS                            $39
7D20   << RESULT1% >>                 ________
7D21   << RESULT2% >>                 ________
```

7.14 When you RUN this program, you will find that RESULT1% contains $FB (251 decimal). This is the value which terminates the inner loop on each round and is therefore the value remaining when the inner loop terminates for the last time. Similarly, $05 will be the value which terminates the outer loop and, sure enough, you'll find it at RESULT2%. So, there you have it - a means of looping more than 256 times. There is a problem, however, in that you might want to loop by a number of times which is prime - you can't divide it by ANYTHING!! What do you do there? The answer is to use 2 loops but this time keep them separate. First, you find out how often 256 goes into the loop number and what the remainder is. You will then perform a nested loop like the one we have just done, where the inner loop goes from 0 to 256 and the outer loop goes from 0 to the dividend. Think, now - how can we detect 256 in a single byte? The answer is that it will wrap round to zero again. So, if the inner count is zero, it is either starting a loop or it is registering 256 - one and the same thing. When the nested loop system terminates, it must then enter the second of your two loops. This is a simple loop which goes from 0 to the remainder. And that is all there is to it. Of course, if you are actually DOING something inside the loop, that piece of code will have to be duplicated in the remainder loop, too.

APPLICATIONS

7.15 So far, we have concentrated on describing the loop structures and have avoided code to be executed within them. This was simply to keep things simple. Now that you are an expert in going round in circles, we should push the pace up a bit. Let's write a program to calculate the square of a number. First, think just how we calculate the square of a given number - we multiply it by itself, right? The problem is, of course, that we cannot multiply yet in machine code. Yet, what is multiplication but repeated addition? You know how to add in machine code, so all we have to do is to set up some sort of store and a loop and repeatedly add the number to it the requisite number of times. Using a FOR .. NEXT loop, this would be FOR LOOP% = 1 TO NUMBER% STEP 1. Use Accumulator A to hold the loop counter, NUMBER% to hold the value to be squared and SQUARE% to hold the final result. See if you can come up with this code yourself. Do not run it until you have checked it with the suggested solution below.

PROGRAM NAME: "SQUARE"

PURPOSE: This program takes the value stored in NUMBER% and squares it by repeated addition. The result is stored in SQUARE%

```
VARIABLES:    $7D20      NUMBER%
              $7D21      SQUARE%

ORG:          $7D0B
              7DOB       LDA A NUMBER%        $B6 $7D20
              7DOE       LDA B #00            $C6 $00
              7D10       STA B SQUARE%        $F7 $7D21
              7D13       .loop                CLC     $0C
              7D14       ADC B NUMBER%        $F9 $7D20
              7D17       DEC A                $4A
              7D18       CMP A #0             $81 $00
              7D1A       BNE loop             $26 247
              7D1C       STA B  SQUARE%       $F7 $7D21
              7D1F       RTS                  $39
              7D20       << NUMBER% >>        ————
              7D21       << SQUARE% >>        ————
```

7.16 To begin with, try 5 as the number. You should find $19 in SQUARE%. Use other numbers and note the results you get when the SQUARE% is greater than 255. You can see from the above program that I have used a different approach from previous examples (although there are MANY ways to code up this problem). I have elected to DECREMENT the counter instead of incrementing it and have decided not to use the ADC for the STEP since we MUST go in steps of 1.

CONCLUSION

7.17 We have looked at the problem of coding loop structures in machine code and have examined a number of options such as DO .. UNTIL, WHILE .. ENDWH and the "foreign" FOR .. STEP .. NEXT loop. We have seen how to use the CCR as a means of keeping tabs on what is going on inside the CPU and how we can take a number of actions depending on the results of those checks. Before we carry on to look at how we can implement arrays in machine code, try out the following Post Test.

POST TEST

1. Which register do we use in the decision making process at machine code level?

2. Without reference to the text, list the instructions which allow values to be compared and state which areas are compared.

3. I wish to compare an immediate value with the contents of Accumulator A. What is the Assembly code for this?

4. What is Relative Addressing and how is it used in branching instructions?

5. Without reference to the text, list the branch instructions provided by the Hitachi CPU and describe their functions.

6. Describe the method by which the CPU arrives at the actual address to jump to after receiving a relative branch instruction.

7. I wish to jump backwards by 23 bytes using the BNE instruction. What is the complete instruction for this?

Chapter 8

Give me Arrays!!

8: Give me Arrays!!

TRAINING OBJECTIVE:

At the end of this chapter, you will be able to write programs using indexed addressing and array structures.

ENABLING OBJECTIVES:

To enable you to do this, you must be able to:

a. State how Indexed Addressing is implemented in machine code.

b. State how an individual "cell" in a machine code array can be indicated.

c. Describe the meaning and use of a "stack".

d. Describe how to put the contents of a register onto the stack.

e. Describe how to retrieve the contents of a register from the stack.

INTRODUCTION

8.0 The PSION Organiser has its own way of creating arrays using its Operating System. This is a very easy to use method but it is slow and can be memory-hungry in certain applications. We will now turn our attention to the problem of creating machine code arrays and, thereby, handling large areas of the Organiser's memory map.

INDEXED ADDRESSING

8.1 To begin with, let's look at the problem of addressing. Let's suppose you wanted to hold a list of integers. Easy - except that in our scenario arrays have not yet been invented!! You would have to use an individual variable for each and every number. This may not be too much of a problem if you have a lot of memory to spare but what happens when you want to indicate one of them? Which variable do you choose? How do you run down them and list them?

8.2 At this point in our gentle trot through the Black Art of Machine Code Programming, we are in just this position. We can create as many "variables" as we have memory available but, as yet, we cannot skim through them in the same way as we can in OPL. To deal with this sort of problem, the concept of Indexed Addressing was invented. Here we store the address of the first element of our array in the X (Index) Register. An indexed instruction then takes the form of:

OPERATOR DISPLACEMENT,X

For example, if we want to store the contents of Accumulator A in the 5th element of the array (assuming that each element takes up a single byte), we would enter:

STA A 5,X

A load instruction would look just the same - easy - but do note that the offset is a positive, unsigned integer i.e. you can't refer backwards as you do in Relative Addressing. If I were to use the instruction "LDA A 0,X", I would obviously mean to load the value at the base address itself. To scan through the entire array, all I would do is to use the load instruction with an offset of zero, incrementing the X Register on each pass.

8.3 Time for an example, I think. Ever heard of the FIBONACCI series? For those of you who haven't, let me briefly describe it. It consists of an infinite series of numbers which has the property that each element is the sum of the preceding two elements (starting with 0 and 1) i.e. 0,1,1,2,3,5,8,13,21 ..... The reasons for and uses of this series are somewhat outside the scope of this book, so let's just look upon it as an interesting little programming problem and leave it at that. So where does the indexed addressing come in? So far, it looks just like a simple looping problem. Well, I want you to write this program so that it will place the first 10 items in the series in an array which you must set up somewhere in memory. To give you a clue, here is how it could look in OPL:

```
FIBON:

REM Nil Global variables - set up Local variables
LOCAL one%,two%,point%,array%(10)

REM Initialise variables
one%=0
two%=1
array%(1)=one%
array%(2)=two%
point%=3

DO
    array%(point%)=one%+two%
    one%=two%
    two%=array%(point%)
    point%=point%+1
UNTIL point%=11

REM View the array
point%=1
CLS
DO
    PRINT point%;" .... ";array%(point%)
    point%=point%+1
UNTIL point%=11
GET

RETURN
```

Of course, there are more elegant ways to do this, but the approach I have adopted above lends itself reasonably easily to implementation in machine code. Note that you should start your machine code array at ZERO and not ONE, as I have done in the OPL example - OPL does not allow arrays to have a ZERO subscript.

8.4 Remembering the points I made about skipping through a machine code array, have a look at my suggested solution. If yours is not identical, it doesn't matter. What is important is that it runs and gives the correct output. Note also that now we are in the realms of more difficult problems, I have introduced the concept of commenting the suggested solutions. This is done much in the same way as the REM statement of OPL. In machine code, however, we use the backslash or "\". An assembler would ignore all text on the same line after this mark. I STRONGLY advise the use of commenting as programs can become totally unintelligible after a very short time, particularly in machine code where the meaning of the program is not always immediately apparent.

PROGRAM NAME: "FIBONACCI"

PURPOSE: This program is designed to calculate the first 10 elements of the Fibonacci series. The first of the two numbers to be added together is held in the variable ONE% and the second in TWO%. The count controlling the loop is held in Accumulator B.

```
VARIABLES:      $7D3A       ONE%
                $7D3B       TWO%
                $7D3C       ARRAY% \ Base address of the
                array

ORG: $7D0B
7D0B        LDX #ARRAY%     $CE $7D3C       \ Base address of
                                            \ array into X Reg
7D0E        LDA A #00       $86 $00
7D10        STA A ONE%      $B7 $7D3A       \ Zero into ONE%
7D13        STA A 0,X       $A7 $00         \ and into the
                                            \ first element of
                                            \ the array
7D15        INX             $08             \ Point to the next
                                            \ element
7D16        INC A           $4C
7D17        STA A TWO%      $B7 $7D3B       \ One into TWO%
7D1A        STA A 0,X       $A7 $00         \ and into the next
                                            \ element of array
7D1C        INX             $08             \ Increment pointer
7D1D        LDA B #02       $C6 $02         \ Set counter to 2
7D1F .loop  LDA A ONE%      $B6 $7D3A       \ Get the first
                                            \ number
7D22        CLC             $0C             \ Clear Carry Flag
```

```
7D23            ADC A TWO%      $B9 $7D3B       \ Add the second -
7D26            STA A 0,X       $A7 $00         \ and store it in
                                                \ the current cell
                                                \ of the array
7D28 .swap      LDA A TWO%      $B6 $7D3B       \ Put TWO% into
7D2BSTA A ONE%                  $B7 $7D3A       \ ONE% and then
7D2ELDA A 0,X $A6 $00                           \ put current cell
7D30            STA TWO%        $B7 $7D3B       \ into TWO%
7D33 .inc       INX             $08             \ Increment pointer
7D34            INC B           $5C             \ Increment counter
7D35            CMP B #10       $C1 $0A         \ Counter = 10 ?
7D37            BNE -24         $26 230         \ Yes - goto loop
7D39            RTS             $39             \ No - all done.
7D3A            << ONE% >>
7D3B            << TWO% >>
7D3C            <<ARRAY%>>
```

If you managed to come up with a program similar to the above, you are doing well - keep it up!

THE STACK

8.5 So, what's a stack? It sounds like some sort of enormous cooling tower but actually it's much more like the sort of thing you would find in a restaurant or cafeteria. You must have seen the sort of plate warmers in such places where they put plates into a stainless steel cabinet in a vertical pile with a spring at the bottom. As each plate is taken off the top, the column of plate rises up to reveal the next one. This is precisely how a stack works in a computer except that instead of a column of plates, we have a column of data.

8.6 One of the very useful features of a stack is that you don't have to remember exactly WHERE you stored your data. You simply put it on the stack with a single command and take it off again with another. The only thing you must be careful of is to take the data off in the reverse order from that in which you put it on. For example, going back to our catering example, let's suppose that Tom, Dick and Harry each have their own monogrammed plates which they wish to place in the warmer until they heat up (the plates, that is, not Tom, Dick or Harry). Tom Puts his on first, followed by Dick and then Harry. Naturally, when they come back to retrieve them, HARRY goes up first to take his off the stack, since his is on top. Then Dick's plate springs up and lastly Tom's. To put this into computer context, Tom, Dick and Harry are 3 memory locations whose contents you want to stack while you use them to store other things. When you go back to restore the data to the locations you must restore them in the reverse order to avoid putting Tom's data into Harry, for example.

8.7 The Organiser has its own stack of plates, set up as an area of memory. A special register called the Stack Pointer (SP) keeps track of the current free location on the stack. You, the user, can alter the contents of the SP. In fact, many otherwise impossible tricks can be done using this method. However, I must stress that this is an extremely ill-advised thing to do until you are ABSOLUTELY sure of what you are doing. The Organiser uses the stack to hold all sorts of information. Indeed, we could refer to the Organiser as a "Stack-Orientated Machine", since it relies heavily on stack operations to carry out its work. This means that you have to be very careful not to overwrite the stack by ill-conceived machine code programs. There is nothing to stop you actually USING the stack by means of the legitimate instructions but do it with your eyes open and don't allow the effects of your STORE instructions to deliver the dreaded TRAP. As more things are put on the stack, it grows upwards until it meets the ROM area. The operating system constantly checks that there is enough room to meet each operation it is called to carry out in OPL. You may, in fact, have already met the "STACK OVERFLOW" and "STACK UNDERFLOW" errors.

8.8 Let's see how we can put all this into practice. There are 2 commands we need to know. Firstly, the instruction to place the contents of the A Register on the stack is:

PSHA (PuSH the A register onto the stack)

Secondly, we can retrieve the data from the stack by using the instruction:

PULA (PULl the A register from the stack)

The same is, of course, true for the B Register. We can illustrate the use of these instructions by means of a short program. There is a classic little problem in programming involving the need to swap the contents of 2 variables. This would normally require a third variable to hold the contents of one of the variables, temporarily, while the other is moved over into it. The temporary variable is then copied into the first and the process is complete. It is, however, possible to do the job WITHOUT the use of a temporary variable. Since we have been talking about the stack for a little while, now, it will come as no great shock to you to discover that it is involved in the task.

8.9 In OPL, the program might look something like this:

```
SWAP:

REM Nil global variables - all LOCAL
LOCAL first%, second%, temp%
CLS
PRINT"FIRST : ";
INPUT first%
PRINT"SECOND : ";
INPUT second%

TEMP%=SECOND%
SECOND%=FIRST%
FIRST%=TEMP%

CLS
PRINT"FIRST : ";FIRST%
PRINT"SECOND: ";SECOND%

GET
RETURN
```

8.10 The machine code version is very simple indeed, if we assume that the 2 numbers to be swapped are already stored in memory. Try to work out the code for yourself and check it against the following suggested solution:

PROGRAM NAME: "SWAP"

PURPOSE: This program is designed to take the contents of 2 single-byte variables, called FIRST% and SECOND% and to swap their contents.

VARIABLES:	$7D20	FIRST%
	$7D21	SECOND%

```
ORG: $7D0B
   7D0B     LDA A FIRST%      $B6 $7D20    \Load the contents
                                           \of FIRST% into
                                           \Acc A.
   7D0E     LDA B SECOND%     $F6 $7D21    \Load the contents
                                           \of SECOND% into
                                           \Acc B.
   7D11     PSH A             $36          \Stack the contents
                                           \of Acc A.
   7D12     TBA               $17          \Copy Acc B into
                                           \Acc A.
   7D13     PUL B             $33          \Retrieve the data
                                           \from the stack,
                                           \placing it into
                                           \Acc B.
   7D14     STA A FIRST%      $B7 $7D20    \Store Acc A into
                                           \FIRST%.
   7D17     STA B SECOND%     $F7 $7D21    \Store Acc B into
                                           \SECOND%.
   7D1A     RTS               $39          \All Done.
   7D20     FIRST%
   7D21     SECOND%
```

If you use the "View" facility of the Hexloader, you will see that they have in fact been swapped. All this is very interesting but where does it lead ? It leads, in fact, to a very useful facility to be able to implement in machine code - a sorting routine.

USING AN ARRAY TO SORT NUMBERS

8.11 We now know how to set up an array, to fill it with numbers and to swap them about. In the case of the Fibonnaci series, these are already in order. Nevertheless, there are many occasions when we want to sort numbers into either ascending or descending format. So, let's now turn our attention to this sort of problem.

8.12 There are many algorithms designed to sort numbers or strings into some form of order but perhaps the easiest to understand is the Bubble Sort (if you are an old hand at this - bear with me for a little while). Essentially, this form of sort consists of 2 loops - one inside the other. The outer loop is designed to go down the array from the first element to the penultimate one. At each increment of this loop, the inner one makes a complete pass starting at the next element up from the one being indicated by the outer loop and going to the very end of the array. At each step of the inner loop, the element indicated by the inner is compared to that pointed to by the outer. If the inner element is numerically or alphabetically LOWER than the outer, the two are swapped (which, of course, requires a temporary variable) and the inner loop incremented. The procedure continues until the outer loop completes.

8.13 As before, look at how this is implemented in OPL. Here, we set up an array and you are prompted to enter 10 numbers - make sure they are positive and less than 256 (the program could handle numbers outside this range but remember - we are going to implement this in machine code where each number will occupy a single byte). The routine will then sort the set and print them out.

```
SORT:

LOCAL array%(10),temp%,outer%,inner%

CLS
outer%=1
DO
   PRINT "ELEMENT" ;outer%;" ";
   INPUT array%(outer%)
   outer%=outer%+1
UNTIL outer%>10
CLS
PRINT "PRESS ANY KEY"
GET
PRINT "SORTING .. WAIT"

outer%=1
DO
   inner%=outer%+1
   DO
      IF array(inner%)<array%(outer%)
         temp%=array%(outer%)
         array%(outer%)=array%(inner%)
```

```
        array(inner%)=temp%
      ENDIF
      inner%=inner%+1
   UNTIL inner%>10
   outer%=outer%+1
UNTIL outer%>9

CLS
outer%=1
DO
   PRINT "ELEMENT ";outer%;" = ";array%(outer%)
   outer%=outer%+1
UNTIL outer%>10
PRINT "PRESS ANY KEY"
GET
RETURN
```

8.14 Of course, we will not need the section of the program where we insert values into the array - we can do this using the VIEW facility of the Hexloader. Similarly, we can display the sorted contents of the array using the same facility. Note that since you will perhaps need to stack ADDRESSES instead of bytes of information, you may need to look up the instruction to stack the IX Register. I'll leave this up to you as an extra test of your developing abilities in machine code. Right then, all we are interested in is the actual sorting part - see if you can implement it in machine code. The suggested solution is set out below.

PROGRAM NAME: "SORT"

PURPOSE: This program is designed to take the contents of an array, composed of 10 single-byte integers, and sort them into ascending order. Two variables are used - OUTER% and INNER% to hold the sort pointers and the stack to assist in the swapping of array contents.

VARIABLES:	$7D3A	OUTER%
	$7D3C	INNER%
	$7D3E	ARRAY% \Base address of the array
	$7D40	ARRAY ELEMENTS

8.14 Ascending order

```
ORG: $7D0B

7D0B            LDX ARRAY%      $FE $7D3E     \Load IX with array
                                              \address.
7D0E            LDAA OUTER%     $B6 $7D3A     \Load Acc A with
                                              \size of array.
7D11 POINT1:    STAA INNER%     $B7 $7D3C     \Store inner loop.
7D14            PSHX            $3C           \Push the IX onto
                                              \the stack.
7D15            LDAA 0,X        $A6 $00       \Load Acc A with
                                              \the contents of
                                              \cell indicated by
                                              \IX.
7D17 POINT2:    INX             $08           \Increment IX.
7D18            CMPA 0,X        $A1 $00       \Compare the next
                                              \item in the array
                                              \with the greatest
                                              \value so far.
7D1A            BCS POINT3      $25 $05       \If it's greater,
                                              \branch to POINT3.
7D1C            LDAB 0,X        $E6 $00       \Otherwise, load
                                              \Acc B with array
                                              \element.
7D1E            STAA 0,X        $A7 $00       \Store Acc A in the
                                              \array position.
7D20            TBA             $17           \Transfer Acc B to
                                              \Acc A, making it
                                              \the new greatest.
7D21 POINT3:    DEC INNER%      $7A $7D3C     \Decrement inner
                                              \loop.
7D24            BNE POINT2      $26 $F1       \If it's not zero,
                                              \branch to POINT2.
7D26            PULX            $38           \Get the IX value
                                              \from the stack.
7D27            STAA 0,X        $A7 $00       \Store Acc A in the
                                              \array.
7D29            INX             $08           \Increment the IX.
7D2A            DEC OUTER%      $7A $7D3A     \Decrement the
                                              \outer loop.
7D2D            LDAA OUTER%     $B6 $7D3A     \Load Acc A with
                                              \the outer loop.
7D30            BNE POINT1      $26 $DF       \If it's not zero,
                                              \branch to POINT2.
7D32            RTS             $39           \Otherwise, end.
7D3A            OUTER%
7D3C            INNER%
7D3E            ARRAY%
7D40            ARRAY ELEMENTS
7Dxx            END OF ARRAY
```

CONCLUSION

8.15 In this chapter, we have examined the ways in which we can simulate arrays in machine code by means of indexed addressing. We have also come up against the concept of a stack and how to manipulate its contents using the Push and Pull commands. In keeping with the general approach of this book, we have illustrated the new material with examples. So then, before we go on to look at subroutines, try the following Post Test.

POST TEST

1. Which register is used to step through a list of memory locations ?

2. What is a stack ?

3. What is the term for putting an item of data on the stack ?

4. What is the term for taking an item of data off the stack ?

5. What is the machine code instruction for taking data off the stack and putting it :

   a. In Accumulator B.

   b. In the Index Register.

6. Repeat 5. for taking putting data on the stack from

   a. Accumulator B.

   b. Index Register.

Chapter 9

There and Back

9: There and Back

TRAINING OBJECTIVE:

At the end of this chapter, you will be able to write programs using subroutines.

ENABLING OBJECTIVES:

To enable you to do this, you must be able to:

a. State how a machine code program calls a subroutine.

b. State the machine code equivalent of the OPL "return" statement.

c. Describe how the user can pass parameters to a subroutine.

d. Describe how the Organiser knows where to return to after completing a subroutine.

e. Describe how subroutines aid the programmer.

INTRODUCTION

9.0 As you know, the Organiser has the facility to enable the user to code his OPL program as a series of subroutines, called by a main program (which itself is really regarded as a subroutine except that the RETURN is optional). Dividing and conquering like this is good practice and is called MODULAR PROGRAMMING. It enables the user to split up an otherwise complex problems into a series of easier ones. This means that when you return to the program some time later, you would find it easier to understand and, just as important, modify it in the light of changing requirements.

9.1 As I have shown, ALL machine code programs, even the main program, MUST have its equivalent of the RETURN command - RTS - at the end of the code. This is because the machine code simply would not know where to go at the end of the code if there was no RTS. However, what you have not met up until now is how to use the RTS as the end of a true subroutine called from a main one.

CALLING A SUBROUTINE

9.2 The secret of understanding machine code subroutines is to treat them exactly like OPL ones! However, whereas in OPL we would call a subroutine simply by using its name, the machine code programmer has to specify the address of the subroutine instead. To call it, we use the following instruction:

JSR xxxx (Jump to SubRoutine at xxxx)

Notice that the jump address is NOT like that for the branch or jump instructions where the offset is specified as a signed byte i.e. it can be positive or negative. In the case of the JSR instruction the address is just that - an actual hexadecimal address of the start of the subroutine. It can also be expressed in Indexed and Direct addressing modes.

9.3 When the JSR is called, the Organiser automatically stacks the current address where the JSR is located before jumping to the specified subroutine and continuing execution from that point. When the RTS is encountered, the Organiser retrieves the return address, jumps to that point and continues execution until the RTS of the main program is reached. All just like OPL! We can test this out using one of our previous machine code programs as a subroutine and writing a new one to act as its controller. We will use the "LOOP STRUCTURE 2" program in paragraph 7.8. We will place our controlling program at address $7D20. This illustrates an important point - the controller does NOT have to occur before the subroutine. However, it aids readability if the main program does come first. Nevertheless, we will fly in the face of convention - mainly because we can simply enter it as laid out in chapter 7 and add the new bits at the end!

9.4 Passing parameters

PROGRAM NAME: "LOOP STRUCTURE 2"

PURPOSE: This program loops round 100 times. The count is held in Accumulator A and the final value is placed in RESULT%

VARIABLES: $7D16 RESULT%

```
ORG:            $7D0B
     7DOB          LDA A #1           $86 $01
     7D0D .loop    INC A              $4C
     7D0E          CMP A #101         $81 $65
     7D10          BNE loop           $26 251
     7D12          STA A  RESULT%     $B7 $7D16
     7D15          RTS                $39
     7D16          << RESULT% >>      ———
```

PROGRAM NAME: "LOOP STRUCTURE 2 CONTROLLER"

PURPOSE: This program controls the LOOP 2 program outlined above.

VARIABLES: Nil.

```
ORG:            $7D20
      7D20JSR $7D0B        $BD $7D0B      \ Jump to the
                                          \ subroutine.
      7D23                 RTS$39         \ All done.
```

9.4 Do remember to specify $7D20 as the location you want to RUN from. Hopefully, then, you can see that the actual use of the JSR and RTS instructions are very easy to use in your own programs. But what about passing parameters to a subroutine ? Well, one way favoured by the able and confident is to stack any values required by the subroutine prior to executing the JSR instruction. Can you see any problems with that for the inexperienced ? Just before the CPU makes its jump to the subroutine, it STACKS THE CURRENT (RETURN) ADDRESS. This means that the data for the subroutine is underneath the return address on the stack. To some programmers, this is not a problem but I advise you strongly against this practice, however attractive it may seem. We will use a simpler method.

9.5 Those of you who have been weaned on a diet of John Le Carré will recognize the term "Dead Letter Box". This is a hidden location, such as under a tree root, where a documents can be left by one spy for collection at a later date by another. This is precisely what we do in the case of parameter passing. Before we call the subroutine, we place any necessary data in a memory location for reading at the appropriate time. Let's see if we can use another of our previous programs in this way.

9.6 A good example would be the program to square a number. You'll find it at paragraph 7.15. We could allow the controlling program to store the number to be squared at the required location. Look at the definition of program "SQUARE":

```
PROGRAM NAME:  "SQUARE"

PURPOSE:       This program takes the value stored in
               NUMBER% and squares it by repeated addition.
               The result is stored in SQUARE%

VARIABLES:     $7D20          NUMBER%
               $7D21          SQUARE%

ORG: $7D0B

    7DOB       LDA A NUMBER%                $B6 $7D20
    7DOE       LDA B #00      $C6 $00
    7D10       STA B SQUARE%                $F7 $7D21
    7D13 .loop CLC            $0C
    7D14       ADC B NUMBER%                $F9 $7D20
    7D17       DEC A          $4A
    7D18       CMP A #0       $81 $00
    7D1A       BNE loop       $26 247
    7D1C       STA B  SQUARE%               $F7 $7D21
    7D1F       RTS            $39
    7D20       << NUMBER% >>                ---------
    7D21       << SQUARE% >>                ---------
```

Our controlling program simply places the number into location NUMBER%, calls the subroutine and terminates.

PROGRAM NAME: "SQUARE CONTROLLER"

PURPOSE: This program places the number to be squared in location NUMBER% before calling the SQUARE subroutine. This, in turn, squares the number and places it in location SQUARE% before returning to the main program which itself then terminates.

VARIABLES: Nil.

ORG: $7D30

```
7D30    LDA A #03          $86 $03       \Any number.
7D32    STA A NUMBER%      $B6 $7D20     \Store it.
7D35    JSR $7D0B          $BD $7D0B     \Jump to the
                                         \subroutine.
7D38    RTS                $39           \All done.
```

CONCLUSION

9.6 In this short chapter, we have looked at how we can implement subroutines in machine code and how we can call them, with or without parameters. We have seen that programming in modules is good practice since it aids readability and modifiability. Try out the following Post Test before going on to the last chapter.

POST TEST

1. State the machine code instruction to call a subroutine.

2. State the machine code instruction to return from a subroutine.

3. Why should the programmer use subroutines ?

4. How does the programmer pass parameters to a machine code subroutine ?

Chapter 10

Organiser Operating System

10: Organiser Operating System

TRAINING OBJECTIVE:
At the end of this chapter you will be able to write programs which make use of the PSION Organiser's operating system.

ENABLING OBJECTIVES:
To enable you to do this, you must be able to:

a. Describe the functions of an Operating System (OS).

b. State the meaning of an OS call.

c. Describe the means by which an OS call can be invoked.

INTRODUCTION
10.0 Finally, in this the last chapter, we look at the PSION Organiser OS. PSION have packed a very great deal into their firmware and there are many facilities which can be called by the informed user to add flexibility and speed to his programs. These facilities are in fact subroutines stored in ROM. However, instead of accessing them as we would do normal subroutines, we call them by means of OS calls. This is not to say that the unscrupulous could not discover their actual locations and use them directly (indeed there are advantages in speed to this method) but I would advise against any approach of this kind. Firstly, the actual internal workings of the Organiser can and does change from version to version and a program written to PEEK and POKE where it shouldn't is going to come a cropper sooner or later. Using the accepted OS calls means that PSION do all the work in ensuring that the call is routed to the correct location, irrespective of any changes which have been made deeper down. Secondly, PSION have gone to a great deal of trouble to produce a superb OS for the size of the machine. It is flexible and easy to use. It is good programming practice to make use of these facilities.

10.1 Operating systems have grown up due to the increasing complexity of modern computer systems. In the bad old days, all the housekeeping chores were dome by the programmer and the program took complete control of the CPU when it was running. This meant that, unless specifically coded, other things like polling the keyboard, were deactivated on some systems. Operating systems evolved to counter this problem and provide a means by which the system can periodically stop what it is doing and "have a look around" to see if it should be updating a clock or reading a keyboard. In addition, most of them, including the Organiser, provide the user with a suite of pre-written routines which he can call from his own programs.

10.2 Annex G holds details of the PSION Organiser's OS calls and you should use this to code your programs. Calling an OS routine is simplicity itself. The CPU will jump to an OS routine when it encounters the Software Interrupt (SWI) instruction - $3F. It interprets the byte immediately following the SWI as the number of the OS call you wish to enter. The Operating System then takes the CPU to the relevant area in ROM where the routing is located and execution continues from that point. When the routine has completed, the CPU returns to the byte following the OS call number in your main program. Annex G explains this, and how to pass parameters, in more depth.

10.3 I don't intend to work my way through all of these, or even a proportion of them. Most of them are way beyond the stage of the average reader of this book and are included for completeness and the more advanced user using the publication for reference. However, I will give examples of how to use the more common ones. To start off, have a look at G-6 and Vector (or Call) number 13. The function of this routine is to sound the alarm. Notice that its entry requirements are shown as NIL. This means that no parameters need to be passed to it using our "Dead Letter Boxes" of Chapter 9. The functional description tells us what it does and the fact that it disables interrupts. This could have ramifications if we were particularly interested in timing and we would have to take the length of time the alarm was sounding into consideration. For our purposes, though, it is not a problem. So let's try it out by coding a small program to call it.

10.4 Make a sound

PROGRAM NAME: "SOUND ALARM"

PURPOSE: This program calls a software interrupt and passes the Vector number to the OS for execution of the routine.

VARIABLES: Nil

ORG: $7D0B

```
7DOB   SW1#$0D   $3F$0D   \Call the Software Interrupt 13.
7D0D   RTS       $39      \All done.
```

10.4 Quite impressive, yes? For a modicum of code, you have been able to produce a sound which CANNOT be made using OPL. This is the sort of thing which machine code can do. It taps directly into the heart of the machine to make it perform in a way not attainable in a higher level language. The pitfall, of course, is that the code had better be correct! Did you notice that the call only gave a single blast of the alarm? How could we make it give, say, 3 or 4? A loop, of course. Have a look back at 7.7. Here we have a perfect vehicle to hold our OS call. See if you can use this loop to sound the alarm 5 times. HINT: save the loop counter in a suitable variable and load it into Accumulator A each time for testing. This is because the OS call trashes the contents of the Accumulator. The code is shown below but try it yourself, first.

PROGRAM NAME: "ALARM LOOP"

PURPOSE: This program loops around 5 times, calling Vector 13 (Sound the Alarm) each time, before terminating. The loop counter is held in the variable COUNTER% since the OS routine makes its own use of the Accumulator during its operation.

VARIABLES: $7D30 COUNTER%

ORG: $7D0B

```
7DOB        LDA A#0       $86$00       \Initialise counter
7D0D        STA A$7D30    $B7 $7D30    \Store it.
7D10.loop   INC $7D30     $7C$7D30     \Increment it.
```

7D13	SWI#$0D	$3F$0D	\Sound alarm.
7D15	LDA A $7D30	$B6$7D30	\Retrieve it.
7D18	CMP A #05	$81 $05	\At 5?
7D1A	BNE loop	$26 244	\No - go round.
7D1C	RTS	$39	\All done.

10.5 So now you are able to call the Organiser's alarm sound using your very own controlling routine. This itself could be useful in that you can now call your machine code program from an OPL program to produce the sound on request. The same approach goes for Vector 14 - the Beep note but since this is as in OPL, I won't dwell on it.

10.6 Let's move on to a call which requires some sort of parameter. Up until now, we have been unable to display anything on the screen from machine code - now, we can. Look at Vector 16 - Output a Character. This requires you to put the character you want printed into Accumulator A prior to calling the SWI. This will display the character at the cursor position. All characters can be used, so this means that you could clear the screen as well as print a message. A good test would be to see if we could clear the screen and print the word "PSION" - try it.
PROGRAM NAME: "PRINT PSION"

PURPOSE: This program clears the screen and prints the word "PSION" by repeatedly loading Accumulator A with the requisite values and calling SWI 16.

VARIABLES: Nil

ORG: $7D0B

7DOB	LDA A#12	$86$0C	
7D0D	SWI#16	$3F$10	\clear screen
7D0F	LDA A#80	$86 $50	
7D11	SWI #16	$3F$10	\Print "P".
7D13	LDA A#83	$86 $53	
7D15	SWI#16	$3F$10	\Print "S".
7D17	LDA A#73	$86$49	
7D19	SWI#16	$3F$10	\Print "I".
7D1B	LDA A#79	$86$4F	
7D1D	SWI#16	$3F$10	\Print "O".
7D1F	LDA A#78	$86$4E	
7D21	SWI#16	$3F$10	\Print"N".
7D23	RTS	$39	\All done.

10.7 You should be greeted with the word "PSION" at the top left of the screen. After a short pause, this will be replaced by the "ROUTINE DONE" message and the opportunity to run the routine again. All this is very well and good, but it does not help you actually talk to the Organiser. Suppose we wanted to ENTER the word PSION and to have it printed out as a complete string - how would we approach it? Well, the first thing to do is to identify the OS calls which are relevant to the problem. First, we need some way to enter the keypresses into the memory of the Organiser. We can do this by repeated calls to Vector 72 - GET KEY. This will place the ASCII value of the keypress into Accumulator B which we can then store in memory. When we have all five letters (sounds like a count of some sort to me), we must then print it as a string. This requires Vector 17 - PRINT A STRING. Here, we place the number of characters to be printed in Accumulator B and the start address of the string in the IX Register. Remember that you will have to place the number 5 in CHAR% and a suitable address (say, $7D34) in STORE% prior to running the program. The code looks like this:

```
PROGRAM NAME:   "GET PSION"

PURPOSE:        This program clears the screen and prints the word
                "PSION" by getting the word, letter by letter, from
                the keyboard. The address of the string storage
                space is held in STORE% and the number of
                characters to be printed in CHAR%.

VARIABLES:      $7D30        CHAR%
                $7D31        STORE%

ORG: $7D0B
  7DOB       LDA A#12        $86$0C
  7D0D       SWI#16          $3F$10        \clear screen.
  7DOF       LDA A #126      $86$7E
  7D11       SWI#16          $3F$10        \Print arrow.
  7D13       LDA A CHAR%     $B6$7D30      \Load number
                                           \of characters.
  7D16       LDX STORE%      $FE $7D31     \Load address
                                           \of store.
  7D19 loop.SWI#72           $3F$48        \Call Vector number 72.
  7D1B       STA B 0,X       $E7 $00       \Store char.
  7D1D       INX             $08           \Inc store.
```

```
7D1E    DEC A           $4A         \Dec count.
7D1F    CMP A#0         $81 $00     \=0?
7D21    BNE loop        $26 $F6     \No - loop.
7D23    LDA A#12        $86$0C
7D25    SWI #16         $3F $10     \Clear screen.
7D27    LDA B CHAR%     $F6 $7D30   \Get count.
7D2A    LDX STORE%      $FE $7D31   \Get store.
7D2D    SWI #17         $3F$11      \Call Vector number 17.
7D2F    RTS             $39         \All done.
```

10.8 What you should have seen was the screen clearing and the right arrow appearing at the top left of the screen to indicate that you should start typing. Notice that your key presses do NOT appear on the screen. If you want this, you will have to code it in at each iteration of the loop. You already know how to do this (remember Vector 16?). In addition, notice how you did not have to press EXE to enter the string. The word appeared as soon as the fifth character was entered. You could, of course, make it continue to accept characters UNTIL the EXE key was pressed. This would mean that you would have to test for the EXE key being pressed and to keep a count of the number of characters already stored in the STORE% buffer. This number would then be passed to the B Register when it came to printing the string. So you can see that you already know quite a bit and should be able to code some reasonably complex programs of your own.

CONCLUSION

10.9 In this chapter, we have looked at the Organiser OS and described how calls to the various facilities can be made. This chapter also brings to a close this entire book. I hope that it has brought you some way on the rocky road to machine code programming. The secret is to carefully check out your programming ON PAPER before entering it into the machine and running it. Even then, you should check it out first using the disassembler function of the Hexloader. Certainly you should save all your important information to disc or Datapack in case battery removal becomes necessary. If you have followed my instructions faithfully, such disasters will have been minimised but now you are on your own. Have fun, for that's what programming is all about.

POST TEST

1. What is the function of an Operating System?

2. How do we call a specific OS routine?

3. What is the Hexadecimal code for this instruction?

Annex A

Answers to Post Tests

A: Answers to Post Tests

Chapter 1

1. He developed a mechanical gear wheel calculator in the 17th century. (1.2)

2. Leibnitz improved upon the design to enable it to do multiplication and division. (1.2)

3. Clockwork toys and ornaments in vogue particularly in the 18th century.(1.3)

4. He developed a loom whose patterns were determined by punched holes in a series of cards - the first program, in effect.(1.3)

5. Charles Babbage.(1.4)

6. The military requirements of World War II.(1.5)

7. Colossus was a computer used to decrypt signals and ENIAC was employed in calculating ballistic trajectories.(1.5)

8. The invention of the transistor.(1.8)

9. Languages which are more like a subset of English than codes.(1.9)

10. FORTRAN..(1.9)

11. COBOL..(1.9)

Chapter 2

1. A computer on a single chip..(1.10)

2. Central Processing Unit. (2.17)

3. Doing simple arithmetic and controlling the other chips on the board.(2.1)

4. Read-Only Memory.(2.2)

5. FIRMWARE. (2.3)

6. Random Access Memory.(2.4)

7. They convert computer signals into a format which is of use in the outside world and vice versa.(2.7)

8. The Address Bus wakes up the chip required by the CPU and the Data Bus passes data to or takes data from the chip. (2.9,2.10)

9. 255.(2.10)

10. The Oscillator acts as a sort of metronome, keeping time so that all operations within the computer take place in a synchronized manner.

11. The Hitachi HD6303X.(2.13)

12. 192 bytes. (2.20)

13. Standby, Reset, Active, Halt and Sleep.(2.17)

14. Standby, Active and Sleep. In Standby, the machine is under power but switched off. In Active, everything is up and running. In Sleep, the processor ticks over but everything else is dozing to reduce power consumption. (2.17)

15. It acts as a central clearing house and as a time keeper. (2.19)

Chapter 3

1. Decimal, or Base 10. (3.0)

2. Base 2. (3.3)

3.

a. 10000000	b. 11100000	c. 00100010	d. 0011001
e. 01000001	f. 01100101	g. 11001010	h. 11000011
i. 01001101	j. 10000100	k. 11001000	l. 11110000

4.

a. 76	b. 211	c. 45	d. 241
e. 170	f. 85	g. 227	h. 126
i. 129	j. 94	k. 254	l. 127

5. a. 11010111 b. 00101011 c. 11111110 d. 11111011

6. A method by which 2 binary numbers can be subtracted. All the ones and naughts of the number to be subtracted are reversed and the number one is then added to this. The resulting Two's Complement number is added to the number to be subtracted FROM and the result is a subtraction.(3.9)

7. a. 10101001 b. 01101001 c. 11111000 d. 00001011

8. We are only human - mistakes would be made. (3.10)

9. Base 16. (3.10)

10.

a. 80	b. E0	c. 18	d. 32
e. 41	f. 41	g. CA	h. C3
i. 4D	j. 84	k. C8	l. F0

a.4C	b. D3	c. 2D	d. F1
e.AA	f. 55	g. E3	h. 7E
i. 81	j. 5E	k. FE	l. 7F

Chapter 4

1. Speed and Flexibility. (4.4)

2. Bad machine code routines can cause the Organiser to freeze, forcing the user to remove the battery. This would lose all the diary records etc. This can be circumvented by saving all valuable data to Datapack or disc before using any machine code programs. (4.5)

3. Moving the base of the Language Stack to make room for the machine code.(4.7)

4. The *Operator* is the actual coded instruction in machine code. (4.8)

5. The *Operand* is the data on which an operator will work.(4.8)

6. *Assembly language* is a one-to-one correspondence of mnemonics to machine code instructions. These mnemonics make the machine code easier to learn e.g. RTS instead of $39. (4.10)

7. Two eight-bit Registers A and B for arithmetic, 16- bit Register D produced by combining A and B for double-precision arithmetic, 16-bit register IX for addresses, a 16-bit stack pointer (SP), a 16-bit program counter (PC) to hold the address of the current instruction and an 8-bit condition code register (CCR) which holds various status flags. (4.13)

Chapter 5

1. We select an appropriate memory location and use this to hold the data. (5.2)

2. LDA A . (5.6)

3. Stores the contents of Accumulator A in a specified location. (5.7)

4. It can handle 16-bit numbers. Accumulators A and B can only deal with 8-bit numbers. (5.18)

5. $FC. (Annex E)

6. $DD. (Annex E)

Chapter 6

1. ADC A. (6.4)

2. Accumulator D. (6.11)

3. ADD D. (6.11)

4. Signifies if there is an arithmetic carry from a previous calculation to be added in. (6.11)

5. Signifies if a carry from a previous calculation should be subtracted.

6. The ADD D operation does not take any carry from a previous operation into consideration. (6.17)

7. ADC A includes any carry, whereas ADD A ignores it. (6.4)

Chapter 7

1. The Condition Code Register (CCR). (7.4)

2. As per 7.4 a-d. (7.4)

3. If, say, 13 was to be compared, the code would be CMP A #13.(7.6)

4. Relative Addressing involves specifying the size and direction of a jump from the current location in the program on the result of a comparison. (7.5)

5. As per 7.5 a-q. (7.5)

6. The CPU takes the relative jump specified and adds 2 to this number. It then works out where in memory this point is located and carries on execution from that point. (7.6)

7. BNE -25. (7.6)

Chapter 8

1. The IX Register. (8.2)

2. The stack is a data structure where all the items are added to and removed from one end like the plates on a spring loaded warmer. (8.5)

3. Pushing an item onto the stack. (8.8)

4. Popping an item off the stack. (8.8)

5. a. PUL B. b. PULX. (Annex E)

6. a. PSH B b. PSHX. (Annex E)

Chapter 9

1. JSR. (9.2)

2. RTS. (9.3)

3. To encourage modularity of design. This makes the program easier to understand and subsequently modify. It also makes for economical code, where a single sub- routine can be used by many other programs. (9.0)

4. Parameters can either be stacked prior to calling the routine (not recommended) or by placing the data items in memory locations. (9.5)

Chapter 10

1. The Operating System is responsible for maintaining the smooth running of all functions, maintaining time and providing a kernel of faciiities and routines which the programmer can use. (10.1)

2. By executing a Software Interrupt to a specified Vector Number. (10.2)

3. $3F.(10.2)

Annex B

Number Bases Test Program

B: Number Bases Test Program

B.1 This suite of programs allows the user to test out his arithmetic in four different number bases - BINARY, OCTAL, DECIMAL and HEXADECIMAL. It will allow addition, subtraction and the facility to change number base.

B.2 The suite consists of 3 programs:

a. TEST:

b. INTOBASE:

c. FROMBASE:

Enter each and translate them one at a time.

B.3 To use the program, enter the PROG menu and RUN TEST. Alternatively, put TEST in the high-level Organiser menu. This will allow you to select it immediately, without typing. The user is presented with the menu:

```
add     subtract
convert new-base
quit
```

The default base is hexadecimal. To change the base select the new-base option. This will give a second menu:

```
binary   octal
decimal    hex
```

Simply select the base required using either the arrow keys or pressing the first letter of the base.

B.4 To make an addition or subtraction, select the appropriate option from the first menu. The user will be asked for the first and then the second number. The user must enter these and, after a short pause, the answer will appear in the selected base. To convert a number from one base to another, select Convert from the top menu. This will ask the user to enter the number to be converted. This is followed by a request to enter the current base of the number and then the base the user wants the number to be displayed in. After a short pause the number in its new base is displayed on the screen. Pressing any key will return the user to the top menu. Pressing any key will return the user to the first menu. this continues until QUIT is selected.
TEST:

```
GLOBAL
number$(16),convert$(16),number,m1%,m2%,base1,base2,width%,num1,
num2,num1$(8),num2$(8),answer

number$="0123456789ABCDEF"
base1=16.0
width%=4

DO
CLS
m1%=MENU("ADD,SUBTRACT,CONVERT,NEW-BASE,QUIT")

IF m1%=1 OR m1%=2
CLS
PRINT"1st : ";
INPUT num1$
PRINT"2nd : ";
INPUT num2$
FROMBASE:(num1$,base1)
num1=number
FROMBASE:(num2$,base1)
num2=number

IF m1%=1
number=num1+num2
ELSEIF m1%=2
```

```
number=num1-num2
ENDIF

CLS
INTOBASE:(base1,width%*2)
PRINT"ANSWER:"
PRINT convert$;
GET
ELSEIF m1%=3
CLS
PRINT"Number: "
INPUT num1$
CLS
PRINT"PRESS KEY TO"
PRINT"SELECT BASE1"
GET
CLS
m2%=MENU("BINARY,OCTAL,DECIMAL,HEX")
IF m2%=1
base1=2.0
width%=8
ELSEIF m2%=2
base1=8.0
width%=3
ELSEIF m2%=3
base1=10.0
width%=3
ELSEIF m2%=4
base1=16.0
width%=4
ENDIF
FROMBASE:(num1$,base1)
CLS
PRINT"PRESS KEY TO"
PRINT"SELECT BASE2"
GET
CLS
m2%=MENU("BINARY,OCTAL,DECIMAL,HEX")
IF m2%=1
```

```
base2=2.0
width%=8
ELSEIF m2%=2
base2=8.0
width%=3
ELSEIF m2%=3
base2=10.0
width%=3
ELSEIF m2%=4
base2=16.0
width%=4
ENDIF
INTOBASE:(base2,width%)
CLS
PRINT"ANSWER:"
PRINT convert$;
GET

ELSEIF m1%=4
CLS
m2%=MENU("BINARY,OCTAL,DECIMAL,HEX")
IF m2%=1
base1=2.0
width%=8
ELSEIF m2%=2
base1=8.0
width%=3
ELSEIF m2%=3
base1=10.0
width%=3
ELSEIF m2%=4
base1=16.0
width%=4
ENDIF
ENDIF
UNTIL m1%=5
RETURN
```

```
INTOBASE:(b,w%)
LOCAL temp
convert$=""
DO
temp=number
number=INTF(number/b)
temp=temp-number*b
convert$=MID$(number$,temp+1,1)+convert$
UNTIL number<1
convert$=REPT$("0",w%-LEN(convert$))+convert$
RETURN
```

```
FROMBASE:(convert$,base)
LOCAL power%
power%=0 :number=0
DO
number=number+(LOC(number$,MID$(convert$,LEN(convert$)-
power%,1))-1)*(base**(power%))
power%=power%+1
UNTIL power%=LEN(convert$)
number=INTF(number+0.5)
RETURN
```

Annex C

Memory Map

C: Memory Map

$FFFF	System ROM
$8000	Not Used (except LA/OS)
$8000 $6000 $4000 LA/OS XP/OS CM/OS $7F00 $5F00 $3F00	Processor Stack
	Language Stack (grows down) (grows up) Allocated Cells
$2000I	System Variables
$0400I	Not Used (except LA/OS)
$0100-I	Hardware Addresses
$00E0	Transient Application Area
$0040I $0020	System Variables I
$0000-I	Internal Registers

THE CPU RAM

C.1 The following memory locations are shown with their corresponding descriptions and their Read/Write attribute. Note that OPL forbids the use of PEEKs or POKEs affecting locations $00-3F.

INTERNAL CPU RAM ADDRESSES

$01	Port 2 data direction register	W
$02	Port 1	R/W
$03	Port 2	R/W
$04	Port 3 data direction register	W
$05	Not used	
$06	Port 3	R/W
$07	Port 4	R/W
$08	Timer Control/Status	R/W
$09	Free running counter - high	R/W
$0A	Free running counter - low	R/W
$0B	Output compare register - high	R/W
$0C	Output compare register - low	R/W
$0D	Input capture register - high	R
$0E	Input capture register - low	R
$0F	Timer control/Status register 2	R/W
$10	Rate, mode control register	R/W
$11	Tx/Rx control status register	R/W
$12	Receive data register	R
$13	Transmit data register	W
$14	RAM/Port 5 control register	R/W
$15	Port 5	R
$16	Port 6 data direction register	W
$17	Port 6	R/W
$18	Port 7	R/W
$19	Output compare register - high	R/W
$1A	Output compare register - low	R/W
$1B	Timer control/Status register 2	R/W
$1C	Timer constant register	W
$1D	Timer 2 Up counter	R/W
$1E	Not used	-
$1F	Test register (do not use)	-
$20-$3F	Not used	-

ZERO PAGE LOCATIONS OUTSIDE THE CPU

C.2 Zero Page RAM extends from $00 to $FF. Using Zero Page locations speeds up program operation since the addresses consist of a single byte. Users should note, however, that the Operating System uses $40-$DF and the Transient Application goes from $E0 to $FF. These locations are unsafe for the User unless he knows exactly what he is doing!!!

MAIN MEMORY ZERO PAGE LOCATIONS

$40	JMP instruction for vector in UTW_S0
$41	General Word Variable (GWV) 0
$43	GWV 1
$45	GWV 2 [These scratch registers can be used
$47	GWV 3 but their contents could be trashed
$49	GWV 4 by OS calls.]
$4B	GWV 5
$4D	General Word/Byte Variable (GWBV) 0
$4F	GWBV 1
$51	GWBV 2 [The contents of these variables must
$53	GWBV 3 be maintained. To use them for other
$55	GWBV 4 purposes, first PUSH the old values
$57	GWBV 5 and restore them afterwards.]
$59	GWBV 6
$5B	NMI flag, cleared when NMI executes
$5C	Time (in seconds) before auto switch off
$5E	Address of RAMTOP
$60	Run time low battery flag
$61	Reserved
$62	Cursor position (0-31 for Organiser. II or LZ in 2-line mode and
0-79	for 4-line mode LZ)
$63	Cursor status byte
$64	Scrolling line position
$65	Number of characters to scroll
$66	Scroll direction
$67	Save cursor position, used in DP_SAVE
$68	Save cursor status, used in DP_SAVE
$69	Delay when scrolling in ticks (default 4)
$6B	Delay before scrolling in ticks (default 10)
$6D	'Ready to display' timer in ticks [Decremented by one on each keyboard interrupt until its value = 0. Vector 108 uses this variable to time delays]

$6F	Address of scrolling string
$71	Keyboard polling time [Controls the frequency of keyboard interrupts. Default is $B3DD =0.05 secs. If this variable is cleared, lock-up will occur]
$73	Offset in KBT_BUFF to oldest key in buffer
$74	Number of keys in buffer
$75	Previous key pressed
$76	Unget key, zero if no key else the key
$77	Delay before auto-repeating in ticks [Delay before keyboard auto-repeat. Default is 14 = 0.7 sec]
$78	Delay on auto-repeat in ticks [Delay between keys during auto-repeat. Default is 0 which is fastest. A value of 1 gives half normal speed, 2 gives one third and so on]
$79	Keyboard counter
$7A	Offset into keyboard table
$7B	CAPS, NUM and SHIFT lock status [Bit 7 set if SHIFT key pressed, bit 6 for NUM LOCK, 1 for CAP or NUM key and 0 for LOWER CASE LOCK]
$7C	Auto-switch off flag, set for auto-switch off
$7D	Time left in seconds before auto-switch off
$7F	Maximum input length
$80	Prompt length
$81	First editable line
$82	First editable character in first line
$83	Current line edit
$84	Editor cursor status
$85	Current position within line
$87	Offset to current line
$89	Total buffer length
$8B	Pack being looked at
$8C	Actual current pack
$8D	Length of RAM file
$8F	Offset into RAM file
$91	High order byte of pack address
$92	Pack address
$94	Pointer to current pack identifier
$96	Current record type
$97	Current pack

$98	Device being DIR-ed
$99	Next directory record number
$9B	Current record number
$9D	Address of file name
$9F	Number of records
$A1	Current record type
$A2	Current default pack (0-2)
$A3	Which option: FIND, SAVE or ERASE
$A4	Non-zero to mute buzzer
$A5	Run time stack pointer
$A7	Run time frame pointer
$A9	Run time program counter
$AB	Current line being edited
$AD	Current character pointer
$AF	Previous token
$B0	Array index
$B2	Maximum string size
$B4	Pointer to variable
$B6	Temporary constants
$B8	Global O code size
$BA	Current free O code bytes
$BC	Total O code size
$BE	Structure next level
$BF	Next new label number
$C1	General language word
$C3	General language word
$C5	Accumulator : mantissa
$CC	Accumulator : exponent
$CD	Accumulator : sign
$CE	Operand : mantissa
$D5	Operand : exponent
$D6	Operand : sign
$D7	Table program counter
$D9	Table base
$DB	Table stack pointer
$DD	Table flag
$DE	General pointer
$E0 - $F7	Transient application area
$F8 - $FF	Transient application area, trashed on WARM BOOT

OVERLAYS

C.3 The usage of the locations shown in the above table represents their main function. However, to make the most use of available memory, the Organiser doubles up some of the functions of specific locations by allowing other routines to employ them.
This is known as "overlaying against". The following addresses, then, are also used by the indicated facilities.

DIARY VARIABLES

$C5	Year
$C6	Month
$C7	Day
$C8	Hour
$C9	Mins

___ ___ ___ ___ ___

ALARM VARIABLES

$C5-$CB Alarm temporary area

___ ___ ___ ___ ___

RUN TIME VARIABLES

$B0	Escape flag
$B1	Current logical name
$B2	Trap flag
$B3	Current error condition
$B4	Carriage return flag
$B5	Device of top procedure
$B6	General word variables
$B8	
$BA	
$BC	
$BE	
$C0	
$C2	

___ ___ ___ ___ ___

THE SEMI-CUSTOM CHIP

C.4 The Semi-Custom Chip addresses run from $180 to $3FF and, like addresses $00-$3F, OPL will not allow PEEKing or POKEing in this area. This is because the mere act of PEEKing into a location in this area could have unforeseen consequences for the unwary User.

____ ____ ____ ____ ____

SEMI-CUSTOM CHIP ADDRESSES

$0180	Liquid Crystal Display (LCD) control register
$0181	LCD data register
$01C0	Switch off
$0200	Pulse enable
$0240	Pulse disable
$0280	Buzzer on
$02C0	Buzzer off
$0300	keyboard + clock counter reset [used to set all counter lines to zero]
$0340	keyboard+ clock counter - clock once [increments counter address by one]
$0380	Enable NMI to processor
$03C0	Enable NMI to counter
$360	Reset ROM/RAM to bank 0 (LZ)
$3E0	Select next ROM bank (LZ)
$3A0	Select next RAM bank (LZ)

SYSTEM VARIABLES

C.5 The system variables which appear below are guaranteed by PSION to remain correct on all versions above 2.4.

SYSTEM VARIABLES

$2000	Permanent cell
$2002	Top level menu cell
$2004	Diary cell
$2006	Language text cell
$2008	Symbol table cell
$200A	Global record cell
$200C	QCODE output cell
$200E	Field name symbol table 1

$2010	Field name symbol table 2
$2012	Field name symbol table 3
$2014	Field name symbol table 4
$2016	File buffer 1
$2018	File buffer 2
$201A	File buffer 3
$201C	File buffer 4
$201E	Database cell
$2020 - $203E	16 free cells for use by applications
$2040	Top of allocator area
$2042	IRQ2 re-vector address
$2044	CMI re-vector address
$2046	TRAP re-vector address
$2048	SIO re-vector address
$204A	TOI re-vector address
$204C	OCI re-vector address
$204E	ICI re-vector address
$2050	IRQ1 re-vector address
$2052	SWI re-vector address
$2054	NMI re-vector address
$2056	WRM re-vector address
$2058	SWOF re-vector address
$205A	Keyboard poll routine [Points to routine which polls the keyboard and returns the key pressed in the A Register]
$205C	Keyboard translate routine [Points to routine which translates the key number held in the A Register into an ASCII character by using the lookup table.]
$205E	Address of keyboard lookup table [Points to a table of 72 characters representing the ASCII versions of the key number. The user can change this to point to his own table. Such a table must contain 72 items unless SHIFT has been disabled.]
$2060	Frame pointer for ENTER/LEAVE
$2062	Flag to ignore an NMI
$2063	Save interrupt mask while off
$2064	Save TCSR1 while off
$2065	Language stack base

$2067	Save stack pointer while off
$2069	Used in SWI's only
$206B	Used in SWI's only
$206D	Used in SWI's only
$206F	Used in SWI's only
$2070	Top line screen buffer
$2080	Bottom line screen buffer
$2090	Temporary area to save screen
$2092	Number of screen lines (LZ)
$2093	Width of screen (LZ)
$2095	Position of clock on screen (LZ)
$2096	"Clock ready" flag (LZ)
$2099	Border character (LZ)
$209C	"Capitalise menu" flag (LZ)
$20A6	"Daylight saving time" flag (BIT 7) and "24/12 hour flag" (BIT 0) (LZ)
$20A7	Flags to indicate which days of the week are workdays (LZ)
$20A9-$20AB	Addresses of 3 bytes separating the "WEEK VIEW" slots (LZ)
$20AC	"Alarm Prompt" flag (LZ)
$20B0	Type ahead buffer
$20C0	Length of keyboard click [This is the length, in milliseconds, of the keyboard click. The default is 1 but to disable the click entirely, zero should be entered into this variable]
$20C1	Set for pack switch off [This controls whether the packs should be switched off when the keyboard is tested and the buffer is empty.]
$20C2	Caps key [This contains the number of the key which the user wishes to be employed as the CAPS LOCK key. By default it is the UP ARROW key but it can be any of the 36 keys available. To disable CAPS LOCK completely, this variable should b set to any number over 36]
$20C3	Nums key [This works in the same way as the CAPS KEY variable.]

$20C4	Shift key, clear to enable shift key [If this byte is set, the SHIFT key will be disabled and the key will return the "?" symbol.]
$20C5	Current year 0-99
$20C6	Current month 0-11
$20C7	Current day 0-31
$20C8	Current hour 0-23
$20C9	Current minute 0-59
$20CA	Current seconds 0-59
$20CB	Frame counter [This variable is incremented by one on each keyboard interrupt. Maximum value=$FFFF and wraps back to 0.]
$20CD	The auto-switch off time out in seconds
$20CF	Temporary buffer, used in UT_DISP
$20D6	Save interrupt mask while blowing
$20D7	4 pack ID headers, 10 bytes each
$20FF	10 memory slots for calculator (each 8 long)
$214F	$38 byte reserved for I/O drivers
$2184	Mode flag (2-line/4-line)
$2185	"Special keys" flag (LZ)
$2186	"Language in use" flag (LZ)
$2187	Run time buffer length
$2188	Run time buffer ($100 long)
$2288	General purpose buffer for maths + overflow
$22C8	FIND buffer length
$22C9	FIND buffer
$22E9	4 file control blocks (each $04 long)
$22F9	Alarm table, 6 bytes per alarm
$2329	LA/OS only :lowest addr used in low RAM
$232B	LA/OS only : highest addr ... ...
$232E	Flag to enable/disable language selection and second boot (BITS 7 and 0 respectively)
$232D	$2324 reserved to PSION
$2335	If set then alarm checking is enabled
$2336	Temporary variable used checking for alarms
$233C	Temporary variable used checking for alarms
$2342	Temporary variable used checking for alarms
$2348	Temporary variable used checking for alarms
$234A	If set then does alarm check on next interrupt
$234B	Table user vector
$236D	Table stack

$23AD	Saved sign
$23AE	Random number seed
$23B5	Q code offset to stop at
$23B7	External O code size
$23B9	Global & local data sizes
$23BD	Declared variables count
$23C1	Current branch label number
$23C9	Symbol table data pointer
$23CD	End of text pointer
$23CF	Start of current token
$23D1	Saved token for un-lex
$23D2	Saved class for un-lex
$23D3	Function type
$23D4	Decimal places in calculator display
$23D5	Last procedure name length
$23D6	Last procedure name
$23E0	Language type
$23E1	Set to ignore TRAN option after editing
$23E2	Extension O code operator code
$23E4	Return address used in UT_DDSP
$23E6	Overblow factor
$23E7	Vector to vector table
$25DC	Length of paste buffer (LZ)
$25DD	Paste Buffer (LZ)
$7FEA	Editor flags (LZ)
$7FEB	Notepad "Password/No Password" flag (LZ)
$7FEC	Password (LZ)
$7FFD	Number of lines in current notepad (LZ)
$7FFF	Cursor position in current notepad (LZ)
$FFE7	Language byte: $00=English; $01=French; $02=German; $80=11 languages English default $81= English, French, German If BIT 7 is set, indicates multi-lingual machine. This byte shows which languages are *included* in the machine. For indication of which one is *running*, see $2186
$FFE8	Model Byte 1: Bottom 3 BITS = Base model type. This identifies ROM/RAM configuration and Operating System.

Top 5 BITS = Special model type, i.e.:

Value	Model	RAM size	PROM size
0	CM	8K	32K
1	XP(16)	16K	32K
2	XP	32K	32K
5	LP	64K	64K
6	LZ	32K	64K
7	–JUMP TO MODEL BYE 2–		

If Base model type is "7", base model type is given by bottom 3 BITS of Model byte 2. If BIT 3 of Special model type is set, Special model type will be indicated by the top 5 BITS of Model byte 2.

$FFC9 Model byte 2.
Split in the same way as Model byte 1. If BIT 7 is set it indicates a "Lizzie". BIT 6 set indicates a "foreign character" LCD. BITS 3-5 are for extra-special types and the bottom 3 BITS are reserved for future base model types.

$FFE9 Version number.

OVERLAYED AGAINST MATHS AND OVERFLOW BUFFER

$2288 Copy of current time when checking alarms
$228E Time one week from now.

ALLOCATOR CELLS

C.6 An Allocator Cell is a dynamic area of memory reserved for a particular purpose. There are 32 permitted cells the first 16 of which are already used by the Operating System (See $2000-$201E).

C.7 Each cell is identified by a single word which is pointed to by a tag. If the cell has been allocated, this word will point to the cell. Otherwise, it is zero. The size of the cell can be set by using the appropriate OS vector (See Vectors 000-006). Note that the cell can be "grown" or "shrunk" at any time throughout its life. When this occurs, all cells above it move up or down in memory, altering their base addresses. Not only does this mean that the user must recalculate the location of his data in any particular cell if he feels something might have moved it, but frequent expansion and contraction can slow down an application program drastically.

Annex D

The Hitachi HD6303X Microcomputer Unit (MCU)

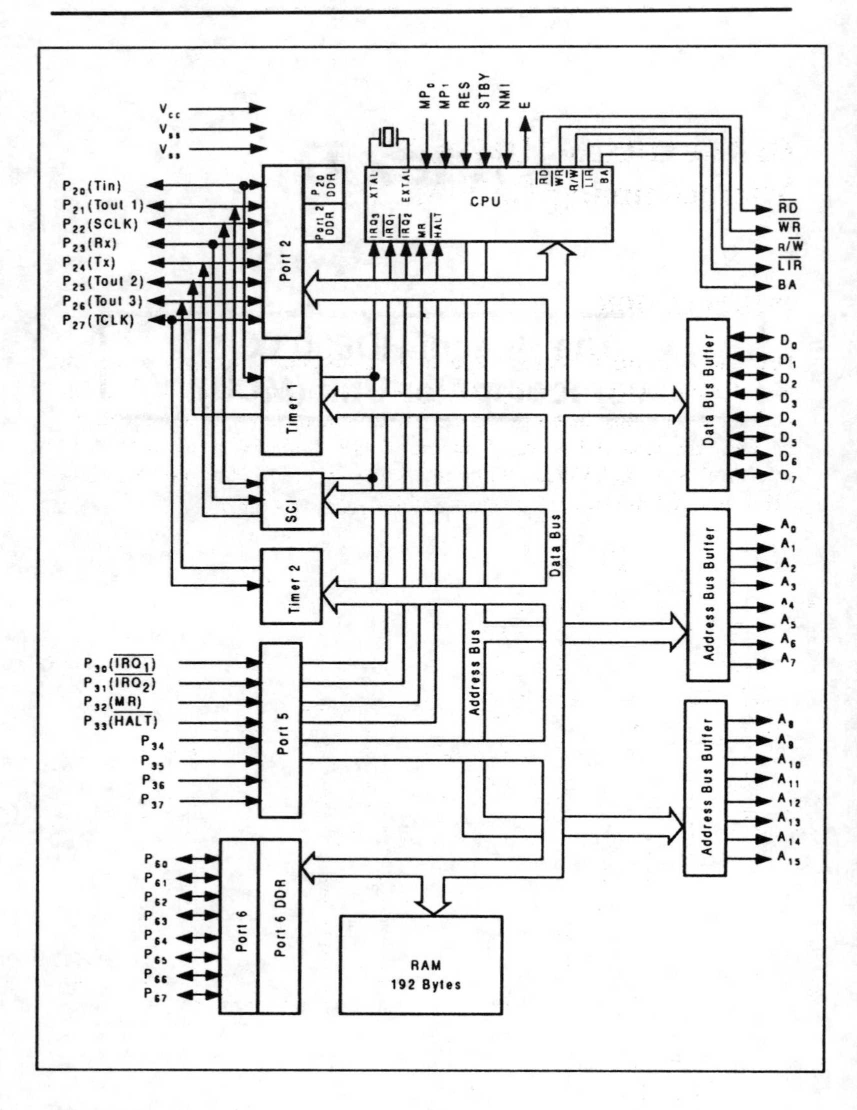

Vcc
Vss
Vss
MP0
MP1
RES
STBY
NMI
E
XTAL
EXTAL
CPU
RD
WR
R/W
LIR
BA
IRQ3
IRQ1
IRQ2
MR
HALT
P20(Tin)
P21(Tout 1)
P22(SCLK)
P23(Rx)
P24(Tx)
P25(Tout 2)
P26(Tout 3)
P27(TCLK)
Port 2
P20 DDR
Port 2 DDR
Timer 1
SCI
Timer 2
Data Bus
Address Bus
Data Bus Buffer
D0
D1
D2
D3
D4
D5
D6
D7
Address Bus Buffer
A0
A1
A2
A3
A4
A5
A6
A7
Address Bus Buffer
A8
A9
A10
A11
A12
A13
A14
A15
P30(IRQ1)
P31(IRQ2)
P32(MR)
P33(HALT)
P34
P35
P36
P37
Port 5
P60
P61
P62
P63
P64
P65
P66
P67
Port 6
Port 6 DDR
RAM
192 Bytes

Diagram 1

D: The Hitachi HD6303X Microcomputer Unit (MCU)

INTRODUCTION

D.1 The HD6303X microcomputer from Hitachi is exactly what the manufacturers claim - a complete computer on a single chip. In common with its sister chips the 6301 and 63701, it contains not only a powerful 8-bit CPU but also 192 bytes of internal RAM, 2 timers, a Serial Comms Interface (SCI) and 53 parallel lines. Moreover, the 6301 and 63701 have 4K of internal ROM, user- programmable in the latter case.

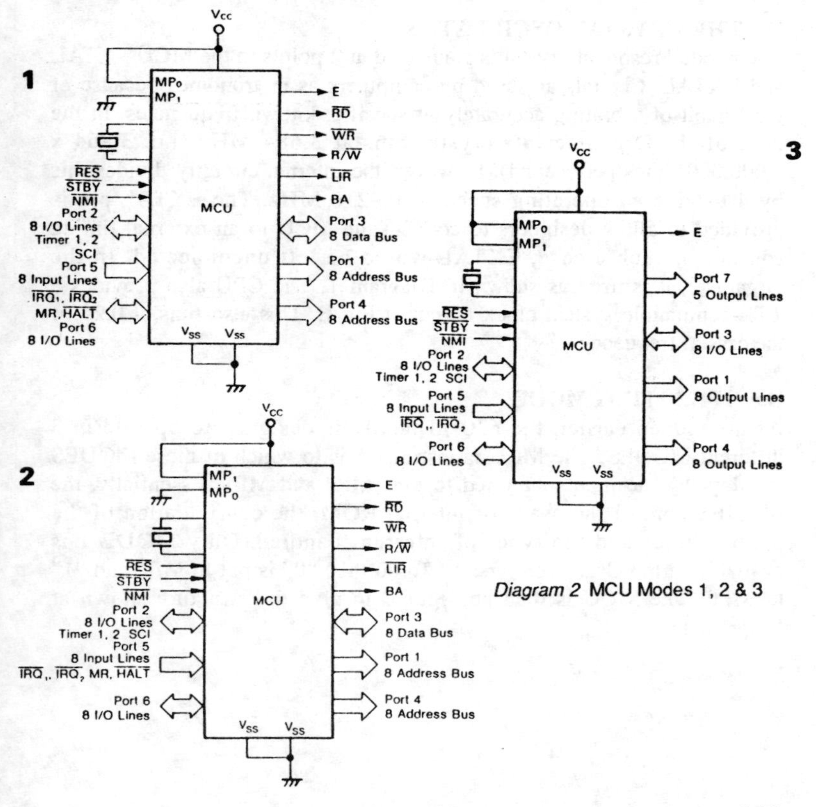

Diagram 2 MCU Modes 1, 2 & 3

D.2 The MPU is designed to work in 3 different configurations. However, only one of these is pertinent to the Organiser application - MODE 1 - and so I will disregard the others. Nevertheless, readers who wish a deeper description than the one offered here should consult the HITACHI 6301/3 FAMILY USER'S MANUAL and the REFERENCE MANUAL. Diagram 1 (courtesy of HITACHI) shows a schematic representation of the internal architecture of the 6303X in MODE 1. The inserts which feature alongside the following functional descriptions relate to the relevant pins in the physical packaging of the chip.

D.3 POWER

Although Diagram 1 shows only 2 types of power connections, shown by the "V", there are in fact 3 points. Vcc receives +5V, plus or minus 10%, Vss is connected to earth, and Vpp collects 21V plus or minus half a volt. This last point is used to program the internal ROM when fitted. Since this is missing in the version used by the Organiser, I will not discuss it further.

D.4 THE CRYSTAL OSCILLATOR

The parallel resonant crystal is connected at 2 points to the MCU - XTAL and EXTAL. Crystals are used by computers as metronomes because of their habit of vibrating accurately at specific, known frequencies. In the case of the Organiser, its crystal runs at 3.684 MHz (i.e. 3.864 x 1,000,000 times per second). However, the internal circuitry divides this by 4 to give an operating speed of 0.9216 MHz. The EXTAL pin is provided to allow designers to connect the MCU to an external timing source. In such a case, EXTAL would be left unconnected. In the Organiser, it is used as shown in Diagram 1. The CPU also provides a TTL-compatible system clock output at Pin E. This also runs at 0.25 of the crystal frequency.

D.5 OPERATING MODE

As mentioned earlier, the 6301/3 family is designed to operate in 3 different MODES. The MCU is instructed as to which of these MODES to adopt by the inputs supplied to pins MP0 and MP1. Essentially, the MODES control the usage of internal ROM, the configuration of the parallel lines and the types of interrupt handled. Only MODE 1 is available in the Organiser version. To do this, "0" is put to MP1 and "1" to MP0. The MCU is then configured to give the structure shown at Diagram 1.

D.6 RESETTING THE MCU

The RES pin is used to reset the internal circuitry of the MCU. Note that when a function is activated on a "0" being supplied to the appropriate pin, it is referred to as being "Active Low". If this is so, the pin mnemonic (RES in this instance) is written with an overscore. Functions which are active high are written without any distinguishing marks.

D.7 STANDBY MODE

Standby Mode is activated by the STNBY pin. All clocks are stopped but power to internal RAM is sustained to allow memory retention. Power consumption in this state is greatly reduced due to the fact that nearly all lines are electronically detached from the CPU. Note that if this pin is active when MP0 and MP1 are both low, the MCU enters its PROM Mode. This allows users of the 63701 to program its internal ROM.

D.8 INTERRUPTS

There are a number of ways in which to interrupt the normal operation of the MCU. These can be hardware or software originated but in either case, the MCU completes the instruction it is currently executing before saving the contents of the Program Counter (PC), Index Register (IR), Accumulators and Condition Code Register (CCR) onto the stack. According to the type of interrupt, the MCU will then branch to a specific location (more properly referred to as a "Vector"), JUMP to the address held at the vector location and begin executing the code found at that location. However, if the Interrupt Mask Bit (IMB) of the CCR is set to "1", no interrupts - with the single exception of the Non-Maskable Interrupt (NMI), which by its name shows that it cannot be ignored - will be serviced. Moreover, if an interrupt IS accepted, the MCU will set the IMB to prevent further interruption. On completion of an interrupt routine, the IMB is cleared.

D.9 The external pins IRQ1 and IRQ2 also double up as lines of PORT 5. Which identity they adopt at any specific instance is determined by the data held in the PORT 5 Control Register, which I will explain soon. In addition, there is a third IRQ. This is activated when an interrupt INTERNAL to the MCU is generated (ICI, OCI, TOI, CMI or SOI). It functions in exactly the same way as IRQs 1 and 2 except that the vector is different.

D.10 Table 1 shows the vectors used by the various interrupts and the priorities accorded to them by the MCU:

VECTOR LOCATION

PRIORITY	*MSB*	*LSB*	*TYPE*
1.	$FFFE	$FFFF	RES
2.	$FFEE	$FFEF	TRAP
3.	$FFFC	$FFFD	NMI
4.	$FFFA	$FFFB	SOFTWARE INTERRUPT (SWI)
5.	$FFF8	$FFF9	IRQ 1
6.	$FFF6	$FFF7	TIMER 1 INPUT CAPTURE (ICI)
7.	$FFF4	$FFF5	TIMER 1 OUTPUT COMPARE (OCI)
8.	$FFF2	$FFF3	TIMER 1 OVERFLOW (TOI)
9.	$FFEC	$FFED	TIMER 2 COUNTER MATCH (CMI)
10.	$FFEA	$FFEB	IRQ 2
11.	$FFF0	$FFF1	SERIAL INTERFACE (SIO)

D.11 READING AND WRITING

The RD and WR outputs are powered to TTL levels and are used to enable the MCU to converse with peripherals using such inputs. The R/W, on the other hand, informs peripherals whether the MCU is in its READ or WRITE state. Normally, this output is set to high i.e. in the READ state.

D.12 INSTRUCTIONS

The Load Instruction Register, or LIR output, informs the Organiser circuit that an instruction opcode is on the data bus.

D.13 BUS AVAILABLE (BA)

The BA output, normally low, is set to high when the MCU releases the busses on accepting a HALT command.

D.14 DATA BUS

Lines D0-D7 in Diagram 1 represent the MCU's 8-bit, bi- directional Data Bus. The direction in force at any particular instant is controlled by the Data Direction Register (DDR), located at $0004. If Bit 0 of the DDR is clear, the bus is configured for output, whereas a "1" will cause the bus to become input.Note that the DDRs are write-only and that instructions such as AIM, OIM and EIM (ANDing, ORing or Exclusive-ORing their contents) cannot be applied to them. DDRs are cleared during RESET.

D.15 ADDRESS BUS

Lines A0-A15 in Diagram 1 make up the Organiser's Address Bus. Bits A0-A7 (the LSB of any address held on the Bus) are regarded by the MCU as PORT 1 and it will place any data for the PORT into the output register at $0002. Bits A8-A15 (the MSB) exit from PORT 4. The appropriate data register is located at $0007 and its operation is as for PORT 1. Note that the MCU, in the MODE used by the Organiser, regards the 2 PORTS as a 16-bit output buffer and that the MCU can internally read both data registers for bit- manipulation purposes.

D.16 INTERNAL RAM

The HD6303X contains 32 bytes of internal RAM from $0000-$001F and a further 192 bytes from $0040-$00FF. Internal registers are held in the first block and the second is used by the Organiser for zero-page processing. The latter has the advantage of speed and efficiency. Readers should consult Annex C for a more detailed examination of the Organiser Memory Map.

D.17 PORT 6

The PORT 6 I/O buffer is made up from lines P60-P67 in Diagram 1. The data register for the PORT is located at $0017 and its DDR (since it is bi-directional) at $0016 Note that each bit in the DDR byte corresponds to the data direction of the respective lines in the PORT (0=output and 1=input).

D.18 PORT 5

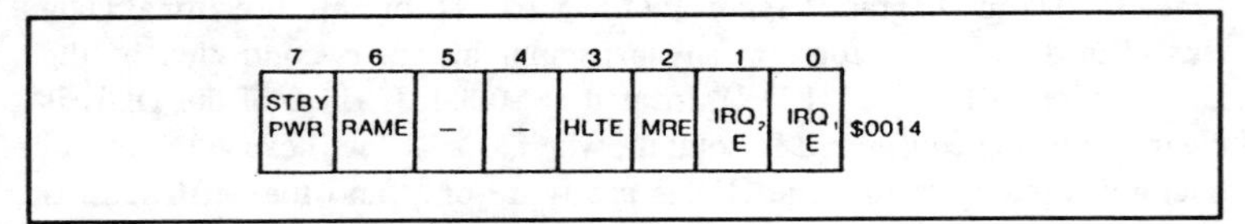

Diagram 3 RAM/Port 5 Control Register

The input-only PORT 5 is supplied by lines P50-P57. In addition, lines P50-P53 double as IRQs 1 and 2, Memory Ready (MR) and HALT. The MR input affects the MCU's speed of operation to allow it to access low-speed peripherals. HALT forces the MCU to complete its current instruction, stop and release the buses, whereupon it sets BA to high and completes a number of other operations. Should an interrupt occur at this time, the MCU will cancel the HALT and service the interrupt. IRQs have already been covered.

D.19 The PORT 5 Control Register, which also affects internal RAM, is located at $0014. It is used as follows:

a. IRQ Enable. Lines P50 and P51 become IRQ 1 and IRQ 2, respectively, when bits 0 and 1 of the Control Register are set. If these bits are cleared, the MCU will disregard external interrupts.

b. MEMORY READ ENABLE (MRE). Line P52 becomes MRE when bit 2 of the Register is set. RESET causes MRE to be initialised to 1.

c. HALT ENABLE (HLTE). When set to 1, bit 3 forces P53 to become the HALT input. HLTE is also initialised to 1 after RESET.

d. RAM ENABLE (RAME). Internal RAM is disabled when bit 6 is cleared. This allows the MCU to access external memory in the range $0040-$00FF. After RESET, RAME is set to allow internal RAM to be used. To protect the contents of internal RAM if the user intends to call Standby MODE, RAME should first be cleared.

e. STANDBY POWER. When power is not supplied in Standby MODE, bit 7 is cleared. If, after setting it prior to calling Standby, it remains 1 on return - power has been maintained to internal RAM and the user can be confident of the integrity of on-chip data.

D.20 TIMER 2

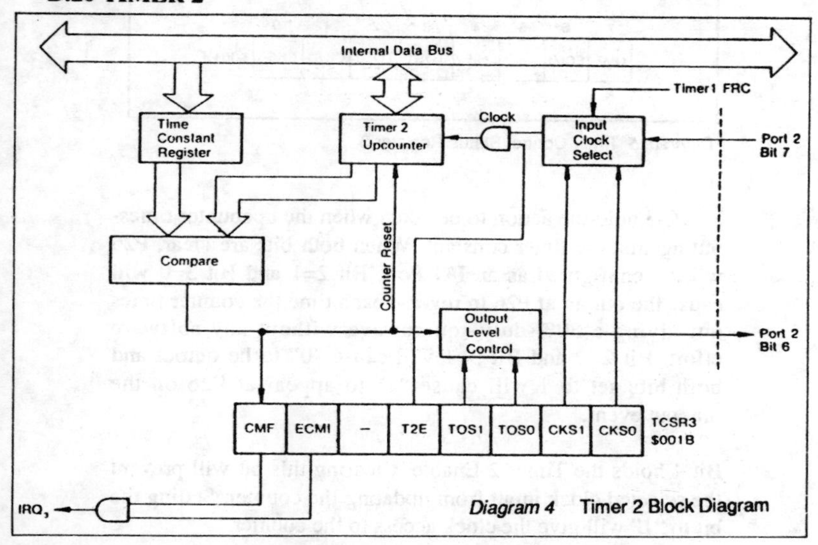

Diagram 4 Timer 2 Block Diagram

Timer 2 is an 8-bit, reloadable counter. It has 3 associated registers:

a. The Timer 2 Upcounter is held at $001D. It is made of 8 bits and can be read or written to at any time without affecting its accuracy.

b. The Time Constant Register. This 8-bit, write-only register is located at $001C. It is the value held in this location which the timer consults. When it matches with the upcounter, it has, in effect, timed out. The up counter would then be zeroed and counting recommenced after P26 despatched the value determined by the condition of bits 2 and 3 of the Timer/Control Status Register.

c. The Control/Status Register. This register is located at $001B and is composed of 7 bits of information as follows:

Bits 0-1 select the type and rate of counter clock. If both bits are set, the clock input arrives via P27. Any other settings make use of the "E" input.

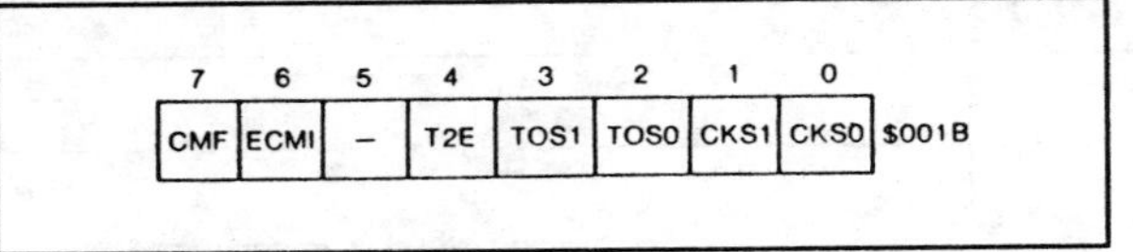

Diagram 5 Timer Control/Status Register 3

Bits 2-3 hold the action to be taken when the upcounter times-out against the timer constant. When both bits are clear, P26 will be configured as an I/O Port. Bit 2=1 and Bit 3=0 will cause the output at P26 to reverse each time the counter times out giving a 50% duty squarewave without any software effort. Bit 2=0 and Bit 3=1 will cause "0" to be output and both bits set to 1 will cause "1" to appear at P26 on the timeout event.

Bit 4 holds the Timer 2 Enable. Clearing this bit will prevent the selected clock input from updating the counter. Setting the bit to "1" will give the clock access to the counter.

Bit 5 is unused.

Bit 6, when set, allows Timer 2 to trigger IRQ3 when a timeout is detected.

Bit 7 holds the Counter Match Flag. This is set to "1" when the current value of the upcounter matches the timer constant. It is cleared by the simple expediency of writing a zero to it.

D.21 SERIAL COMMUNICATIONS INTERFACE (SCI)

The SCI can be operated in asynchronous or clock- synchronous. Asynchronous mode comes in 3 flavours:

a. 1 start bit + 8 data bits + 1 stop bit.

b. 1 start bit + 9 data bits + 1 stop bit.

c. 1 start bit + 8 data bits + 2 stop bits.

Diagram 6 SCI Block Diagram

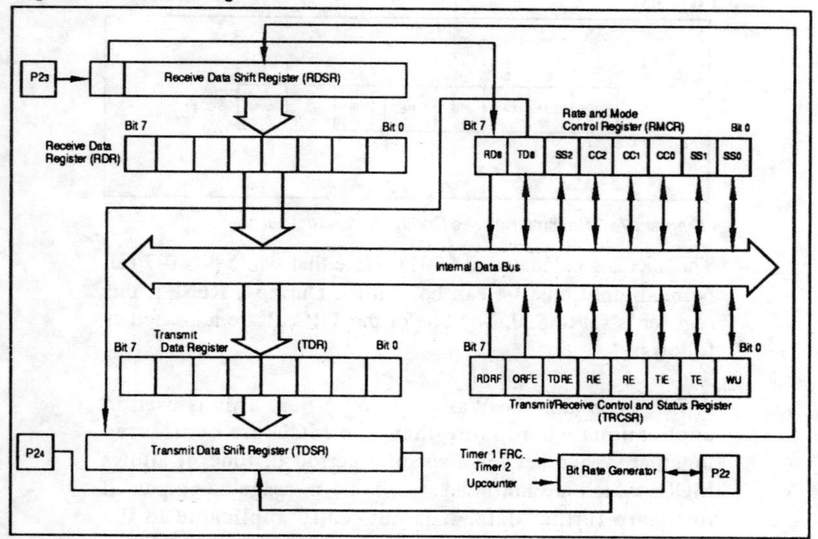

D.22 The SCI has 6 associated registers:

a. Transmit/Receive Control/Status Register (TRCSR).

b. Rate/Mode Control Register (RMCR).

c. Receive Data Register (RDR).

d. Receive Data Shift Register (RDSR).

e. Transmit Data Register (TDR).

f. Transmit Data Shift Register (TDSR).

D.23 TRCSR.

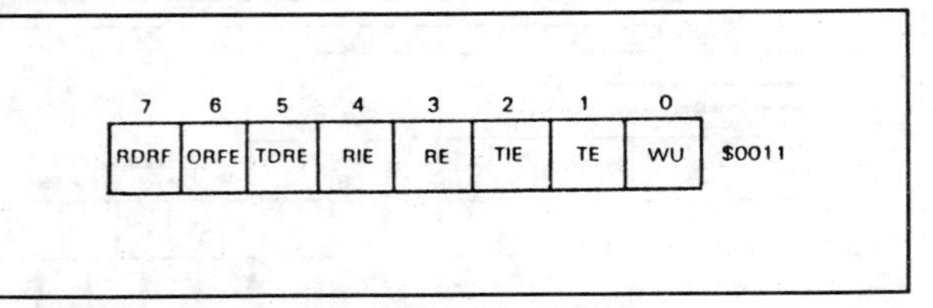

Diagram 7 Transmit/Receive Control Status register

The TRCSR is located at $0011. Note that while bits 0-7 can be read, only bits 0-4 can be written. During a RESET, this register is set to $20. The bits of the TRCSR are allocated as follows:

a. Bit 0 contains the Wake Up (WU) flag. This is used in applications where more than one MCU are configured together. When set for a specific period of time, it allows MCUs which are not interested in the message being passed to ignore further data. It is not really applicable to the Organiser application.

b. Bit 1 specifies the Transmit Enable (TE) status. When it is set, data will emerge from P24. If the SCI is operating in synchronous mode, data will appear immediately. If, however, asynchronous mode is in force, data will appear after a 1-frame preamble of 10 bits (for an 8-bit format) or 11 bits (for a 9-bit format). P24 is the serial output, regardless of the PORT 2 DDR. P24 remains unaffected by serial I/O when TE is cleared.

c. Bit 2 holds the Transmit Interrupt Enable (TIE). When set, the TIE enables bit 5 to set off an IRQ3. The reverse holds true.

d. Bit 3 is the Receive Enable (RE). When set, RE allows data from P23 to be accepted, regardless of the state of the PORT 2 DDR. Clearing the flag exempts P23 from further serial I/O activity.

e. Bit 4 is the Receive Interrupt Enable (RIE). If this is set, bits 6 or 7 can generate an IRQ3. The reverse holds true.

f. Bit 5, which is read-only, holds the Transmit Data Register Empty (TDRE) flag. Asynchronous mode will cause this flag to be set when data is passed from the TDR to the TDSR. In synchronous mode, however, this will happen when the TDSR is itself cleared. Since this bit is read-only, it is cleared by reading the TRCSR and writing data to the TDR. After RESET, the TDRE is set.

g. Bit 6, which is affected only in asynchronous mode and cleared after RESET, is the Overrun/Framing Error (ORFE) flag. Like bit 5, this flag is read-only. It is set to 1 when incoming data is ready to be transmitted to the RDR while the RDRF is still set. The ORFE can be cleared when the RDR is read after reading the TRCSR.

h. Bit 7 holds the Receive Data Register Full (RDRF) flag. It is read-only and is set when the contents of the RDSR are moved to the RDR. The RDRF can be cleared by reading the RDR after the TRCSR or by a RESET.

D.24 RMCR.

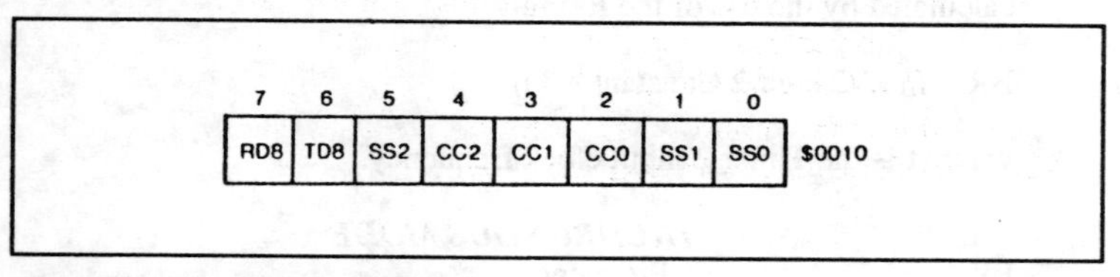

Diagram 8 Tranfer Rate/Mode Control Register

The RMCR is held at $0010. All bits can be read and, with the single exception of bit 7, all bits can be written to. It controls the following aspects of serial I/O:

a. Baud rate.
b. Clock source.
c. Data format.
d. The configuration of P22.
e. Storage of the ninth bit in 9-bit asynchronous I/O.

D.25 The 8 bits of the RMCR are configured like so:

a. Bits 0,1 and 5 control the Baud Rate (BR). For readers unfamiliar with the term, the BR is the rate at which data is received and transmitted serially. The BR is determined as per the table 1.

TABLE 1

ASYNCHRONOUS MODE

Bit 0	Bit 1	Bit 5	Frequency
0	0	0	E/16
0	0	1	E/128
0	1	0	E/1024
0	1	1	E/4096

Note that when Bit 5 is set, the Timer 2 Upcounter acts as the BR generator dependent on the Timer 2 constant. The BR can then be calculated by the use of the formula:

BR = f/(32(Timer 2 Constant + 1))

where f is the Timer 2 input clock frequency.

SYNCHRONOUS MODE

Bit 0	Bit 1	Bit 5	Frequency
0	0	0	E/2
0	0	1	E/16
0	1	0	E/128
0	1	1	E/512

When Bit 5 is set, Timer 2 becomes the SCI clock giving a bit rate determined by:

Bit rate (micro-seconds/bit) = 4(Timer 2 Constant+1)/f

where f = Timer 2 clock frequency.

b. Bits 2,3 and 4 (cleared during RESET) control the clock source and data format as follows:

Bit 2 3 4	Format	Mode	Clock Source	P22
0 0 0	8-bit	Sync	External	Clock Input
0 0 1	8-bit	Async	Internal	Unused
0 1 0	8-bit	Async	Internal	Clock Output
0 1 1	8-bit	Async	External	Clock Input
1 0 0	8-bit	Sync	Internal	Clock Output
1 0 1	9-bit	Async	Internal	Unused
1 1 0	9-bit	Async	Internal	Clock Output
1 1 1	9-bit	Async	External	Clock Input

c. Bit 6 stores the ninth bit of asynchronous 9-bit transmissions. This bit should be written PRIOR to writing the remainder of the byte into the TDR.

d. Bit 7 is the Receive equivalent of Bit 6. This bit should be read before reading the rest of the byte in the RDR.

D.26 RDR. The RDR is located at $0012.
D.27 RDSR. The RDSR is an internal SCI register.
D.28 TDR. The TDR is located at $0013.
D.29 TDSR. The TDSR is an internal SCI register.

INITIALIZATION

D.30 The SCI is initialized by software. This takes the form of writing the required mode to the RMCR and the TRCSR. Note that you can only set the TE and RE bits when P23 and P24 are configured in the serial I/O mode. In addition, TE and RE must be clear when the BR and operating mode are to be set. To set or reset the TE and RE must take more than one BR cycle or a receive/transmit failure may occur.

ASYNCHRONOUS OPERATION

TRANSMISSION

D.31 Simultaneous reception and transmission of data is possible since it has a fully independent transmitter and receiver. The SCI is configured in asynchronous transmission mode when the transmit enable bit of the TRCSR is set. This then switches P24 to become a serial output line. The contents of the PORT 2 DDR have no effect on this situation. The TRCSR and RMCR should then be set to achieve the desired operating conditions as described above. When enabled a 10- or 11-bit preamble will be sent, during which time synchronization will settle down. Data is then sent from the TDR to the TDSR for onward transmission unless the TDR is empty, in which case 1's will be sent to indicate the idling state.

D.32 Depending on the format chosen, data is sent as a leading 0 followed by 8 or 9 bits of data with a stop bit of 1 bringing up the rear. Note that the SCI will set the TDRE bit if the TDR empties. Should the CPU fail to respond in time for the next transmission, a series of 1's will be sent until a suitable response is made. In fact, the transmitter will not send a 0 while the TDRE flag is set.

RECEPTION

D.33 P23 becomes the serial input port, regardless of the state of its DDR bit when the RE bit of the TRCSR is enabled.the reception configuration is selected as for transmission. The first 0 sets everything in motion and the receiver will assume a framing error if the stop bit is not a 1. In such a case, the ORFE flag will be set and the offending data transferred to the RDR. In this way, the CPU can examine the data which caused the error.

D.34 If, however, the information is good the RDRF flag is set to enable an interrupt. Should this flag still be set when the next stop bit arrives, the SCI will assume an over-run. Note that when the CPU examines the RDR in response to either an ORFE or a RDRF, the causal flag is cleared.

SYNCHRONOUS OPERATION

TRANSMISSION

D.35 In synchronous mode, data movement is synchronized by pulses of the system clock. Unlike asynchronous operation, the SCI is unable to handle simultaneous reception and transmission since only one clock I/O pin is provided - P22. The synchronous output port is P24 when the TE of the TRCSR is set. Once again, the PORT 2 DDR has no say in the matter. Set the required operating parameters using the RMCR and TRCSR. Data is transmitted from bit zero and the TDRE flag is set when the TDSR is emptied.

RECEPTION

D.36 The RE flag is set to 1 to allow reception to take place via P23. The PORT 2 DDR is irrelevant. The operating conditions are set as above. Eight external clock pulses enter by P22, while the data bits come in through P23. At each clock pulse, the SCI moves the newly-arrived bit into the RDSR and sets the RDRF flag when it is full. Further pulses are ignored. The RDRF is cleared when the CPU reads the data. Note that the RDRF should be cleared when P22 is high.

D.37 TIMER 1

Diagram9 Timer 1 Block Diagram

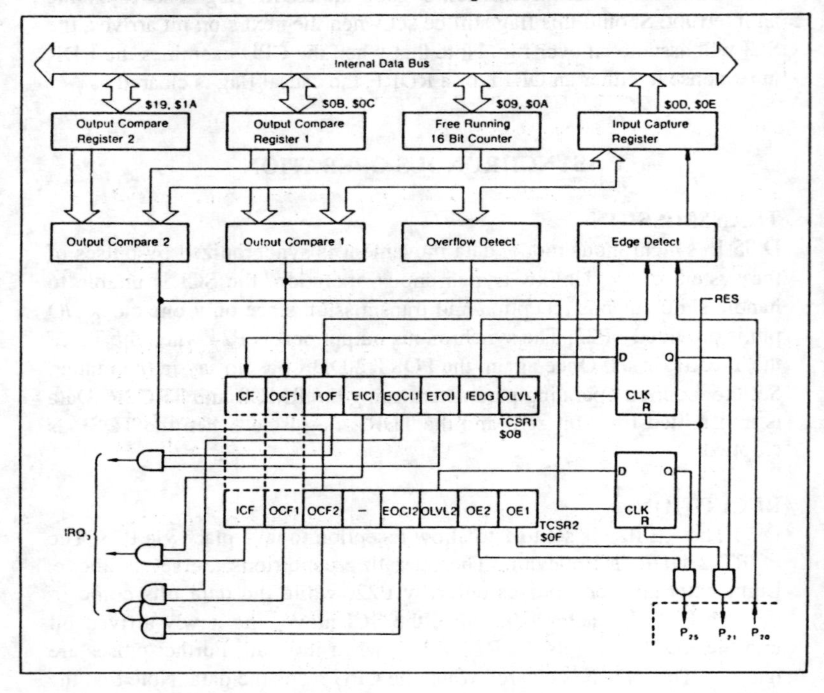

Timer 1 is a 16-bit programmable timer which can accept an input waveform and generate 2 independent waveforms using the original as a base. It has 6 major components:

a. An 8-bit Timer Control/Status Register (TCSR1).

b. A 7-bit TCSR2.

c. A 16-bit Free-Running Counter (FRC).

d. A 16-Bit Output Compare Register (OCR).

e. A second, 16-bit OCR.

f. A 16-bit Input Capture Register (ICR).

D.38 TCSR1.

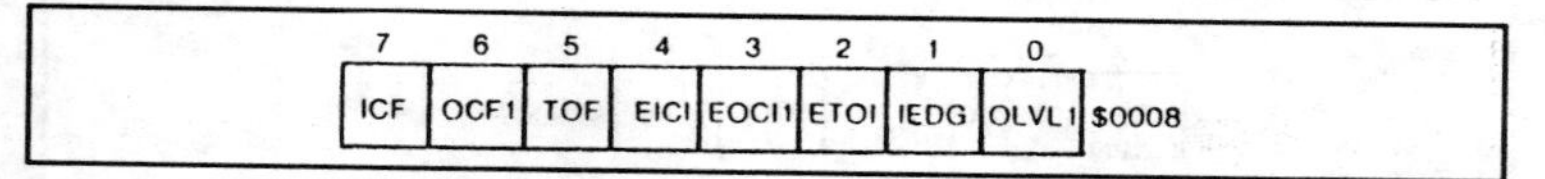

Diagram 10 Timer Control/Status Register 1

This 8-bit register is located at $0018 and is composed of the following components:

a. Bit 0 - The contents of bit 0, known as OLVL1, is output at bit 1 of PORT 2 when a match is made between the OCR1 and the FRC while bit 0 of TCSR2 is set.

b. Bit 1 - The Input Edge (IEDG) is used to determine whether the rising edge or falling edge of P20 will determine the point at which data will be transferred from the FRC to the ICR. A "0" specifies a falling edge and vice versa. Note that bit 0 of PORT 2 must be cleared before IEDG will have any effect.

c. Bit 2 - The Enable Timer Overflow Interrupt (ETOI), when set, allows an IRQ3 to be generated by the Timer Overflow Interrupt (TOI). Clearing this flag inhibits the use of IRQ3.

d. Bit 3 - The Enable Output Compare Interrupt 1 (EOCI1) enables the Output Compare Interrupt 1 (OCI1) to set off an IRQ3. Clearing the flag inhibits this function.

e. Bit 4 - The Enable Input Capture Interrupt (EICI) allows the Input Capture Interrupt to generate an IRQ3. Clearing the flag Inhibits this function.

f. Bit 5 - The Timer Overflow Flag (TOF), which is read-only, is set when the counter moves from $FFF to $0000. When the CPU reads the TCSR1, the TOF and the FRC's high byte are cleared.

g. Bit 6 - The Output Compare Flag 1 (OCF1), which is read-only, is set when the FCR and OCR1 agree. It is cleared by writing to the OCR1 after reading either of the TCSRs.

h. Bit 7 - The Input Capture Flag (ICF), which is read-only, is set when the FRC transfers its data to the ICR. It can be cleared by reading the ICR high byte after reading either of the TCSRs.

D.39 TCSR2.

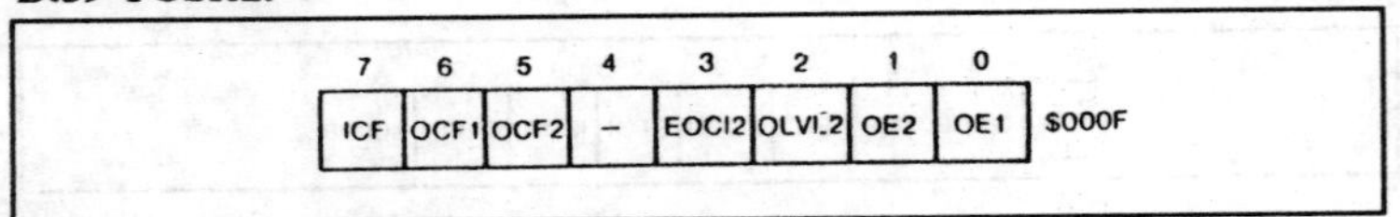

Diagram 11 Timer Control /Status Register 2

This is a 7-bit register held at $000F and is composed of the following items:

a. Bit 0 - Output Enable 1 (OE1), when set, allows bit 0 of TCSR1 to be output at P21 under the conditions already stated. If this flag is cleared, P21 becomes an I/O port.

b. Bit 1 - Setting OE2 allows OVLV2 to be output at P25 when the FRC and OCR2 agree. On the other hand, clearing this bit configures P25 as an I/O port.

c. Bit 2 - OVLV2. This is transferred to P25 under the above conditions.

d. Bit 3 - This contains the EOCI2 and controls OCI2 as per above.

e. Bit 6 - The OCF2, a read-only flag, signals a match between the FRC and the OCR2. It is cleared in a similar manner to OCF1.

f. Bit 7 - By virtue of partial decoding, the CPU can place OCF1 and ICF into bits 6 and 7 after reading the TCSRs.

FRC

D.40 The FRC is a 16-bit free-running counter held at $0009 and $000A. It is cleared on RESET and is incremented by the system clock. The CPU writes the constant $FFF8 to both bytes of the counter when it writes to the high byte first. If the low byte is written to before the high byte, the data is entered. The second method is employed by double byte store instructions.

OCRs

D.41 The OCRs, which are set to $FFFF on RESET, control the nature of the output waveforms. OCr1 is located at $000B-$000C and OCR2 at $0019-$001A. They are constantly being compared to the FRC to find a match. When this occurs, the OCF is set and, if it is enabled, the respective OVLV will appear at its designated point of PORT 2.

D.42 PORT 2

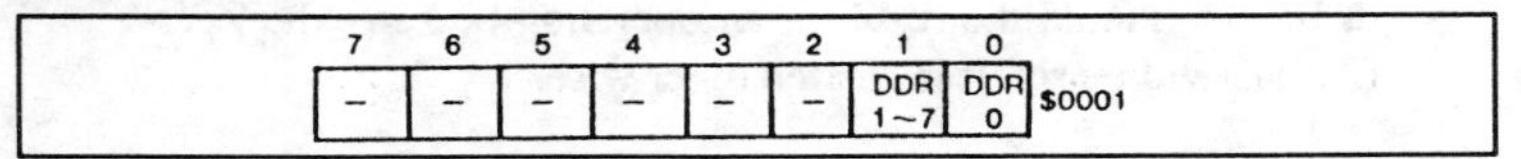

Diagram 12 Port 2 Data Direction Register

PORT 2 is an 8-bit I/O port controlled by its DDR, which is cleared at RESET, at location $0001. Bit 0 of the DDR specifies the direction of P20, while bit 1 configures the direction of P1-P7. The remaining bits of the DDR are unused. As previously mentioned, PORT 2 lines also function as I/O pins for the Timers and SCI. Note that in such a case, with the exception of P20, the state of the DDR has no effect on PORT 2 data direction.

INTERNAL CPU OPERATION

D.43 The HD6303X has three 8-bit registers, three 16-bit registers and 7 distinct modes of addressing. The 8-bit registers are made up of two 8-bit accumulators, ACCA and ACCB, which handle arithmetic and/or logical work. The third is the Condition Code Register, or CCR. The lower 6 bits of this register are relevant :

a. Bit 0 - This holds the Half Carry Flag (H) which is set if a carry at bit 3 or 4 happens during an ADD,ABA or ADA operation. It is cleared otherwise.

b. Bit 1 - The Interrupt Mask (I) is stored here. When set, it disables all interrupts with the exception of the NMI.

c. Bit 2 - The Negative (N) flag is set is the MSB of any operation is 1 and is cleared otherwise.

d. Bit 3 - Should the result of an operation be zero, the Zero (Z) flag will be set. It is cleared other wise.

e. Bit 4 - If a Two's Complement Overflow occurs, the Overflow (V) flag is set. It is cleared otherwise.

f. Bit 5 - The Carry (C) flag is set if a carry or a borrow is generated from the MSB. It is otherwise cleared.

D.44 The first 16-bit register is the Index Register or IX. This register can be used for any purpose but its main function is for indexed addressing. Secondly, the Stack Pointer (SP) holds the 16-bit address of a stack. As with the IX, it can also be used for more mundane purposes. Finally, a 16-bit Program Counter (PC) indicates the address of the instruction currently being executed. Note that the user cannot access this register by software. In addition, a fourth 16-bit register can be made up by combining ACCA and ACCB. It is then, for some inexplicable reason, referred to as ACCD. Note that when ACCA and ACCB are used as a single 16-bit register, the original contents of the 8- bit versions are trashed.

ADDRESSING

D.45 The CPU makes use of 7 types of addressing:

a. Accumulator Addressing. ACCA or ACCB are involved. This type of operation takes a single byte.

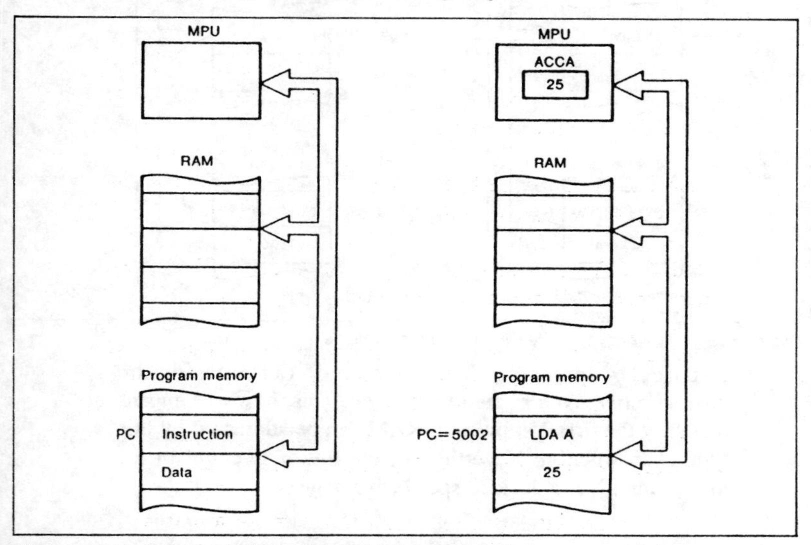

Diagram 14 Data Activity in the Immediate Addressing Mode

b. Immediate Addressing. The data for the operation is given in the second byte of the instruction. However, in the case of LDS or LDX, the second and third bytes are used.

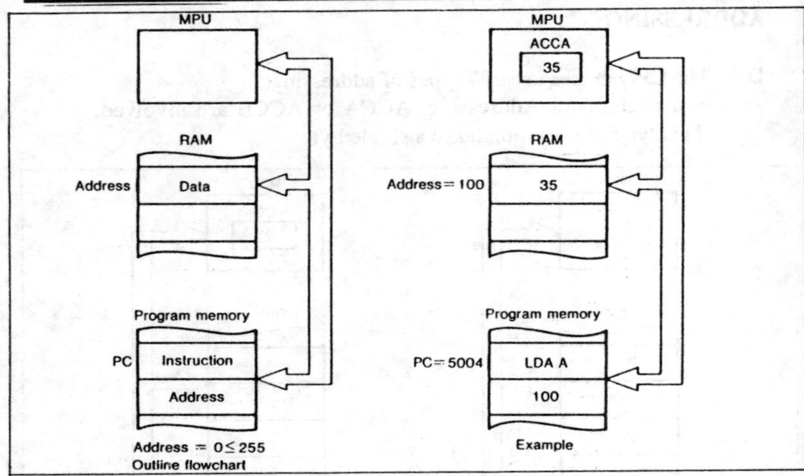

Diagram 15 **Data Activity in the Direct Addressing Mode**

c. Direct Addressing. The address of the data for the instruction is given in the second byte. This, however, means that only the first 256 bytes of RAM can be addressed by this type of instruction. Nevertheless, the low byte count in the instruction gives a decided speed advantage.

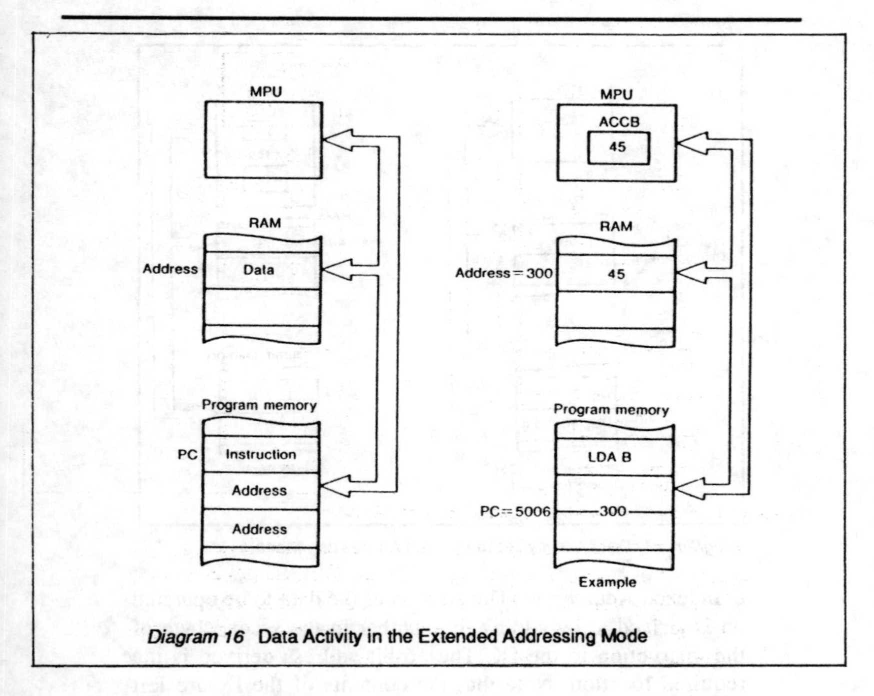

Diagram 16 Data Activity in the Extended Addressing Mode

d. Extended Addressing. This is as for Direct Addressing except that the address is given in the following 2 bytes, MSB first and LSB last.

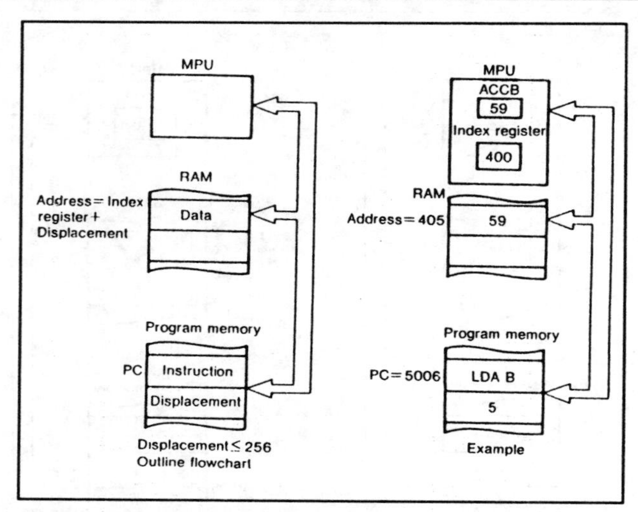

Diagram 17 Data Activity in the Indexed Addressing Mode

e. Indexed Addressing. The address of the data to be operated on is arrived at by adding the number in the second byte of the instruction to the IX. The 16-bit address derived is the required location. Note that the contents of the IX are left unchanged by this operation.

f. Implied Addressing. In this type of instruction, the nature of the task specifies the address. Taking a single byte, they are extremely fast.

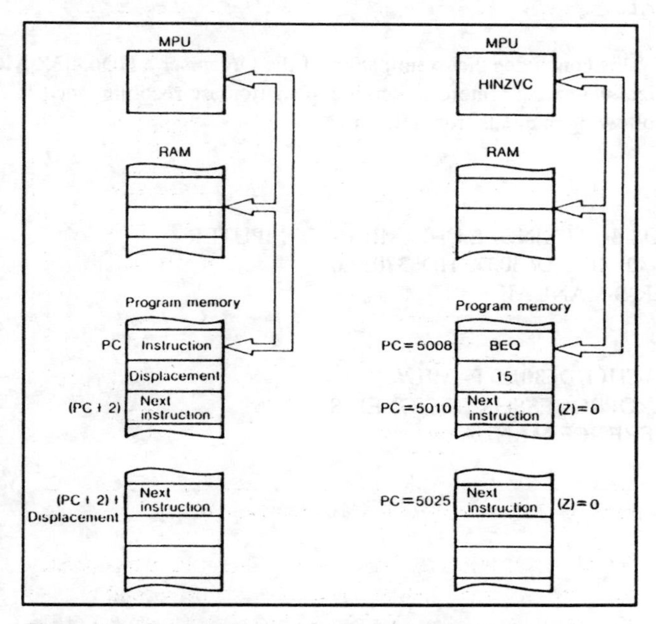

Diagram 18 Data Activity in the Relative Addressing Mode

g. Relative Addressing. In this form of addressing the second byte of the instruction, which is interpreted as lying in the range -126 to +129, is added to the PC to give the address required. This acts in the manner of a GOTO or GOSUB in BASIC.

FINALLY

D.46 This concludes the examination of the Organiser's HD6303X MCU. Readers who wish a more in-depth explanation are recommended to read the following manuals from Hitachi:

CMOS 8-BIT SINGLE CHIP MICROCOMPUTER
HD6301X0, HD6303X, HD63701X0
USER'S MANUAL

HITACHI HD6301/3 FAMILY
MICROPROCESSOR DESIGNER'S
REFERENCE MANUAL

Annex E

HD6303 X Instruction Set

E: HD6303X Instruction Set Arranged Alphabetically

ABA

MNEMONIC FUNCTION: Adds the contents of Acc B to Acc A, storing the result in Acc A.

CCR H: H=1 when bit 3 carry. Cleared otherwise.
CCR I: I is unaffected.
CCR N: Set if MSB of result=1. Cleared otherwise.
CCR Z: Set if result=0. Cleared otherwise.
CCR V: Set if result overflows. Cleared otherwise.
CCR C: Set if carry from MSB. Cleared otherwise.

ADDRESSING MODES	FORMAT	BYTES	CODE
1) Implied	ABA	1	1B

ABX IX

MNEMONIC FUNCTION: Adds the contents of Acc B to the IX, taking account of any carry from the LSB. The result is stored in the IX.

CCR H: Unaffected.
CCR I: Unaffected.
CCR N: Unaffected.
CCR Z: Unaffected.
CCR V: Unaffected.
CCR C: Unaffected.

ADDRESSING MODES	FORMAT	BYTES	CODE
1) Implied	ABX	1	3A

ADC A

MNEMONIC FUNCTION: Adds the contents of a memory location or immediate data, taking into account any carry, to the specified Acc. The result is then stored in the Acc.

CCR H: H=1 if bit 3 carries. Cleared otherwise.
CCR I: Unaffected.
CCR N: Set if MSB of result=1. Cleared otherwise.
CCR Z: Set if result=0. Cleared otherwise.
CCR V: Set if result overflows. Cleared otherwise.
CCR C: Set if MSB carries. Cleared otherwise.

ADDRESSING MODES	FORMAT	BYTES	CODE
1) Immediate	ADC A #Imm	2	89
2) Direct	ADC A M	2	99
3) Extended	ADC A MM	3	B9
4) Indexed	ADC A Disp,X	2	A9

ADC B

MNEMONIC FUNCTION: Adds the contents of a memory location or immediate data, taking into account any carry, to the specified Acc. The result is then stored in the Acc.

CCR H: H=1 if bit 3 carries. Cleared otherwise.
CCR I: Unaffected.
CCR N: Set if MSB of result=1. Cleared otherwise.
CCR Z: Set if result=0. Cleared otherwise.
CCR V: Set if result overflows. Cleared otherwise.
CCR C: Set if MSB carries. Cleared otherwise.

ADDRESSING MODES	FORMAT	BYTES	CODE
1) Immediate	ADC B #Imm	2	C9
2) Direct	ADC B M	2	D9
3) Extended	ADC B MM	3	F9
4) Indexed	ADC B Disp,X	2	E9

ADD A

MNEMONIC FUNCTION: Adds the contents of a memory location or immediate data, ignoring any carry, to the specified Acc. The result is then stored in the Acc.

CCR H: H=1 if bit 3 carries. Cleared otherwise.
CCR I: Unaffected.
CCR N: Set if MSB of result=1. Cleared otherwise.
CCR Z: Set if result=0. Cleared otherwise.
CCR V: Set if result overflows. Cleared otherwise.
CCR C: Set if MSB carries. Cleared otherwise.

ADDRESSING MODES	FORMAT	BYTES	CODE
1) Immediate	ADD A #Imm	2	8B
2) Direct	ADD A M	2	9B
3) Extended	ADD A MM	3	BB
4) Indexed	ADD A Disp,X	2	AB

ADD B

MNEMONIC FUNCTION: Adds the contents of a memory location or immediate data, ignoring any carry, to the specified Acc. The result is then stored in the Acc.

CCR H: H=1 if bit 3 carries. Cleared otherwise.
CCR I: Unaffected.
CCR N: Set if MSB of result=1. Cleared otherwise.
CCR Z: Set if result=0. Cleared otherwise.
CCR V: Set if result overflows. Cleared otherwise.
CCR C: Set if MSB carries. Cleared otherwise.

ADDRESSING MODES	FORMAT	BYTES	CODE
1) Immediate	ADD B #Imm	2	CB
2) Direct	ADD B M	2	DB
3) Extended	ADD B MM	3	FB
4) Indexed	ADD B Disp,X	2	EB

ADD D

MNEMONIC FUNCTION: Adds the double-byte contents of a memory location or immediate data to the contents of Acc D, storing the result in the Acc.

CCR H: Unaffected.
CCR I: Unaffected.
CCR N: Set if MSB of result=1. Cleared otherwise.
CCR Z: Set if result=0. Cleared otherwise.
CCR V: Set if result overflows. Cleared otherwise.
CCR C: Set if MSB carries. Cleared otherwise.

ADDRESSING MODES	FORMAT	BYTES	CODE
1) Immediate	ADD D #Ih Il	3	C3
2) Direct	ADD D M	2	D3
3) Extended	ADD D MM	3	F3
4) Indexed	ADD D Disp,X	2	E3

AIM

MNEMONIC FUNCTION: ANDs the contents of a specified location with an immediate value and stores the result at the memory location.

CCR H: Unaffected.
CCR I: Unaffected.
CCR N: Set if MSB of result=1. Cleared otherwise.
CCR Z: Set if result=0. Cleared otherwise.
CCR V: Cleared.
CCR C: Unaffected.

ADDRESSING MODES	FORMAT	BYTES	CODE
1) Direct	AIM #Imm,M	3	71
2) Indexed	AIM #Imm,Disp,X	3	61

AND A

MNEMONIC FUNCTION: ANDs the contents of a memory location or immediate data with a specified Acc and stores the result in the Acc.

CCR H: Unaffected.
CCR I: Unaffected.
CCR N: Set if MSB of result=1. Cleared otherwise.
CCR Z: Set if result=0. Cleared otherwise.
CCR V: Cleared.
CCR C: Unaffected.

ADDRESSING MODES	FORMAT	BYTES	CODE
1) Immediate	AND A #Imm	2	84
2) Direct	AND A M	2	94
3) Extended	AND A MM	3	B4
4) Indexed	AND A Disp,X	2	A4

AND B

MNEMONIC FUNCTION: ANDs the contents of a memory location or immediate data with a specified Acc and stores the result in the Acc.

CCR H: Unaffected.
CCR I: Unaffected.
CCR N: Set if MSB of result=1. Cleared otherwise.
CCR Z: Set if result=0. Cleared otherwise.
CCR V: Cleared.
CCR C: Unaffected.

ADDRESSING MODES	FORMAT	BYTES	CODE
1) Immediate	AND B #Imm	2	C4
2) Direct	AND B M	2	D4
3) Extended	AND B MM	3	F4
4) Indexed	AND B Disp,X	2	E4

ASL

MNEMONIC FUNCTION: Shifts all the bits of a specified Acc or memory contents one place to the left. The MSB is displaced into the carry and a 0 is inserted into bit 0.

CCR H: Unaffected.
CCR I: Unaffected.
CCR N: Set if MSB of result=1. Cleared otherwise.
CCR Z: set if result=0. Cleared otherwise.
CCR V: If (N=1 and C=0) or (N=0 and C=1) after shift then V=1. Cleared otherwise.
CCR C: Set if MSB of byte=1 BEFORE the shift. Cleared otherwise.

ASLD

ADDRESSING MODES	FORMAT	BYTES	CODE
1) Accumulator	ASL A	1	48
2) Accumulator	ASL B	1	58
3) Extended	ASL MM	3	78
4) Indexed	ASL Disp,X	2	68

ASLD

MNEMONIC FUNCTION: Shifts double-byte Acc one place to the left. The MSB goes into the Carry and bit 0 receives a zero.

CCR H: Unaffected.
CCR I: Unaffected.
CCR N: Set if MSB=1. Cleared otherwise.
CCR Z: Set if result=0. Cleared otherwise.
CCR V: Set if (N=1 and C=0) or (N=1 and C=1). Cleared otherwise
CCR C: Set if MSB of AB=1 before shift. Cleared otherwise.

ADDRESSING MODES	FORMAT	BYTES	CODE
1) Implied	ASLD	1	05

ASR

MNEMONIC FUNCTION: Shifts the contents of a specified Acc or memory location by one place to the right. The Carry receives bit 0 and bit 7 is unaffected.

CCR H: Unaffected.
CCR I: Unaffected.
CCR N: Set if MSB of result=1. Cleared otherwise.
CCR Z: Set if result=0. Cleared otherwise.
CCR V: Set if (N=1 and C=0) or (N=0 and C=1) after shift. Cleared otherwise.
CCR C: Set if LSB is 1 BEFORE shift. Cleared otherwise.

ADDRESSING MODES	FORMAT	BYTES	CODE
1) Accumulator	ASR A	1	47
2) Accumulator	ASR B	1	57
3) Extended	ASR MM	3	77
4) Indexed	ASR Disp,X	2	67

BCC

MNEMONIC FUNCTION: Tests the Carry flag of the CCR. If it is clear, a branch will be made.

CCR H: Unaffected.
CCR I: Unaffected.
CCR N: Unaffected.
CCR Z: Unaffected.
CCR V: Unaffected.
CCR C: Unaffected.

ADDRESSING MODES	FORMAT	BYTES	CODE
1) Relative	BBC rel	2	24

BCLR

MNEMONIC FUNCTION: Clears the specified bit of the contents of a named location. Users should note that the machine code for this instruction is identical to that for AIM.

CCR H: Unaffected.
CCR I: Unaffected.
CCR N: Set if MSB of result=1. Cleared otherwise.
CCR Z: Set if result=0. Cleared otherwise.
CCR V: Cleared.
CCR C: Unaffected.

ADDRESSING MODES	FORMAT	BYTES	CODE
1) Direct	BCLR 0,M	3	71 FE
1) Direct	BCLR 1.M	3	71 FD
1) Direct	BCLR 2.M	3	71 FB
1) Direct	BCLR 3,M	3	71 F7
1) Direct	BCLR 4,M	3	71 EF
1) Direct	BCLR 5,M	3	71 DF
1) Direct	BCLR 6,M	3	71 BF
1) Direct	BCLR 7,M	3	71 7F
2) Indexed	BCLR 0,Disp,X	3	61 FE
2) Indexed	BCLR 1,Disp,X	3	61 FD
2) Indexed	BCLR 2,Disp,X	3	61 FB
2) Indexed	BCLR 3,Disp,X	3	61 F7
2) Indexed	BCLR 4,Disp,X	3	61 EF
2) Indexed	BCLR 5,Disp,X	3	61 DF
2) Indexed	BCLR 6,Disp,X	3	61 BF
2) Indexed	BCLR 7,Disp,X	3	61 7F

BCS

MNEMONIC FUNCTION: Examines the state of the Carry flag and causes a branch if it is set.CCR H: Unaffected.

CCR I: Unaffected.
CCR N: Unaffected.
CCR Z: Unaffected.
CCR V: Unaffected.
CCR C: Unaffected.

ADDRESSING MODES	FORMAT	BYTES	CODE
1) Relative	BCS Rel	2	25

BEQ
MNEMONIC FUNCTION: Examines the state of the Zero flag and causes a branch if it is set.

CCR H: Unaffected.
CCR I: Unaffected.
CCR N: Unaffected.
CCR Z: Unaffected.
CCR V: Unaffected.
CCR C: Unaffected.

ADDRESSING MODES	FORMAT	BYTES	CODE
1) Relative	BEQ Rel	2	27

BGE
MNEMONIC FUNCTION: If employed immediately after an instruction such as SUB, SBA, CMP or CBA, the BGE instruction will cause a branch if the minuend is greater than or equal to the subtractor as a Two's Complement number. That is, if (N=1 and V=1) or (N=0 and V=0).

CCR H: Unaffected.
CCR I: Unaffected.
CCR N: Unaffected.
CCR Z: Unaffected.
CCR V: Unaffected.
CCR C: Unaffected.

ADDRESSING MODES	FORMAT	BYTES	CODE
1) Relative	BGE Rel	2	2C

BGT

MNEMONIC FUNCTION: If employed immediately after an instruction such as SUB, SBA, CMP or CBA, the BGT instruction will cause a branch if the minuend is greater than the subtractor as a Two's Complement number. That is, if (Z=0 and N AND V=1) or (Z=0 and N AND V=0)

CCR H: Unaffected.
CCR I: Unaffected.
CCR N: Unaffected.
CCR Z: Unaffected.
CCR V: Unaffected.
CCR C: Unaffected.

ADDRESSING MODES	FORMAT	BYTES	CODE
1) Relative	BGT Rel	2	2E

BHI

MNEMONIC FUNCTION: If employed immediately after an instruction such as SUB, SBA, CMP or CBA, the BHI instruction will cause a branch if the minuend is greater than the subtractor as an unsigned binary number. That is, if C=0 and Z=0.

CCR H: Unaffected.
CCR I: Unaffected.
CCR N: Unaffected.
CCR Z: Unaffected.

CCR V: Unaffected.
CCR C: Unaffected.

ADDRESSING MODES	FORMAT	BYTES	CODE
1) Relative	BHI Rel	2	22

BIT A

MNEMONIC FUNCTION: Carries out a logical ANDing of the contents of the specified Acc and that of a memory location or immediate data. Note that only the CCR is affected, The actual contents of the Acc and the memory location remain unchanged.

CCR H: Unaffected.
CCR I: Unaffected.
CCR N: Set if MSB of result=1. Cleared otherwise.
CCR Z: Set if all bits of result=0. Cleared otherwise.
CCR V: Cleared.
CCR C: Unaffected.

ADDRESSING MODES	FORMAT	BYTES	CODE
1) Immediate	BIT A #Imm	2	85
2) Direct	BIT A M	2	95
3) Extended	BIT A MM	3	B5
4) Indexed	BIT A Disp,X	2	A5

BIT B

MNEMONIC FUNCTION: Carries out a logical ANDing of the contents of the specified Acc and that of a memory location or immediate data. Note that only the CCR is affected, The actual contents of the Acc and the memory location remain unchanged.

CCR H: Unaffected.
CCR I: Unaffected.
CCR N: Set if MSB of result=1. Cleared otherwise.
CCR Z: Set if all bits of result=0. Cleared otherwise.
CCR V: Cleared.
CCR C: Unaffected.

ADDRESSING MODES	FORMAT	BYTES	CODE
1) Immediate	BIT B #Imm	2	C5
2) Direct	BIT B M	2	D5
3) Extended	BIT B MM	3	F5
4) Indexed	BIT B Disp,X	2	E5

BLE

MNEMONIC FUNCTION: If employed immediately after an instruction such as SUB, SBA, CMP or CBA, the BLE instruction will cause a branch if the minuend is smaller than or equal to the subtractor as a Two's Complement number. That is, if Z=1 or (N=1 and V=0) or (N=0 and V=1).

CCR H: Unaffected.
CCR I: Unaffected.
CCR N: Unaffected.
CCR Z: Unaffected.
CCR V: Unaffected.
CCR C: Unaffected.

ADDRESSING MODES	FORMAT	BYTES	CODE
1) Relative	BLE Rel	2	2F

BLS

MNEMONIC FUNCTION: If employed immediately after an instruction such as SUB, SBA, CMP or CBA, the BLS instruction will cause a branch if the minuend is smaller than or equal to the subtractor as an unsigned binary number. That is, if Z=1 or C=1.

CCR H: Unaffected.
CCR I: Unaffected.
CCR N: Unaffected.
CCR Z: Unaffected.
CCR V: Unaffected.
CCR C: Unaffected.

ADDRESSING MODES	FORMAT	BYTES	CODE
1) Relative	BLS Rel	2	23

BLT

MNEMONIC FUNCTION: If employed immediately after an instruction such as SUB, SBA, CMP or CBA, the BLT instruction will cause a branch if the minuend is smaller than the subtractor as a Two's Complement number. That is, if (N=1 and V=0) or (N=0 and V=1).

CCR H: Unaffected.
CCR I: Unaffected.
CCR N: Unaffected.
CCR Z: Unaffected.
CCR V: Unaffected.
CCR C: Unaffected.

ADDRESSING MODES	FORMAT	BYTES	CODE
1) Relative	BLT Rel	2	2D

BMI

MNEMONIC FUNCTION: Tests the N flag and branches if it is set.

CCR H: Unaffected.
CCR I: Unaffected.
CCR N: Unaffected.
CCR Z: Unaffected.
CCR V: Unaffected.
CCR C: Unaffected.

ADDRESSING MODES	FORMAT	BYTES	CODE
1) Relative	BMI Rel	2	2B

BNE

MNEMONIC FUNCTION: Tests the Z flag and branches if it is clear.

CCR H: Unaffected.
CCR I: Unaffected.
CCR N: Unaffected.
CCR Z: Unaffected.
CCR V: Unaffected.
CCR C: Unaffected.

ADDRESSING MODES	FORMAT	BYTES	CODE
1) Relative	BNE Rel	2	26

BPL

MNEMONIC FUNCTION: Tests the N flag and branches if it is clear.

CCR H: Unaffected.
CCR I: Unaffected.
CCR N: Unaffected.
CCR Z: Unaffected.
CCR V: Unaffected.
CCR C: Unaffected.

ADDRESSING MODES	FORMAT	BYTES	CODE
1) Relative	BPL Rel	2	2A

BRA

MNEMONIC FUNCTION: Always branches, irrespective of prevailing conditions. Jump address is calculated as the contents of the PC+2+the Relative jump which is given by the user as a Two's Complement number in the second byte of the branch instruction.

CCR H: Unaffected.
CCR I: Unaffected.
CCR N: Unaffected.
CCR Z: Unaffected.
CCR V: Unaffected.

CCR C: Unaffected.

ADDRESSING MODES	FORMAT	BYTES	CODE
1) Relative	BRA Rel	2	20

BRN

MNEMONIC FUNCTION: Equivalent to the NOP instruction and the opposite of BRA.

CCR H: Unaffected.
CCR I: Unaffected.
CCR N: Unaffected.
CCR Z: Unaffected.
CCR V: Unaffected.
CCR C: Unaffected.

ADDRESSING MODES	FORMAT	BYTES	CODE
1) Relative	BRN Rel	2	21

BSET

MNEMONIC FUNCTION: Sets the specified bit of the contents of a named location. Users should note that the machine code for this instruction is identical to that for OIM.

CCR H: Unaffected.
CCR I: Unaffected.
CCR N: Set if MSB of result=1. Cleared otherwise.
CCR Z: Set if result=0. Cleared otherwise.
CCR V: Cleared.
CCR C: Unaffected.

ADDRESSING MODES	FORMAT	BYTES	CODE
1) Direct	BSET 0,M	3	72 01
1) Direct	BSET 1.M	3	72 02
1) Direct	BSET 2.M	3	72 04
1) Direct	BSET3,M	3	72 08
1) Direct	BSET 4,M	3	71 10
1) Direct	BSET 5,M	3	72 20
1) Direct	BSET 6,M	3	72 40
1) Direct	BSET 7,M	3	72 40
2) Indexed	BSET 0,Disp,X	3	62 01
2) Indexed	BSET 1,Disp,X	3	62 02
2) Indexed	BSET 2,Disp,X	3	62 04
2) Indexed	BSET 3,Disp,X	3	62 08
2) Indexed	BSET 4,Disp,X	3	62 10
2) Indexed	BSET 5,Disp,X	3	62 20
2) Indexed	BSET 6,Disp,X	3	62 40
2) Indexed	BSET 7,Disp,X	3	62 80

BSR

MNEMONIC FUNCTION: This instruction provides the same sort of function as a procedure call in OPL. Before jumping to the required point, the CPU increments the PC by 2 and stacks it, incrementing the SP appropriately. It then branches to the address indicated.

CCR H: Unaffected.
CCR I: Unaffected.
CCR N: Unaffected.
CCR Z: Unaffected.
CCR V: Unaffected.
CCR C: Unaffected.

ADDRESSING MODES	FORMAT	BYTES	CODE
1) Relative	BSR Rel	2	8D

BTGL

MNEMONIC FUNCTION: Inverts the specified bit of the contents of a named location. Users should note that the machine code for this instruction is identical to that for EIM.

CCR H: Unaffected.
CCR I: Unaffected.
CCR N: Set if MSB of result=1. Cleared otherwise.
CCR Z: Set if result=0. Cleared otherwise.
CCR V: Cleared.
CCR C: Unaffected.

ADDRESSING MODES	FORMAT	BYTES	CODE
1) Direct	BTGL 0,M	3	75 01
1) Direct	BTGL 1.M	3	75 02
1) Direct	BTGL 2.M	3	75 04
1) Direct	BTGL 3,M	3	75 08
1) Direct	BTGL 4,M	3	75 10
1) Direct	BTGL 5,M	3	75 20
1) Direct	BTGL 6,M	3	75 40
1) Direct	BTGL 7,M	3	75 80
2) Indexed	BTGL 0,Disp,X	3	65 01
2) Indexed	BTGL 1,Disp,X	3	65 02

(BTGL cont.)

ADDRESSING MODES	FORMAT	BYTES	CODE
2) Indexed	BTGL 2,Disp,X	3	65 04
2) Indexed	BTGL 3,Disp,X	3	65 08
2) Indexed	BTGL 4,Disp,X	3	65 10
2) Indexed	BTGL 5,Disp,X	3	65 20
2) Indexed	BTGL 6,Disp,X	3	65 40
2) Indexed	BTGL 7,Disp,X	3	65 80

BTST

MNEMONIC FUNCTION: ANDs the specified bit of the contents of a named location with 1 and changes the CCR appropriately. Users should note that the machine code for this instruction is identical to that for TIM.

CCR H: Unaffected.
CCR I: Unaffected.
CCR N: Set if MSB of result=1. Cleared otherwise.
CCR Z: Set if result=0. Cleared otherwise.
CCR V: Cleared.
CCR C: Unaffected.

ADDRESSING MODES	FORMAT	BYTES	CODE
1) Direct	BTST 0,M	3	7B 01
1) Direct	BTST 1.M	3	7B 02
1) Direct	BTST 2.M	3	7B 04
1) Direct	BTST 3,M	3	7B 08
1) Direct	BTST 4,M	3	7B 10
1) Direct	BTST 5,M	3	7B 20
1) Direct	BTST 6,M	3	7B 40
1) Direct	BTST 7,M	3	7B 80
2) Indexed	BTST 0,Disp,X	3	6B 01
2) Indexed	BTST 1,Disp,X	3	6B 02
2) Indexed	BTST 2,Disp,X	3	6B 04
2) Indexed	BTST 3,Disp,X	3	6B 08
2) Indexed	BTST 4,Disp,X	3	6B 10
2) Indexed	BTST 5,Disp,X	3	6B 20
2) Indexed	BTST 6,Disp,X	3	6B 40
2) Indexed	BTST 7,Disp,X	3	6B 80

BVC

MNEMONIC FUNCTION: Tests the V flag and branches if it is clear.

CCR H: Unaffected.
CCR I: Unaffected.
CCR N: Unaffected.
CCR Z: Unaffected.
CCR V: Unaffected.
CCR C: Unaffected.

ADDRESSING MODES	FORMAT	BYTES	CODE
1) Relative	BVC Rel	2	28

BVS

MNEMONIC FUNCTION: Tests the V flag and branches if it is set.

CCR H: Unaffected.
CCR I: Unaffected.
CCR N: Unaffected.
CCR Z: Unaffected.
CCR V: Unaffected.
CCR C: Unaffected.

ADDRESSING MODES	FORMAT	BYTES	CODE
1) Relative	BVS Rel	2	29

CBA

MNEMONIC FUNCTION: Compares the contents of Acc A and Acc B, setting the CCR appropriately. This operation is used as the basis for branching operations. Note that neither Acc is affected by this instruction.

CCR H: Unaffected.
CCR I: Unaffected.
CCR N: Set if MSB of result=1. Cleared otherwise.
CCR Z: Set if the result=0. Cleared otherwise.
CCR V: Set if the result overflows. Cleared otherwise.
CCR C: Set if borrow occurs. Cleared otherwise.

ADDRESSING MODES	FORMAT	BYTES	CODE
1) Implied	CBA	1	11

CLC

MNEMONIC FUNCTION: Clears the Carry flag in the CCR.

CCR H: Unaffected.
CCR I: Unaffected.
CCR N: Unaffected.
CCR Z: Unaffected.
CCR V: Unaffected.
CCR C: Cleared.

ADDRESSING MODES	FORMAT	BYTES	CODE
1) Implied	CLC	1	OC

CLI

MNEMONIC FUNCTION: Clears the interrupt mask flag of the CCR.

CCR H: Unaffected.
CCR I: Cleared.
CCR N: Unaffected.
CCR Z: Unaffected.
CCR V: Unaffected.
CCR C: Unaffected.

ADDRESSING MODES	FORMAT	BYTES	CODE
1) Implied	CLI	1	0E

CLR

MNEMONIC FUNCTION: Clears The contents of a specified Acc or memory location.

CCR H: Unaffected.
CCR I: Unaffected.
CCR N: Cleared.
CCR Z: Set.
CCR V: Cleared.
CCR C: Cleared.

ADDRESSING MODES	FORMAT	BYTES	CODE
1) Accumulator	CLR A	1	4F
2) Accumulator	CLR B	1	5F
3) Extended	CLR MM	3	7F
4) Indexed	CLR Disp,X	2	6F

CLV
MNEMONIC FUNCTION: Clears the V flag of the CCR.

CCR H: Unaffected.
CCR I: Unaffected.
CCR N: Unaffected.
CCR Z: Unaffected.
CCR V: Cleared.
CCR C: Unaffected.

ADDRESSING MODES	FORMAT	BYTES	CODE
1) Implied	CLV	1	0A

CMP A
MNEMONIC FUNCTION: Compares the contents of the specified Acc with immediate data or the contents of a memory location and alters the CCR appropriately. This type of instruction is usually the precursor of a branch-type manoeuvre. Note that the data being compared is not changed in any way.

CCR H: Unaffected.
CCR I: Unaffected.
CCR N: Set if the MSB of the result=1. Cleared otherwise.
CCR Z: Cleared if the result=0. Cleared otherwise.
CCR V: Set if the result overflows. Cleared otherwise.
CCR C: Set if data is greater than that of the specified Acc.

ADDRESSING MODES	FORMAT	BYTES	CODE
1) Immediate	CMP A #Imm	2	81
2) Direct	CMP A M	2	91
3) Extended	CMP A MM	3	B1
4) Indexed	CMP A Disp,X	2	A1

CMP B

MNEMONIC FUNCTION: Compares the contents of the specified Acc with immediate data or the contents of a memory location and alters the CCR appropriately. This type of instruction is usually the precursor of a branch-type manoeuvre. Note that the data being compared is not changed in any way.

CCR H: Unaffected.
CCR I: Unaffected.
CCR N: Set if the MSB of the result=1. Cleared otherwise.
CCR Z: Cleared if the result=0. Cleared otherwise.
CCR V: Set if the result overflows. Cleared otherwise.
CCR C: Set if data is greater than that of the specified Acc.

ADDRESSING MODES	FORMAT	BYTES	CODE
1) Immediate	CMP B #Imm	2	C1
2) Direct	CMP B M	2	D1
3) Extended	CMP B MM	3	F1
4) Indexed	CMP B Disp,X	2	E1

COM

MNEMONIC FUNCTION: Replaces the contents of the specified Acc or a memory location with its One's Complement.

CCR H: Unaffected.
CCR I: Unaffected.
CCR N: Set if MSB of result=1. Cleared otherwise.
CCR Z: Set if result=0. Cleared otherwise.
CCR V: Cleared.
CCR C: Set.

ADDRESSING MODES	FORMAT	BYTES	CODE
1) Accumulator	COM A	1	43
2) Accumulator	COM B	1	53
3) Extended	COM MM	3	73
4) Indexed	COM Disp,X	2	63

CPX

MNEMONIC FUNCTION: Compares the contents of the IX to immediate data or to the word-contents of a memory location and sets the CCR appropriately.

CCR H: Unaffected.
CCR I: Unaffected.
CCR N: Set if MSB of result=1. Cleared otherwise.
CCR Z: Set if result=0. Cleared otherwise.
CCR V: Set if result overflows. Cleared otherwise.
CCR C: Set if data greater than contents of IX. Cleared otherwise.

ADDRESSING MODES	FORMAT	BYTES	CODE
1) Immediate	CPX #Ih Il	3	8C
2) Direct	CPX M	2	9C
3) Extended	CPX MM	3	BC
4) Indexed	CPX Disp,X	2	AC

DAA

MNEMONIC FUNCTION: Decimal adjusts the contents of Acc A.

CCR H: Unaffected.
CCR I: Unaffected.
CCR N: Set if MSB of result=1. Cleared otherwise.
CCR Z: Set if result=0. Cleared otherwise.
CCR V: Set if result overflows. Cleared otherwise.
CCR C: Set following BCD addition.

ADDRESSING MODES	FORMAT	BYTES	CODE
1) Implied	DAA	1	19

DEC

MNEMONIC FUNCTION: Subtracts 1 from the contents of the specified Acc or memory location.

CCR H: Not affected.
CCR I: Not affected.
CCR N: Set if MSB of result=1. Cleared otherwise.
CCR Z: Set if result=0. Cleared otherwise.
CCR V: Set if result overflows. Cleared otherwise. Note that if the data was 80 prior to the instruction, an overflow will occur.
CCR C: Unaffected.

ADDRESSING MODES	FORMAT	BYTES	CODE
1) Accumulator	DEC A	1	4A
2) Accumulator	DEC B	1	5A
3) Extended	DEC MM	3	7A
4) Indexed	DEC Disp,X	2	6A

DES

MNEMONIC FUNCTION: Subtracts 1 from the SP.

CCR H: Unaffected.
CCR I: Unaffected.
CCR N: Unaffected.
CCR Z: Unaffected.
CCR V: Unaffected.
CCR C: Unaffected.

ADDRESSING MODES	FORMAT	BYTES	CODE
1) Implied	DES	1	34

DEX
MNEMONIC FUNCTION: Subtracts 1 from the IX.
CCR H: Unaffected.
CCR I: Unaffected.
CCR N: Unaffected.
CCR Z: Set if result=0. Cleared otherwise.
CCR V: Unaffected.
CCR C: Unaffected.

ADDRESSING MODES	FORMAT	BYTES	CODE
1) Implied	DEX	1	09

EIM
MNEMONIC FUNCTION: ORs the immediate value with the memory contents and stores the result in memory.

CCR H: Unaffected.
CCR I: Unaffected.
CCR N: Set if MSB of the memory location=1. Cleared otherwise.
CCR Z: Set if contents of memory location=0. Cleared otherwise.
CCR V: Cleared.
CCR C: Unaffected.

ADDRESSING MODES	FORMAT	BYTES	CODE
1) Direct	EIM #Imm,M	3	75
2)Indexed	EIM #Imm,Disp,X	3	65

EOR A
MNEMONIC FUNCTION: EORs the contents of the specified Acc with the immediate data or a memory location and stores the result in the Acc.

CCR H: Unaffected.
CCR I: Unaffected.
CCR N: Set if MSB of result=1. Cleared otherwise.
CCR Z: Set if result=1. Cleared otherwise.
CCR V: Cleared.
CCR C: Unaffected.

ADDRESSING MODES	FORMAT	BYTES	CODE
1) Immediate	EOR A #Imm	2	88
2) Direct	EOR A M	2	98
3) Extended	EOR A MM	3	B8
4) Indexed	EOR A Disp,X	2	A8

EOR B

MNEMONIC FUNCTION: EORs the contents of the specified Acc with the immediate data or a memory location and stores the result in the Acc.

CCR H: Unaffected.
CCR I: Unaffected.
CCR N: Set if MSB of result=1. Cleared otherwise.
CCR Z: Set if result=1. Cleared otherwise.
CCR V: Cleared.
CCR C: Unaffected.

ADDRESSING MODES	FORMAT	BYTES	CODE
1) Immediate	EOR B #Imm	2	C8
2) Direct	EOR B M	2	D8
3) Extended	EOR B MM	3	F8
4) Indexed	EOR B Disp,X	2	E8

INC

MNEMONIC FUNCTION: Increments the contents of the specified Acc or memory location by 1.

CCR H: Unaffected.
CCR I: Unaffected.
CCR N: Set if MSB of result=1. Cleared otherwise.
CCR Z: Set if result=0. Cleared otherwise.
CCR V: Set if result overflows. Cleared otherwise. Note that if the data was 7F BEFORE the operation, then an overflow will occur.
CCR C: Unaffected.

ADDRESSING MODES	FORMAT	BYTES	CODE
1) Accumulator.	INC A	1	4C
2) Accumulator	INC B	1	5C
3) Extended	INC MM	3	7C
4) Indexed	INC Disp,X	2	6C

INS

MNEMONIC FUNCTION: Increments the SP by 1.

CCR H: Unaffected.
CCR I: Unaffected.
CCR N: Unaffected.
CCR Z: Unaffected.
CCR V: Unaffected.
CCR C: Unaffected.

ADDRESSING MODES	FORMAT	BYTES	CODE
1) Implied	INS	1	31

INX

MNEMONIC FUNCTION: Increments the IX by 1.

CCR H: Unaffected.
CCR I: Unaffected.
CCR N: Unaffected.
CCR Z: Set if all 16 bits=0. Cleared otherwise.
CCR V: Unaffected.
CCR C: Unaffected.

ADDRESSING MODES	FORMAT	BYTES	CODE
1) Implied	INX	1	08

JMP

MNEMONIC FUNCTION: Branches to the double-byte address given.

CCR H: Unaffected.
CCR I: Unaffected.
CCR N: Unaffected.
CCR Z: Unaffected.
CCR V: Unaffected.
CCR C: Unaffected.

ADDRESSING MODES	FORMAT	BYTES	CODE
1) Extended	JMP MM	3	7E
2) Indexed	JMP Disp,X	2	6E

JSR

MNEMONIC FUNCTION: Increments the SP appropriately and branches to the address specified.

CCR H: Unaffected.
CCR I: Unaffected.
CCR N: Unaffected.
CCR Z: Unaffected.
CCR V: Unaffected.
CCR C: Unaffected

ADDRESSING MODES	FORMAT	BYTES	CODE
1) Extended	JSR MM	3	BD
2) Indexed	JSR Disp,X	2	AD
3) Direct	JSR M	2	9D

LDA A

MNEMONIC FUNCTION: Loads the immediate data or contents of memory location into the specified Acc.

CCR H: Unaffected.
CCR I: Unaffected.
CCR N: Set if MSB of result=1. Cleared otherwise.
CCR Z: Set if result=0. Cleared otherwise.
CCR V: Cleared.
CCR C: Unaffected.

ADDRESSING MODES	FORMAT	BYTES	CODE
1) Immediate	LDA A #Imm	2	86
2) Direct	LDA A M	2	96
3) Extended	LDA A MM	3	B6
4) Indexed	LDA A Disp,X	2	A6

LDA B

MNEMONIC FUNCTION: Loads the immediate data or contents of memory location into the specified Acc.

CCR H: Unaffected.
CCR I: Unaffected.
CCR N: Set if MSB of result=1. Cleared otherwise.
CCR Z: Set if result=0. Cleared otherwise.
CCR V: Cleared.
CCR C: Unaffected.

ADDRESSING MODES	FORMAT	BYTES	CODE
1) Immediate	LDA B #Imm	2	C6
2) Direct	LDA B M	2	D6
3) Extended	LDA B MM	3	F6
4) Indexed	LDA B Disp,X	2	E6

LDD

MNEMONIC FUNCTION: Load the double-byte contents of a memory location or immediate data into Acc D.

CCR H: Unaffected..
CCR I: Unaffected.
CCR N: Set if MSB of result=1. Cleared otherwise.
CCR Z: Set if result=0. Cleared otherwise.
CCR V: Cleared.
CCR C: Unaffected.

ADDRESSING MODES	FORMAT	BYTES	CODE
1) Immediate	LDD #Ih Il	3	CC
2) Direct	LDD M	2	DC
3) Extended	LDD MM	3	FC
4) Indexed	LDD Disp,X	2	EC

LDS

MNEMONIC FUNCTION: Loads immediate data or the double-byte contents of a memory location into the SP. The first byte goes to the MSB and the second to the LSB of the SP.

CCR H: Unaffected.
CCR I: Unaffected.
CCR N: Set if MSB of result=1. Cleared otherwise.
CCR Z: Set if all SP bits=0. Cleared otherwise.
CCR V: Cleared.
CCR C: Unaffected.

ADDRESSING MODES	FORMAT	BYTES	CODE
1) Immediate	LDS #Ih Il	3	8E
2) Direct	LDS M	2	9E
3) Extended	LDS MM	3	BE
4) Extended	LDS Disp,X	2	AE

LDX

MNEMONIC FUNCTION: Loads immediate data or the double-byte contents of a memory location into the IX. The first byte goes to the MSB and the second to the LSB of the IX.

CCR H: Unaffected.
CCR I: Unaffected.
CCR N: Set if MSB of result=1. Cleared otherwise.
CCR Z: Set if all IX bits=0. Cleared otherwise.
CCR V: Cleared.
CCR C: Unaffected.

ADDRESSING MODES	FORMAT	BYTES	CODE
1) Immediate	LDX #Ih Il	3	CE
2) Direct	LDX M	2	DE
3) Extended	LDX MM	3	FE
4) Extended	LDX Disp,X	2	EE

LSR

MNEMONIC FUNCTION: Shifts the specified Acc or the contents of the memory location one bit to the right. Bit 0 is transferred into the Carry flag of the CCR and 0 is placed into bit 7.

CCR H: Unaffected.
CCR I: Unaffected.
CCR N: Cleared.
CCR Z: Set if result=0. Cleared otherwise.
CCR V: Set if (N=1 and C=0) or (N=0 and C=1). Cleared otherwise.
CCR C: Set if bit 0 of the byte=1 BEFORE the shift. Cleared otherwise.

ADDRESSING MODES	FORMAT	BYTES	CODE
1) Accumulator	LSR A	1	44
2) Accumulator	LSR B	1	54
3) Extended	LSR MM	3	74
4) Indexed	LSR Disp,X	2	64

LSRD

MNEMONIC FUNCTION: Shifts the contents of Acc D one bit to the right. Bit 0 is transferred into the Carry flag of the CCR and bit 15 receives a 0.

CCR H: Unaffected.
CCR I: Unaffected.
CCR N: Cleared.
CCR Z: Set if result=0. Cleared otherwise.
CCR V: Set if (N=1 and C=0) or (N=0 and C=1). Cleared otherwise.
CCR C: Set if bit 0 of Acc D is 1 BEFORE the shift. Cleared otherwise.

ADDRESSING MODES	FORMAT	BYTES	CODE
1) Implied	LSRD	1	04

MUL

MNEMONIC FUNCTION: Multiplies the contents of Acc A and Acc B together and deposits the 16-bit unsigned result into Acc D, the MSB going to Acc A.

CCR H: Unaffected.
CCR I: Unaffected.
CCR N: Unaffected.
CCR Z: Unaffected.
CCR V: Unaffected.
CCR C: Set if bit 7 of result=1. Cleared otherwise.

ADDRESSING MODES	FORMAT	BYTES	CODE
1) Implied	MUL	1	3D

NEG

MNEMONIC FUNCTION: Takes the contents of the specified Acc or memory location, calculates the Two's Complement and restores it to its origin. Note that if the original number was -128, no action will be taken.

CCR H: Unaffected.
CCR I: Unaffected.
CCR N: Set if MSB of result=1. Cleared otherwise.
CCR Z: Set if result=0. Cleared otherwise.
CCR V: Set if result overflows. Cleared otherwise. Note that the bit is set when the data is equal to -128.
CCR C: Set if borrow occurs. Cleared otherwise. Bit is set when data is not equal to 0.

ADDRESSING MODES	FORMAT	BYTES	CODE
1) Accumulator	NEG A	1	40
2) Accumulator	NEG B	1	50
3) Extended	NEG MM	3	70
4) Indexed	NEG Disp,X	2	60

NOP

MNEMONIC FUNCTION: This instruction simply increments the PC and has no other function. It does not affect the CCR.

CCR H: Unaffected.
CCR I: Unaffected.
CCR N: Unaffected.
CCR Z: Unaffected.
CCR V: Unaffected.
CCR C: Unaffected.

ADDRESSING MODES	FORMAT	BYTES	CODE
1) Implied	NOP	1	01

OIM

MNEMONIC FUNCTION: Takes the immediate data, the contents of a specified memory location and ORs them, storing the result in the memory location.

CCR H: Unaffected.
CCR I: Unaffected.
CCR N: Set if MSB of result=1. Cleared otherwise.
CCR Z: Set if result=0. Cleared otherwise.
CCR V: Cleared.
CCR C: Unaffected.

ADDRESSING MODES	FORMAT	BYTES	CODE
1) Direct	OIM #Imm,M	3	72
2) Indexed	OIM #Imm,Disp,X3		62

ORA A

MNEMONIC FUNCTION: Takes the contents of the specified Acc, the contents of a memory location (or immediate data) and ORs them, placing the result in the Acc.

CCR H: Unaffected.
CCR I: Unaffected.
CCR N: Set if MSB or result=1. Cleared otherwise.
CCR Z: Set if all bits=0. Cleared otherwise.
CCR V: Cleared.
CCR C: Unaffected.

ADDRESSING MODES	FORMAT	BYTES	CODE
1) Immediate	ORA A #Imm	2	8A
2) Direct	ORA A M	2	9A
3) Extended	ORA A MM	3	BA
4) Indexed	ORA A Disp,X	2	AA

ORA B

MNEMONIC FUNCTION: Takes the contents of the specified Acc, the contents of a memory location (or immediate data) and ORs them, placing the result in the Acc.

CCR H: Unaffected.
CCR I: Unaffected.
CCR N: Set if MSB or result=1. Cleared otherwise.
CCR Z: Set if all bits=0. Cleared otherwise.
CCR V: Cleared.
CCR C: Unaffected.

ADDRESSING MODES	FORMAT	BYTES	CODE
1) Immediate	ORA B #Imm	2	CA
2) Direct	ORA B M	2	DA
3) Extended	ORA B MM	3	FA
4) Indexed	ORA B Disp,X	2	EA

PSH

MNEMONIC FUNCTION: Takes the contents of the specified Acc and stores it on the stack as indicated by the SP. The SP is then decremented by 1.

CCR H: Unaffected.
CCR I: Unaffected.
CCR N: Unaffected.
CCR Z: Unaffected.
CCR V: Unaffected.
CCR C: Unaffected.

ADDRESSING MODES	FORMAT	BYTES	CODE
1) Accumulator	PSH A	1	36
2) Accumulator	PSH B	1	37

PSHX

MNEMONIC FUNCTION: Takes the contents of the IX and stores it on the stack as indicated by the SP. Because the IX is a 16-bit Acc, the SP is then decremented by 2.

CCR H: Unaffected.
CCR I: Unaffected.
CCR N: Unaffected.
CCR Z: Unaffected.
CCR V: Unaffected.
CCR C: Unaffected.

ADDRESSING MODES	FORMAT	BYTES	CODE
1) Implied	PSHX	1	3C

PUL

MNEMONIC FUNCTION: The contents of the stack, as indicated by the SP, is removed and placed in the specified Acc. The SP is then incremented by 1.

CCR H: Unaffected.
CCR I: Unaffected.
CCR N: Unaffected.
CCR Z: Unaffected.
CCR V: Unaffected.
CCR C: Unaffected.

ADDRESSING MODES	FORMAT	BYTES	CODE
1) Accumulator	PUL A	1	32
2) Accumulator	PUL B	1	33

PULX

MNEMONIC FUNCTION: Loads the IX with the double-byte contents of the stack, as indicated by the SP. The SP is then incremented by 2.

CCR H: Unaffected.
CCR I: Unaffected.
CCR N: Unaffected.
CCR Z: Unaffected.
CCR V: Unaffected.
CCR C: Unaffected.

ADDRESSING MODES	FORMAT	BYTES	CODE
1) Implied	PULX	1	38

ROL

MNEMONIC FUNCTION: Shifts the contents of the specified Acc or memory location one place to the left. The Carry flag is inserted into bit 0 and bit 7 is then placed in the Carry bit of the CCR.

CCR H: Unaffected.
CCR I: Unaffected.
CCR N: Set if MSB of result=1. Cleared otherwise.
CCR Z: Set if all bits of result=0. Cleared otherwise.
CCR V: Set if (N=1 and C=0) or (N=0 and C=1) after the shift. Cleared otherwise.
CCR C: Set if MSB of data=1 before the shift. Cleared otherwise.

ADDRESSING MODES	FORMAT	BYTES	CODE
1) Accumulator	ROL A	1	49
2) Accumulator	ROL B	1	59
3) Extended	ROL MM	3	79
4) Indexed	ROL Disp,X	2	69

ROR

MNEMONIC FUNCTION: Shifts the contents of the specified Acc or memory location one place to the right. The Carry flag is inserted into bit 7 and bit 0 is then placed in the Carry bit of the CCR.

CCR H: Unaffected.
CCR I: Unaffected.
CCR N: Set if MSB of result=1. Cleared otherwise.
CCR Z: Set if all bits of result=0. Cleared otherwise.
CCR V: Set if (N=1 and C=0) or (N=0 and C=1) after the shift. Cleared otherwise.
CCR C: Set if LSB of data=1 before the shift. Cleared otherwise.

ADDRESSING MODES	FORMAT	BYTES	CODE
1) Accumulator	ROR A	1	46
2) Accumulator	ROR B	1	56
3) Extended	ROR MM	3	76
4) Indexed	ROR Disp,X	2	66

RTI

MNEMONIC FUNCTION: The contents of the stack are restored to the various registers as they were before servicing the interrupt. Data is removed in the following order, incrementing the SP at each operation:

a. The CCR.
b. Accumulator A.
c. Accumulator B.
d. The high byte of the IX.
e. The low byte of the IX.
f. The high byte of the PC.
g. The low byte of the PC.

CCR H: As returned.
CCR I: As returned.
CCR N: As returned.
CCR Z: As returned.
CCR V: As returned.
CCR C: As returned.

ADDRESSING MODES	FORMAT	BYTES	CODE
1) Implied	RTI	1	3B

RTS

MNEMONIC FUNCTION: After incrementing the SP by 1, the new return address is pulled off the stack, high order byte first, and returned to the PC.

CCR H: Unaffected.
CCR I: Unaffected.
CCR N: Unaffected.
CCR Z: Unaffected.
CCR V: Unaffected.
CCR C: Unaffected.

ADDRESSING MODES	FORMAT	BYTES	CODE
1) Implied	RTS	1	39

SBA

MNEMONIC FUNCTION: Subtracts the contents of Acc B from those of Acc B, storing the result in Acc A and leaving Acc B unaltered.

CCR H: Unaffected.
CCR I: Unaffected.
CCR N: Set if MSB of result=1. Cleared otherwise.
CCR Z: Set if result=0. Cleared otherwise.
CCR V: Set if overflow occurs. Cleared otherwise.
CCR C: Set if the absolute value of Acc B is greater than that of Acc A. Cleared otherwise.

ADDRESSING MODES	FORMAT	BYTES	CODE
1) Implied	SBA	1	10

SBC A

MNEMONIC FUNCTION: Subtracts the immediate value (or the contents of a memory location), including the Carry flag, from the specified Acc and stores the result in the Acc.

CCR H: Unaffected.
CCR I: Unaffected.
CCR N: Set if MSB of result=1. Cleared otherwise.
CCR Z: Set if result=0. Cleared otherwise.
CCR V: Set if result overflows. Cleared otherwise.
CCR C: Set if absolute value of data plus Carry is greater than the contents of the Acc. Cleared otherwise.

ADDRESSING MODES	FORMAT	BYTES	CODE
1) Immediate	SBC A #Imm	2	82
2) Direct	SBC A M	2	92
3) Extended	SBC A MM	3	B2
4) Indexed	SBC A Disp,X	2	A2

SBC B

MNEMONIC FUNCTION: Subtracts the immediate value (or the contents of a memory location), including the Carry flag, from the specified Acc and stores the result in the Acc.

CCR H: Unaffected.
CCR I: Unaffected.
CCR N: Set if MSB of result=1. Cleared otherwise.
CCR Z: Set if result=0. Cleared otherwise.
CCR V: Set if result overflows. Cleared otherwise.
CCR C: Set if absolute value of data plus Carry is greater than the contents of the Acc. Cleared otherwise.

ADDRESSING MODES	FORMAT	BYTES	CODE
1) Immediate	SBC B #Imm	2	C2
2) Direct	SBC B M	2	D2
3) Extended	SBC B MM	3	F2
4) Indexed	SBC B Disp,X	2	E2

SEC

MNEMONIC FUNCTION: Sets the Carry flag of the CCR to 1.

CCR H: Unaffected.
CCR I: Unaffected.
CCR N: Unaffected.
CCR Z: Unaffected.
CCR V: Unaffected.
CCR C: Set.

ADDRESSING MODES	FORMAT	BYTES	CODE
1) Implied	SEC	1	0D

SEI

MNEMONIC FUNCTION: Sets the Interrupt Mask flag of the CCR. In this state, all interrupts, with the single exception of the NMI, are disabled.

CCR H: Unaffected.
CCR I: Set.
CCR N: Unaffected.
CCR Z: Unaffected.
CCR V: Unaffected.
CCR C: unaffected.

ADDRESSING MODES	FORMAT	BYTES	CODE
1) Implied	SEI	1	0F

SEV

MNEMONIC FUNCTION: Sets the Two's Complement flag in the CCR.

CCR H: Unaffected.
CCR I: Unaffected.
CCR N: Unaffected.
CCR Z: Unaffected.
CCR V: Set.
CCR C: Unaffected.

ADDRESSING MODES	FORMAT	BYTES	CODE
1) Implied	SEV	1	0B

SLP

MNEMONIC FUNCTION: The SLP instruction stops the CPU but maintains the internal registers. All timers run as normal. An IRQ can cancel the instruction. Once released from Sleep, the system will continue working as before if the Interrupt Mask is set. If it is clear, the CPU will set it and load the interrupt vector address into the PC. Program execution will then recommence at that address.

CCR H: Unaffected.
CCR I: Unaffected.
CCR N: Unaffected.
CCR Z: Unaffected.
CCR V: Unaffected.
CCR C: Unaffected.

ADDRESSING MODES	FORMAT	BYTES	CODE
1) Implied	SLP	1	1A

STA A

MNEMONIC FUNCTION: Stores the contents of the specified Acc into the required memory location, leaving the original contents of the Acc intact.

CCR H: Unaffected.
CCR I: Unaffected.
CCR N: Set if MSB of Acc=1. Cleared otherwise.
CCR Z: Set if contents of Acc=0. Cleared otherwise.
CCR V: Cleared.
CCR C: Unaffected.

ADDRESSING MODES	FORMAT	BYTES	CODE
1) Direct	STA A M	2	97
2) Extended	STA A MM	3	B7
3) Indexed	STA A Disp,X	2	A7

STA B

MNEMONIC FUNCTION: Stores the contents of the specified Acc into the required memory location, leaving theoriginal contents of the Acc intact.

CCR H: Unaffected.
CCR I: Unaffected.
CCR N: Set if MSB of Acc=1. Cleared otherwise.
CCR Z: Set if contents of Acc=0. Cleared otherwise.
CCR V: Cleared.
CCR C: Unaffected.

ADDRESSING MODES	FORMAT	BYTES	CODE
1) Direct	STA B M	2	D7
2) Extended	STA B MM	3	F7
3) Indexed	STA B Disp,X	2	E7

STD

MNEMONIC FUNCTION: Stores the double-byte contents of Acc D into a double-byte memory location, leaving the original contents of Acc D unchanged.

CCR H: Unaffected.
CCR I: Unaffected.
CCR N: Set if MSB of Acc D=1. Cleared otherwise.
CCR Z: Set if contents of Acc D=0. Cleared otherwise.
CCR V: Cleared.
CCR C: Unaffected.

ADDRESSING MODES	FORMAT	BYTES	CODE
1) Direct	STD M	2	DD
2) Extended	STD MM	3	FD
3) Indexed	STD Disp,X	2	ED

STS

MNEMONIC FUNCTION: Stores the SP into a specified memory location, high order byte first.

CCR H: Unaffected.
CCR I: Unaffected.
CCR N: Set if MSB of SP=1. Cleared otherwise.
CCR Z: Set if SP=0. Cleared otherwise.
CCR V: Cleared.
CCR C: Unaffected.

ADDRESSING MODES	FORMAT	BYTES	CODE
1) Direct	STS M	2	9F
2) Extended	STS MM	3	BF
3) Indexed	STS Disp,X	2	AF

STX

MNEMONIC FUNCTION: Stores the IX into a specified memory location, high order byte first.

CCR H: Unaffected.
CCR I: Unaffected.
CCR N: Set if MSB of IX=1. Cleared otherwise.
CCR Z: Set if IX=0. Cleared otherwise.
CCR V: Cleared.
CCR C: Unaffected.

ADDRESSING MODES	FORMAT	BYTES	CODE
1) Direct	STX M	2	DF
2) Extended	STX MM	3	FF
3) Indexed	STX Disp,X	2	EF

SUB A

MNEMONIC FUNCTION: Subtracts the immediate data or the contents of a memory location from the specified Acc and deposits the result in the Acc.

CCR H: Unaffected.
CCR I: unaffected.
CCR N: Set if MSB of result=1. Cleared otherwise.
CCR Z: Set if result=0. Cleared otherwise.
CCR V: Set if result overflows. Cleared otherwise.
CCR C: Set if absolute value of data is greater than that of the Acc. Cleared otherwise.

ADDRESSING MODES	FORMAT	BYTES	CODE
1) Immediate	SUB A #Imm	2	80
2) Direct	SUB A M	2	90
3) Extended	SUB A MM	3	B0
4) Indexed	SUB A Disp,X	2	A0

SUB B

MNEMONIC FUNCTION: Subtracts the immediate data or the contents of a memory location from the specified Acc and deposits the result in the Acc.

CCR H: Unaffected.
CCR I: unaffected.
CCR N: Set if MSB of result=1. Cleared otherwise.
CCR Z: Set if result=0. Cleared otherwise.
CCR V: Set if result overflows. Cleared otherwise.
CCR C: Set if absolute value of data is greater than that of the Acc. Cleared otherwise.

ADDRESSING MODES	FORMAT	BYTES	CODE
1) Immediate	SUB B #Imm	2	C0
2) Direct	SUB B M	2	D0
3) Extended	SUB B MM	3	F0
4) Indexed	SUB B Disp,X	2	E0

SUB D

MNEMONIC FUNCTION: Subtracts the double-byte immediate data or memory contents from Acc D and deposits the result in Acc D.

CCR H: Unaffected.
CCR I: Unaffected.
CCR N: Set if MSB of result=1. Cleared otherwise.
CCR Z: Set if result=0. Cleared otherwise.
CCR V: Set if result overflows. Cleared otherwise.
CCR C: Set if absolute value of data is greater than that of Acc D. Cleared otherwise.

ADDRESSING MODES	FORMAT	BYTES	CODE
1) Immediate	SUBD #Ih Il	3	83
2) Direct	SUBD M	2	93
3) Extended	SUBD MM	3	B3
4) Indexed	SUBD Disp,X	2	A3

SWI

MNEMONIC FUNCTION: The PC is incremented by 1. Internal registers are stacked in the order PC, IX, AccA, AccB and CCR, decrementing the SP after each byte. Note that double-byte registers are saved low-byte first and that the instruction sets bits 6 and 7 of the CCR before stacking. The interrupt mask is then set and the double-byte contents of $FFFA is loaded into the PC.

CCR H: Unaffected.
CCR I: Set.
CCR N: Unaffected.
CCR Z: Unaffected.
CCR V: Unaffected.
CCR C: Unaffected.

ADDRESSING MODES	FORMAT	BYTES	CODE
1) Implied	SWI	1	3F

TAB

MNEMONIC FUNCTION: Transfers the contents of Acc A into Acc B, leaving the original contents of Acc A untouched.

CCR H: Unaffected.
CCR I: Unaffected.
CCR N: Set if MSB of Acc A=1. Cleared otherwise.
CCR Z: Set if Acc A=0. Cleared otherwise.
CCR V: Cleared.
CCR C: Unaffected.

ADDRESSING MODES	FORMAT	BYTES	CODE
1) Implied	TAB	1	16

TAP

MNEMONIC FUNCTION: Transfers bits 0-5 of Acc A into the corresponding positions in the CCR, leaving the contents of Acc A unchanged.

CCR H: Bit 5 of Acc A.
CCR I: Bit 4 of Acc A.
CCR N: Bit 3 of Acc A.
CCR Z: Bit 2 of Acc A.
CCR V: Bit 1 of Acc A.
CCR C: Bit 0 of Acc A.

ADDRESSING MODES	FORMAT	BYTES	CODE
1) Implied	TAP	1	06

TBA

MNEMONIC FUNCTION: Transfers the contents of Acc B into Acc A, leaving the original contents of Acc B unchanged.

CCR H: Unaffected.
CCR I: Unaffected.
CCR N: Set if MSB of Acc B=1. Cleared otherwise.
CCR Z: Set if Acc B=0. Cleared otherwise.
CCR V: Cleared.
CCR C: Unaffected.

ADDRESSING MODES	FORMAT	BYTES	CODE
1) Implied	TBA	1	17

TIM

MNEMONIC FUNCTION: Takes immediate data and the contents of a specified memory location and ANDs them together with the object of changing the CCR. Note that both operands remain unaffected by this operation.

CCR H: Unaffected.
CCR I: Unaffected.
CCR N: Set if MSB of result=1. Cleared otherwise.
CCR Z: Set if result=0. Cleared otherwise.
CCR V: Cleared.
CCR C: Unaffected.

ADDRESSING MODES	FORMAT	BYTES	CODE
1) Direct	TIM #Imm,M	3	7B
2) Indexed	TIM #Imm,Disp,X	3	6B

TPA

MNEMONIC FUNCTION: Transfers bits 0-5 of the CCR into Acc A, leaving the original contents of the CCR unchanged.

CCR H: Unaffected.
CCR I: Unaffected.
CCR N: Unaffected.
CCR Z: Unaffected.
CCR V: Unaffected.
CCR C: Unaffected.

ADDRESSING MODES	FORMAT	BYTES	CODE
1) Implied	TPA	1	07

TST

MNEMONIC FUNCTION: Examines the contents of the specified Acc or memory location and sets the N or Z flag of the CCR accordingly.

CCR H: Unaffected.
CCR I: Unaffected.
CCR N: Set if MSB of data=1. Cleared otherwise.
CCR Z: Set if data=0. Cleared otherwise.
CCR V: Cleared.
CCR C: Cleared.

ADDRESSING MODES	FORMAT	BYTES	CODE
1) Accumulator	TST A	1	4D
2) Accumulator	TST B	1	5D
3) Extended	TST MM	3	7D
4) Indexed	TST Disp,X	2	6D

TSX

MNEMONIC FUNCTION: Increments the SP by 1 and transfers it into the IX, leaving the SP unchanged.

CCR H: Unaffected.
CCR I: Unaffected.
CCR N: Unaffected.
CCR Z: Unaffected.
CCR V: Unaffected.
CCR C: Unaffected.

ADDRESSING MODES	FORMAT	BYTES	CODE
1) Implied	TSX	1	30

TXS

MNEMONIC FUNCTION: Decrements the IX by 1 and transfers it to the SP, leaving the IX unchanged.

CCR H: Unaffected.
CCR I: Unaffected.
CCR N: Unaffected.
CCR Z: Unaffected.
CCR V: Unaffected.
CCR C: Unaffected.

ADDRESSING MODES	FORMAT	BYTES	CODE
1) Implied	TXS	1	35

WAI

MNEMONIC FUNCTION: Increments the PC by 1 and stacks the PC, IX Acc A, Acc B and CCR, in that order, decrementing the SP by 1 at each byte. Note that double-byte registers are stored low byte first and that bits 6-7 of the CCR are stacked as binary 11. The program then stops and waits for an interrupt from a peripheral. If the interrupt mask bit is 0 prior to the interrupt occurring, it will be set on the interrupt and the vector lead to the PC.

CCR H: Unaffected.
CCR I: Unaffected until interrupt. If=0 on interrupt, it is set.
CCR N: Unaffected.
CCR Z: Unaffected.
CCR V: Unaffected.
CCR C: Unaffected.

ADDRESSING MODES	FORMAT	BYTES	CODE
1) Implied	WAI	1	3E

XGDX
MNEMONIC FUNCTION: Exchanges the IX and Acc D registers.

CCR H: Unaffected.
CCR I: Unaffected.
CCR N: Unaffected.
CCR Z: Unaffected.
CCR V: Unaffected.
CCR C: Unaffected.

ADDRESSING MODES	FORMAT	BYTES	CODE
1) Implied	XGDX	1	18

Arranged Numerically

Note that AIM, BSET, BTST and BTGL have codes identical with BCLR, OIM, TIM and EIM, respectively.

00 ——	01 NOP	02 ——
03 ——	04 LSR D	05 ASL D
06 TAP	07 TPA	08 INX
09 DEX	0A CLV	0B SEV
0C CLC	0D SEC	0E CLI
0F SEI	10 SBA	11 CBA
12 ——	13 ——	14 ——
15 ——	16 TAB	17 TBA
18 XGDX	19 DAA	1A SLP
1B ABA	1C ——	1D ——
1E ——	1F ——	20 BRA REL
21 BRN REL	22 BHI REL	23 BLS REL
24 BCC REL	25 BCS REL	26 BNE REL
27 BEQ REL	28 BVC REL	29 BVS REL
2A BPL REL	2B BMI REL	2C BGE REL
2D BLT REL	2E BGT REL	2F BLE REL
30 TSX	31 INS	32 PUL A
33 PUL B	34 DES	35 TXS
36 PSH A	37 PSH B	38 PUL X
39 RTS	3A ABX	3B RTI
3C PSH X	3D MUL	3E WAI
3F SWI	40 NEG A	41 ——
42 ——	43 COM A	44 LSR A
45 ——	46 ROR A	47 ASR A
48 ASL A	49 ROL A	4A DEC A
4B ——	4C INC A	4D TST A
4E ——	4F CLR A	50 NEG B
51 ——	52 ——	53 COM B
54 LSR B	55 ——	56 ROR B
57 ASR B	58 ASL B	59 ROL B
5A DEC B	5B ——	5C INC B
5D TST B	5E ——	5F CLR B
60 NEG DISP,X	61 AIM #IMM,DISP,X	61 BCLR BIT,DISP,X
62 BSET BIT,DISP,X	62 OIM #IMM,DISP,X	63 COM DISP,X
64 LSR DISP,X	65 BTGL BIT,DISP,X	65 EIM #IMM,DISP,X
66 ROR DISP,X	67 ASR DISP,X	68 ASL DISP,X
69 ROL DISP,X	6A DEC DISP,X	6B BTST BIT,DISP,X

6B TIM #IMM,DISP,X
6C INC DISP,X
6D TST DISP,X
6E JMP DISP,X
6F CLR DISP,X
70 NEG MM
71 AIM #IMM,M
71 BCLR BIT,M
72 BSET BIT,M
72 OIM #IMM,M
73 COM MM
74 LSR MM
75 BTGL BIT,M
75 EIM #IMM,M
76 ROR MM
77 ASR MM
78 ASL MM
79 ROL MM
7A DEC MM
7B BTST BIT,M
7B TIM #IMM,M
7C INC MM
7D TST MM
7E JMP MM
7F CLR MM
80 SUB A #IMM
81 CMP A #IMM
82 SBC A #IMM
83 SUB D #IH IL
84 AND A #IMM
85 BIT A #IMM
86 LDA A #IMM
87 ——
88 EOR A #IMM
89 ADC A #IMM
8A ORA A #IMM
8B ADD A #IMM
8C CPX #IMM
8D BSR REL
8E LDS #IH IL
8F ——
90 SUB A M
91 CMP A M
92 SBC A M
93 SUB D M
94 AND A M
95 BIT A M
96 LDA A M
97 STAA M
98 EOR A M
99 ADC A M
9A ORA A M
9B ADD A M
9C CPX M
9D JSR M
9E LDS M
9F STS M
A0 SUB A DISP,X
A1 CMP A DISP,X
A2 SBC A DISP,X
A3 SUB D DISP,X
A4 AND A DISP,X
A5 BIT A DISP,X
A6 LDA A DISP,X
A7 STA A DISP,X
A8 EOR A DISP,X
A9 ADCA DISP,X
AA ORA A DISP,X
AB ADD A DISP,X
AC CPX DISP,X
AD JSR DISP,X
AE LDS DISP,X
AF STS DISP,X
B0 SUB A MM
B1 CMP A MM
B2 SBC A MM
B3 SUB D MM
B4 AND A MM
B5 BIT A MM
B6 LDA A MM
B7 STA A MM
B8 EOR A MM
B9 ADC A MM
BA ORA A MM
BB ADD A MM
BC CPX MM
BD JSR MM
BE LDS MM
BF STS MM
C0 SUB B #IMM
C1 CMP B #IMM
C2 SBC B #IMM
C3 ADD D #IH IL
C4 AND B #IMM
C5 BIT B #IMM
C6 LDA B #IMM
C7 ——
C8 EOR B #IMM
C9 ADC B #IMM
CA ORA B #IMM
CB ADD B #IMM
CC LDD #IH IL
CD ——
CE LDX #IH IL
CF ——
D0 SUB B M
D1 CMP B M
D2 SBC B M
D3 ADD D M
D4 AND B M
D5 BIT B M
D6 LDA B M
D7 STA B M
D8 EOR B M
D9 ADC B M
DA ORA B M
DB ADD B M
DC LDD M
DD STD M
DE LDX M
DF STX M
E0 SUB B DISP,X
E1 CMP B DISP,X
E2 SBC B DISP,X
E3 ADD D DISP,X
E4 AND B DISP,X
E5 BIT B DISP,X
E6 LDA B DISP,X
E7 STA B DISP,X
E8 EOR B DISP,X
E9 ADC B DISP,X
EA ORA B DISP,X

EB ADD B DISP,X
EC LDD DISP,X
ED STD DISP,X
EE LDX DISP,X
EF STX DISP,X
F0 SUB B MM
F1 CMP B MM
F2 SBC B MM
F3 ADD D MM
F4 AND B MM
F5 BIT B MM
F6 LDA B MM
F7 STA B MM
F8 EOR B MM
F9 ADC B MM
FA ORA B MM
FB ADD B MM
FC LDD MM
FD STD MM
FE LDX MM
FF STX MM

Annex F

Hexloader for the *Psion Organiser*

F:Hexloader for the *Psion Organiser*

F.0 Introduction. Enter each of the routines listed below one at a time, translating and saving each one as you go. You would be wise to omit the REM statements. Their purpose is to give some clarity to the code and thereby allow you to make your own modifications. However, they take up a great deal of space and contribute nothing to the actual performance of the hexloader. You would therefore be better to omit them from your code.

F.1 Making Room For Machine Code. As I mentioned in paragraph 4.7, we must make some space into which we can place our machine code. There are a number of ways in which we could do this but ideally our choice should take into consideration:

a. That the area chosen must not interfere with the workings of the Organiser.
b. That the area must be static and not subject to movement under the whim of the Operating System.
c. That the area must not be trashed by the Operating System.

F.2 It would be inappropriate at this point to go through all the pros and cons of each and every possibility. Suffice it to say that the best choice in my opinion is to lower the baseline of the stack to the level we want. The space created between the default level and the new is ours to do with pretty much as we please. Have a look at Annex C. This shows the memory map of the Organiser. Near the top, you can see the line dividing the processor and language stacks. The former grows no further than the line itself but the latter starts AT the line and grows downwards. The actual address of the line is held as a 2-byte word at location $2065. Lowering the number held in $2065 will give us the space we need.

F.3 The Hexloader consists of the following 21 routines:

a. MC:
b. NEW:
c. VIEW:
d. DECODE:
e. RUN:
f. FILES:
g. SPACE:
h. INFO:
j. GETNUM:
k. CENTRAL:
l. INTOBASE:
m. FROMBASE:
n. CHECK:
p. BADNEWS:
q. ORGLOAD:
r. ORGSAVE:
s. ORGDIR
t. ORGKILL:
u. PCLOAD:
v. PCSAVE:
w. SCREEN:
x. MODIFY:

F.4 Together, these routines swallow up a great deal of space. Those readers who have less memory to play with can do without the "DECODE:" routine, which disassembles the code. Since this routine makes use of a sizeable mnemonic look-up table, the table itself can also be dispensed with. Just make sure that you remove the call to "DECODE:" in the main program ("MC:"). For those of you who would like the disassembler, you must construct a mnemonic file. This can be done in one of 2 ways:

a. Word Processor. Those readers fortunate enough to have a PC at their command can simply type the mnemonics into an ASCII file. Each mnemonic consists of 2 single-digit numbers and a string. Each of these must be separated by a <TAB> character and each complete 3 must be terminated by the

<CR> key. You would then end up with a file consisting of 256 lines, each of which contains two items. You may vall this PC file anything you wish as long as its file extension is ".ODB". To load it into the Organiser, use the "RECEIVE" option in the "COMMS" menu and select "FILE". Give the file the Organiser internal name "MNEMONIC". That's all there is to it.

b. No Word Processor. Those of you who do not have access to a micro or a serial link can use the routine "TYPEMNEM:". This program expects the user to type in the data, following the prompts. As I pointed out in the sub-para above, each line consists of 3 items. The first of these is the "addressing mode", the second indicates the number of bytes in the instruction and the string holds the assembly language mnemonic for that instruction. The routine will prompt you for each of these in turn, allowing you to view your entry and correct mistakes before storing it in "MNEMONIC:". Note that there is no need to use the <TAB> key. This routine can be deleted to save space when the file construction is complete.

F.5 Calling The Hexloader. The best way to start the Hexloader, is by including it in the top level menu. Refer to your Organiser manual if you are unsure how to do this. Simply put "MC" at the desired point in the menu. Selecting this option will cause the Organiser to jump immediately to the Hexloader and start running the routines.

F.6 Using The Hexloader. On calling "MC:", the program checks for the existence of a "MNEMONIC" file. If this is not present, a warning beep is issued and the fact made known to the user:

<< WARNING >>
No mnemonic file

This remains on the screen for a short while and is then replaced by:

-< PROBLEMS >-
Continue <Y/N>

This is to allow the user the opportunity to escape from the program to create or load the file. It is not strictly necessary to have the file in memory but its absence is required if the user wants to disassemble any area of memory. If it is not needed, the user should reply <Y> to the enquiry. When this is done (or, indeed, if the "MNEMONIC" file IS present), the user is presented with a title screen, requesting him to press a key to begin. This leads to the main menu, offering the following options:

a. NEW
b. VIEW
c. DECODE
d. RUN
e. FILES
f. SPACE
g. INFO
h. QUIT

F.7 NEW. The "NEW" option allows the user to enter a new program. Note carefully that you should not enter anything without first clearing some space for your machine code program using the "SPACE" option in the main menu. Calling the "NEW" option clears the screen and offers the user a screen showing:

-START ADDRESS-
Value: [$....]

The user is expected to enter the hexadecimal address of the start of the new routine. Note that the SHIFT key is unnecessary, since a routine allows the user to press only the "hex alphabet"
keys. Simply pressing the <EXE> key without entering an address, will cause the Organiser to return to the main menu. If, for example, the address "$7D0B" is entered, the screen will change and be replaced by:

- CELL $7D0B -
Value: [$..]

A 2-digit hexadecimal number is expected and can be input in the same way as the address. This number will then be POKEd into the memory cell, the cell will be incremented and the screen will be redrawn with the new address at the top centre. This continues until the <EXE> key is pressed without entering a value. The main menu will re-appear and you have entered your first program.

F.8 VIEW. The "VIEW" option allows the user to view the contents of any memory location. Note that this option does not take into account "bank switching". It is intended, as is the disassembler, to allow the user to examine his program, NOT to take the Organiser Operating System apart. On calling the routine, the user will get the following screen:

- VIEW START -
Value: [$....]

The routine expects the user to enter the address where the memory dump is to start. This number must be in hexadecimal and can be entered without the aid of the SHIFT key. Once this number is entered, the screen will clear to give:

LZ Model	CM/XP Model
7D13 B6 7D 30 FE	7D0B 86 0C 3F 10
7D0F 86 7E 3F 10	[..?.]
7D0B 86 0C 3F 10	
[..?...?...0.]	

The user can scroll up/down the memory map using the up/down arrow keys. This will advance the memory by one "line's worth". To move a little faster, the user can move 16 bytes at a time, using the left arrow to decrement and the right arrow to increment. If any byte on screen needs to be altered, the "MODE" key should be pressed. This will produce a left-arrow symbol at the first byte. This can be scrolled around the screen until it indicates the offending byte. Pressing <EXE> at this juncture will clear the screen and display:

- NEW CONTENTS -
Value: [$....]

Enter the new value for that location or just press the <EXE> key on its own to leave the current value unchanged. The screen will change once more and be replaced by the memory dump. If any alteration has been entered, its effect should now be visible. To exit from the "VIEW" option, press <ON/CLEAR>.

F.9 DECODE. The "DECODE" option is very simple to use. The user is presented with an entry screen like so:

-START ADDRESS-
Value: [$....]

Enter the start address where the disassembly is to take place. Let's assume that the address $9003 has been chosen. The screen would look something like this:

$9003
STA A $2351

Pressing the <EXE> key will advance to the next mnemonic. Note that it is not possible to scroll up and down memory as with the "VIEW" option. When the disassembly is no longer required, pressing the <ON/CLEAR> key will terminate and return to the main menu.

F.10 RUN. The "RUN" option executes programs which the user has stored in memory. The routine enquires after the start address of the routine. This must be the address at which execution of the program must begin. It is perfectly possible to have data and other sub-routines below the actual main machine code program. The address requested is the location of the code at which the user wants to start execution. The entry is done via a screen like the following:

-EXECUTE BINARY-
Value: [$....]

Pressing the <ON/CLEAR> key will escape from the routine without executing any code. However, having entered the correct address (and assuming the user's code is correct!!) the screen will clear after execution and present the user with:

- ROUTINE DONE -
Another <Y/N>

Pressing <Y> will repeat the routine, while <N> will terminate and return to the main menu.

F.11 FILES. The "FILES" option is, in fact, the gateway to another menu which offers:

a. ORGLOAD
b. ORGSAVE
c. ORGDIR
d. ORGKILL
e. PCLOAD
f. PCSAVE
g. QUIT

F.12 ORGSAVE. Taking the "ORGSAVE" option first, it provides the user with a means by which his binary program stored in memory can be turned into hexadecimal TEXT and saved into a user-named file. The importance of this step is that several files of programs can reside within the Organiser simultaneously and that they can be loaded/saved to/from PC in the same way as for ordinary files. This routine asks the user to give the name of the file where the code is to be stored. If there is already a file of that name it will be deleted. the entry screen looks like this:

-SAVE TO PSION-
File:

Entering a null filename will cause the routine to terminate and return to the FILES sub-menu. Otherwise, the next screen will appear:

-START ADDRESS-
Value: [$....]

This is a standard address entry vehicle and is intended to set the bottom address of the code to be saved. Pressing <ON/CLEAR> or entering a null string will terminate the routine. If a valid address is entered, the next screen will appear:

- END ADDRESS -
Value: [$....]

This is entered under the same conditions as for the start address. If an end address has been entered which is greater than the start address, the routine will beep a warning and return to the FILES sub-menu. Otherwise, the screen will clear to show:

- ORGSAVE -

under which is shown a growing, grey bar indicating the percentage of the file which has been translated into text. When the save is complete, the user is returned to the FILES sub-menu.

F.13 ORGLOAD. The "ORGLOAD" routine, then, is the reverse of "ORGSAVE". The user is prompted:

LOAD FROM PSION
File:

If a null filename or a file which does not exist is entered, the routine will give a warning before returning to the FILES sub- menu. If all is well, the user will see:

- LOAD ADDRESS -
Value: [$....]

Enter the address at which you wish the routine to be loaded. Be vary careful here. Ideally, the user should load the code to the address from which it was originally stored. This is because jumps may specify exact addresses. If the code contains no jumps or location-specific instructions, then it does not matter where it goes. The user should beware, however. Pressing the ,ON/CLEAR> key or entering a null address string will terminate the routine and return to the FILES sub-menu. If all is well, the screen will change to:

- ORGLOAD -

with a growing, grey bar underneath to show the storage progress. Once complete, the FILES sub-menu will re-appear.

F.14 ORGDIR. The "ORGDIR" routine allows the user to view the currently held files. Pressing any key displays the next file stored until either the end of files is reached or the <ON/CLEAR> key is pressed. The program will then return to the FILES sub- menu.

F.15 ORGKILL. The "ORGKILL" routine deletes old program files which are no longer required. The user is prompted with the screen:

- ORGKILL -
File:

Entering a null filename or a non-existent one will cause the routine to terminate and return to the FILES sub-menu. Let's suppose we wished to delete the "MNEMONIC" file to make some more room. The user would see:

-KILL MNEMONIC-
Patience ...

and, when the deletion was complete, the screen would change to:

-KILL MNEMONIC-
Deleted

The screen would then pause for approximately 4 seconds before returning to the FILES sub-menu.

F.15 PCLOAD. This routine is very easy to use. The user is first asked for the full name (including drive and path) of the file on the PC:

- PCLOAD -
Remote:

and then the name of the file as it is to appear in the Organiser:

- PCLOAD -
Local:

Once both are entered, they are checked. If either are null, the routine terminates and the program returns to the FILES sub-menu. If everything is as it should be the screen will change to:

-READY TO LOAD-
Press any key

This gives the user the opportunity to check that the COMMS side of things is ready. Pressing any key causes the transfer to begin. When complete, the program returns to the FILES sub-menu.

F.16 PCSAVE. This routine is the exact corollary of "PCLOAD" except that traffic is going in the other direction. Its description is as for F.15.

F.17 QUIT. Selecting "QUIT" causes the FILES sub-menu to terminate and the program returns to the main menu.

F.18 SPACE. This routine is essential if the user's machine code programs are to be successfully loaded and run. It is responsible for reserving an area into which the code can be POKEd. The user sees:

- NEW MEMBASE -
Value: [$....]

This is a straightforward entry screen. The point at which you require the new memory base to be set must now be entered. BE CAREFUL!! Follow the instructions in the book until you are familiar enough with the Organiser memory map to do do anything exotic. Pressing <ON/CLEAR> or entering a null string will terminate the routine with a beep and return the user to the main menu without doing anything unfortunate. If, however, a valid address is entered, the new memory base will be set. This can be checked using the "INFO" option.

F.19 INFO. Using this option, the user can check the current level of the memory base or, just as importantly, if his use of "SPACE" has worked. It will display, for example:

- MC LOADER -
Membase= $7D0B

This display will remain on screen until the user presses any key. The main menu will then re-appear.

F.20 QUIT. Selecting "QUIT" from the main menu will terminate the Hexloader. If the program has been called from the Organiser's TOP LEVEL MENU, the user will be returned to it. Otherwise, he will find himself in the PROG menu.

Entering a Program

F.21 So, in summary, entering a program is very simple. First, ensure that there is enough space reserved for the code. Check this by calling the "INFO" option. If no memory has been reserved or there is insufficient for his requirements, the user should enter the "SPACE" routine and set the memory base to a new level. In most of the program examples in this book, a memory level of $7D0B is used. This reserves about 500 bytes of space - ample for the needs of the material in this book. When this is done, the code itself can be entered by using the "NEW" routine. This will ask for the start address (which should normally be the memory base) and then repeatedly request bytes of code until <ON/CLEAR> is pressed or <EXE> without entering any data. This will cause a return to the main menu. The code should then be checked using "VIEW" to ensure that no finger trouble intervened. Remember - more than in any other walk of life, Murphy's Law Rule the careless in TRAPper's country. If any small mistakes of a byte or so have been made, they can be altered by using the modify facility, called by pressing <MODE>. When the user is satisfied that the code is 100% correct (wry smile), it can be executed using the "RUN" option. Finally, the good code can be saved to an Organiser file and from there to a PC file, if desired. Similarly, stored code can be re-entered into memory by virtue of the "ORGLOAD" option.

F.22 Conclusion. That concludes the description of the Hexloader. The code follows next, including the "TYPEMNEM:" to enter the mnemonics directly into the Organiser, and then the HD6303 mnemonics themselves for the mnemonic file. Note that each routine begins with a header block describing the code. In addition, each routine is terminated by another, shorter block. These form no part of the code and should not be entered into the Organiser.

```
REM ***************************************************
REM          //// MAIN PROGRAM BEGINS \\\\
REM ***************************************************
mc:
GLOBAL width%,lines%,number$(4),number,tnum,nomnem%
LOCAL keypres$(1),option%

REM Initialise variables.
lines%=2 :REM "4" FOR LZ
width%=16 :REM "20" FOR LZ
nomnem%=0
REM "Welcome" Screen.
CLS
central:("-< MC  LOADER >-",1)
central:("Press any key",2)
GET

REM Check for existence of Mnemonic file. If not present, issue
REM warning and set "nomnem" flag.
IF NOT EXIST("A:MNEMONIC")
  CLS
  central:("<< WARNING >>",1)
  central:("No mnemonic file",2)
  badnews:
  PAUSE 40
  nomnem%=1
REM Otherwise, open the Mnemonic file.
ELSE
  OPEN"A:mnemonic",A,mode%,bytes%,mnem$
ENDIF
REM If the Mnemonic file is not present, off the chance to REM
terminate operation.
IF nomnem%=1
  CLS
  central:("-< PROBLEMS >-",1)
  central:("Continue <Y/N>",2)
  keypres$=UPPER$(GET$)
  IF keypres$="N"
    RETURN
  ENDIF
ENDIF

REM Main Loop
```

```
DO

 REM Main Menu
option%=MENU("NEW,VIEW,DECODE,RUN,FILES,SPACE,INFO,QU
IT")

 REM Call chosen option.
 IF option%=1
  new:
 ELSEIF option%=2
  view:
 ELSEIF option%=3
  decode:   ELSEIF option%=4
  run:
 ELSEIF option%=5
  files:
 ELSEIF option%=6
  space:
 ELSEIF option%=7
  info:
 ENDIF
UNTIL option%=8

REM If Mnemonic file WAS present, close it.
IF nomnem%=0
 USE A :CLOSE
ENDIF

REM Finished.
RETURN
REM ********************************************************
REM              //// MAIN PROGRAM ENDS \\\\
REM ********************************************************
```

```
REM ******************************************************
REM                    //// SUBROUTINE "NEW" \\\\
REM ******************************************************

new:
LOCAL cell,address

REM Get start address where code is to be stored, exiting if a REM null
string is entered.
CLS
getnum:("-START  ADDRESS-",4)
IF number$=""
  RETURN
ENDIF

REM Make temporary store of address.
cell=number

CLS

REM "Entry" loop.
DO
  number=cell

  REM Check that address is a legal integer.
  check:
  address=tnum

  REM Convert it to a hexadecimal string.
  intobase:(4)

  REM Get byte for storage.
  getnum:("- CELL $"+number$+" -",4)
  check:

  REM If byte is not a null string, size it and poke it as a word   REM or a
byte, as appropriate.
  IF number$<>""
    IF LEN(number$)<3
```

```
    POKEB address,tnum
    cell=cell+1 :REM Increment memory address by 1 byte
  ELSE
    POKEW address,tnum
    cell=cell+2 :REM Increment memory address by 1 word
  ENDIF
 ENDIF

REM Loop until a null string is received.
UNTIL number$=""

REM Finished.
RETURN

REM ********************************************************
REM            //// END OF SUBROUTINE "NEW" \\\\
REM ********************************************************
```

```
REM ****************************************************
REM              //// SUBROUTINE "VIEW" \\\\
REM ****************************************************

view:

REM The following 2 lines should be one long one!!!
LOCAL legal$(7),up$(1),down$(1),lefft$(1),rite$(1),onclear$(1),
                    mode$(1),start,keypres$(1)

REM Set variables and constants to initial values.
onclear$=CHR$(1)
mode$=CHR$(2)
up$=CHR$(3)
down$=CHR$(4)
lefft$=CHR$(5)
rite$=CHR$(6)
legal$=onclear$+mode$+up$+down$+lefft$+rite$

REM Get start address for viewing, exiting if a null  string is REM input.
getnum:("-  VIEW START  -",4)
IF number$=""
 RETURN
ENDIF

CLS

REM Copy address to temporary storage.
start=number

REM "View" loop.
DO
 number=start

 REM Check address is a legal integer.
 check:
 start=number

 REM Draw a "screenful" of memory contents.
```

```
 screen:

 REM Get a legal key.
 DO
  keypres$=UPPER$(GET$)
 UNTIL LOC(legal$,keypres$)>0

 REM Alter memory address, enter modification routine or exit,   REM
according to the key entered.
 IF keypres$=up$
  start=start+4
 ELSEIF keypres$=down$
  start=start-4
 ELSEIF keypres$=lefft$
  start=start-16
 ELSEIF keypres$=rite$
  start=start+16
 ELSEIF keypres$=mode$     number=start
  modify:
 ENDIF

UNTIL keypres$=onclear$

REM Finished.
RETURN

REM ******************************************************
REM            ////END OF SUBROUTINE "VIEW" \\\\
REM ******************************************************
```

```
REM ************************************************
REM              //// SUBROUTINE "DECODE" \\\\
REM ************************************************

decode:
LOCAL byte%,decode$(40),mode%,hash$(1),temp

hash$=CHR$(35)

REM Ensure Mnemonic file is current.
USE A

CLS

REM Get start address for disassembly, exiting if null string is REM
entered.
getnum:("-START  ADDRESS-",4)
IF number$=""
 badnews:
 RETURN
ENDIF

REM "Decode" loop.
DO
 CLS

 REM Ensure that address is legal integer.
 check:

 REM Convert address to hexadecimal string.
 intobase:(4)

 REM Get contents of memory location.
 byte%=PEEKB(tnum)

 REM Display memory address in hex.
 central:("$"+number$,1)

 REM Find the relevant mnemonic in the file.
```

```
POSITION byte%+1
decode$=A.mnem$+" "

REM Increment the memory address and ensure legal integer.
number=number+1
check:

REM make temporary copy of address.
temp=number

REM Add appropriate "text" to mnemonic.
IF A.mode%=2 OR A.mode%=3 OR (A.mode%=5 AND A.bytes%=3)
 decode$=decode$+hash$+"$"
ELSEIF A.mode%=4 OR (A.mode%=5 AND A.bytes%=2)
 decode$=decode$+" $"
ENDIF

REM PEEK the appropriate bytes, incrementing the memory  REM
location.  IF A.mode%=3 OR A.mode%=4 OR (A.mode%=5 AND
A.bytes%=3)
 number=PEEKW(tnum)
 intobase:(4)
 temp=temp+2
ELSEIF A.mode%=2 OR (A.mode%=5 AND A.bytes%=2) OR
A.mode%=7
 number=PEEKB(tnum)
 intobase:(2)
 temp=temp+1
ENDIF

IF A.mode%=2 OR A.mode%=3 OR A.mode%=4
 decode$=decode$+number$
ELSEIF A.mode%=5 AND A.bytes%=2
 decode$=decode$+number$+",X"
ELSEIF A.mode%=5 AND A.bytes%=3

decode$=decode$+LEFT$(number$,2)+",$"+RIGHT$(number$,2)+",X"

REM Relative jump.
```

```
 ELSEIF A.mode%=7
  number=number+2
  IF number>129
   number=number-256
  ENDIF
  decode$=decode$+GEN$(number,4)
 ENDIF


 REM Display complete mnemonic.
 central:(decode$,2)
 number=temp

REM Keep going until <ON/CLEAR> pressed.
UNTIL GET$=CHR$(1)

REM Finished.
RETURN

REM ****************************************************
REM          //// END OF SUBROUTINE "DECODE" \\\\
REM ****************************************************
```

```
REM ********************************************************
REM                  //// SUBROUTINE "RUN" \\\\
REM ********************************************************
run:
LOCAL byte%,keypres$(1)

REM "Run" loop
DO

 REM Get execution address, terminating if a null string is
 REM entered.
 getnum:("-EXECUTE BINARY-",4)
 IF number$=""
  badnews:
  RETURN
 ENDIF

 REM Ensure address is a legal integer.
 check:

 REM Call routine.
 byte%=USR(tnum,0)

 REM Pause to allow user to view last screen display before
 REM clearing screen.
 PAUSE 40
 CLS

 REM Offer repeat performance.
 central:("- ROUTINE DONE -",1)
 central:("Another  <Y/N>",2)
 keypres$=UPPER$(GET$)

REM No more routines required.
UNTIL keypres$="N"

REM Finished.
RETURN
REM ********************************************************
REM            //// END OF SUBROUTINE "RUN" \\\\
REM ********************************************************
```

```
REM ****************************************************
REM                //// SUBROUTINE "FILES" \\\\
REM ****************************************************

files:
LOCAL option%

REM "Files" loop
DO

 REM "Files" sub-menu.

option%=MENU("ORGLOAD,ORGSAVE,ORGDIR,ORGKILL,PCLOA
D,PCSAVE,QUIT")

 REM Call selected routine.
 IF option%=1
  orgload:
 ELSEIF option%=2
  orgsave:
 ELSEIF option%=3
  orgdir:
 ELSEIF option%=4
  orgkill:
 ELSEIF option%=5
  pcload:
 ELSEIF option%=6
  pcsave:
 ENDIF

REM "QUIT" selected.
UNTIL option%=7

REM Finished.
RETURN

REM ****************************************************
REM            //// END OF SUBROUTINE "FILES" \\\\
REM ****************************************************
```

```
REM ********************************************************
REM                  //// SUBROUTINE "SPACE" \\\\
REM ********************************************************

space:

REM Get new memory base, exiting if null address string entered.
CLS
getnum:("- NEW  MEMBASE -",4)
IF number$=""
 RETURN
ENDIF

REM POKE new memory base into system variable.
POKEW $2065,number

REM Finished.
RETURN

REM ********************************************************
REM             //// END OF SUBROUTINE "SPACE" \\\\
REM ********************************************************
```

```
REM ****************************************************
REM                //// SUBROUTINE "INFO" \\\\
REM ****************************************************

info:

REM Display title.
central:("- MC  LOADER -",1)

REM Get current memory base from system variable.
number=PEEKW($2065)

REM Convert address into hexadecimal string.
intobase:(4)

REM Display memory base.
central:("Membase= $"+number$,2)

REM Wait for keypress.
GET

REM Finished.
RETURN

REM ****************************************************
REM          //// END OF SUBROUTINE "INFO" \\\\
REM ****************************************************
```

```
REM ********************************************************
REM                //// SUBROUTINE "GETNUM" \\\\
REM ********************************************************

GETNUM:(prompt$,length%)
LOCAL legal$(19),convert$(19),keypres$(1),temp$(14)

REM Initialise variables.
convert$="YUVWOPQIJKABCDEF"+CHR$(1)+CHR$(8)+CHR$(13)
legal$="0123456789ABCDEF"+CHR$(1)+CHR$(8)+CHR$(13)
number$=""
number=0

REM Display prompt passed as parameter.
central:(prompt$,1)

REM "Getnum" loop.
DO

  REM Construct bottom line display (this could be done in a  REM single
line but has been split over 2 to avoid word   REM processor-induced
misunderstandings).
  temp$="Value:"+CHR$(91)+"$"
  temp$=temp$+number$+REPT$(".",length%LEN(number$))+-
CHR$(93)

  REM Display bottom line.
  central:(temp$,2)

  REM Repeatedly get a keypress until it is one of the legal  REM values.
  DO
    keypres$=UPPER$(GET$)
  UNTIL LOC(convert$,keypres$)>0

  REM Now convert the keypress to its hex equivalent.
  keypres$=MID$(legal$,LOC(convert$,keypres$),1)

  REM If the key was <DEL>, and the string is not null, delete  REM the
last chracter.
```

```
 IF ASC(keypres$)=8 AND LEN(number$)>0
  number$=LEFT$(number$,LEN(number$)-1)

 REM If the key was <ON/CLEAR>, wipe the string, make a beep and
REM terminate.
 ELSEIF keypres$=CHR$(1)
  badnews:
  number$=""
  RETURN

 REM If the key was not <EXE> and the string is not at maximum  REM
length, add the key character to the string.
 ELSEIF keypres$<>CHR$(13) AND LEN(number$)<length%
  number$=number$+keypres$
 ENDIF

 REM Keep doing the above until <EXE> is pressed.
 UNTIL keypres$=CHR$(13)

 REM If not a null string, convert it into a decimal number.
 IF number$<>""
  frombase:
 ENDIF

REM Finished.
RETURN

REM ****************************************************
REM          //// END OF SUBROUTINE "GETNUM" \\\\
REM ****************************************************
```

```
REM *******************************************************
REM             //// SUBROUTINE "CENTRAL" \\\\
REM *******************************************************

central:(text$,row%)

REM Move the cursor to the centre of the line passed as a REM
parameter.
AT ((width%-LEN(text$))/2)+1,row%

REM Display the test string passed as a paramenter.
PRINT text$

REM Finished.
RETURN

REM *******************************************************
REM          //// END OF SUBROUTINE "CENTRAL" \\\\
REM *******************************************************
```

```
REM ****************************************************
REM              //// SUBROUTINE "INTOBASE" \\\\
REM ****************************************************

intobase:(length%)
LOCAL legal$(16),temp1,temp2

REM Initialise variables.
legal$="0123456789ABCDEF"
temp1=number
number$=""

REM "Intobase" loop.
DO

  REM Copy number to temporary store.
  temp2=number

  REM Get the whole number result of number divided by 16.
  number=INTF(number/16)

  REM Now get the remainder.
  temp2=temp2-number*16

  REM Add the remainder number to the string.
  number$=MID$(legal$,temp2+1,1)+number$

REM Continue until the original number is exhausted.
UNTIL number<1

REM Pack out the string with leading zeros to make up the length REM
passed as a parameter.
number$=REPT$("0",length%-LEN(number$))+number$

REM Restore the original contents of the number variable.
number=temp1
REM Finished.
RETURN
REM ****************************************************
REM           //// END OF SUBROUTINE "INTOBASE" \\\\
REM ****************************************************
```

```
REM ********************************************************
REM//// SUBROUTINE "FROMBASE" \\\\
REM ********************************************************

frombase:

LOCAL p,legal$(16)

REM Initialise variables.
legal$="0123456789ABCDEF"
p=0
number=0

REM "Frombase" loop.
DO

  REM Get the decimal value of the currently sliced hex digit and   REM
add it to the number variable. Note that this operation is
  REM split over 2 lines to avoid word-processor originated
  REM misunderstandings. They can be put togther.
  number=number+(LOC(legal$,MID$(number$,LEN(number$)-p,1))-1)
  number=number*(16**p)

  REM Increment the "power" variable.
  p=p+1

REM Continue until the end of the string.
UNTIL p=LEN(number$)

REM Round off the number.
number=INTF(number+0.5)

REM Finished.
RETURN

REM ********************************************************
REM        //// END OF SUBROUTINE "FROMBASE" \\\\
REM ********************************************************
```

```
REM ******************************************************
REM                //// SUBROUTINE "CHECK" \\\\
REM ******************************************************

check:

REM Check for wrap-round.
IF number>65535
 number=number-65536
ELSEIF number<0
 number=65536+number
ENDIF

REM Check for legal PEEK/POKE value.
IF number>32767
 tnum=number-65536
ELSE
 tnum=number
ENDIF

REM Finished.
RETURN

REM ******************************************************
REM            //// END OF SUBROUTINE "CHECK" \\\\
REM ******************************************************
```

```
REM ************************************************************
REM             //// SUBROUTINE "BADNEWS" \\\\
REM ************************************************************

badnews:

REM Emit 2 beeps.
BEEP 100,1000
BEEP 200,1200

REM Finished.
RETURN

REM ************************************************************
REM         //// END OF SUBROUTINE "BADNEWS" \\\\
REM ************************************************************
```

```
REM ******************************************************
REM            //// SUBROUTINE "ORGLOAD" \\\\
REM ******************************************************

orgload:

LOCAL name$(8),start,record,extent,address$(4)

REM Display title and request file name.
central:("LOAD FROM PSION",1)
AT (width%-14)/2,2
PRINT"File: ";
INPUT name$

REM Exit if filename is null string.
IF name$=""
 badnews:
 RETURN
ENDIF

REM Exit with warning if file does not exist.
IF NOT EXIST("A:"+name$)
 badnews:
 CLS
 central:("— PROBLEMS —",1)
 central:("- No such file -",2)
 PAUSE 40
 RETURN

REM Otherwise, open the file.
ELSE
 OPEN "A:"+name$,B,byte$
ENDIF

REM Get the start address for the load, exiting if a null string REM is
entered.
CLS
getnum:("- LOAD ADDRESS -",4)
IF number$=""
```

```
 badnews:
 RETURN
ENDIF

REM Make a temporary copy of the start address.
start=number

REM Initialise the record variable and set the current file REM handle.
record=0
USE B

REM Establish the size of the file.
LAST
extent=POS
FIRST

CLS

REM "Orgload" loop.
DO
 number=start

 REM Ensure that the address is a legal integer.
 check:

 REM Convert the address to a hexadecimal string.
 intobase:(4)

 REM Display the title and memory location.
 address$=number$
 central:("- ORGLOAD -",1)
 central:(REPT$(CHR$(255),(width%*(record/(extent+1)))+1),2)

 REM Get the byte string from the file.
 number$=B.byte$

 REM Convert string to decimal number.
 frombase:
```

```
  REM POKE into the memory location.
  POKEB tnum,number

  REM Point to the next record in the file.
  NEXT

  REM Increment the address and the record counter.
  start=start+1
  record=record+1

REM Continue until all records have been read.
UNTIL record=extent

REM Finished.
RETURN

REM ***********************************************************
REM        //// END OF SUBROUTINE "ORGLOAD" \\\\
REM ***********************************************************
```

```
REM ******************************************************
REM              //// SUBROUTINE "ORGSAVE" \\\\
REM ******************************************************

orgsave:

LOCAL name$(8),start,end,b

REM Display title and request filename.
central:("-SAVE TO PSION-",1)
AT (width%-14)/2+1,2
PRINT"File: ";
INPUT name$

REM Exit if nul filename entered.
IF name$=""
 badnews:
 RETURN
ENDIF

REM Get start address, exiting if null string entered.
CLS
getnum:("-START  ADDRESS-",4)
IF number$=""
 RETURN
ENDIF
start=number

REM Get end address, exiting if null string entered.
getnum:("- END  ADDRESS -",4)
IF number$=""
 RETURN
ENDIF
end=number

REM Exit if end address is greater than the start address.
IF start>end
 badnews:
 RETURN
```

```
ENDIF

REM If the file already exists, delete it.
IF EXIST(name$)
 DELETE "A:"+name$
ENDIF

REM Create the file.
CREATE "A:"+name$,B,byte$
USE B

REM Set the baseline address.
b=start

CLS

REM "Orgsave" loop
DO
 number=start
  REM Convert address to hexadecimal string.
 intobase:(4)

 REM Display title and progress bar.
 central:("- ORGSAVE -",1)
 central:(REPT$(CHR$(255),width%*((start-b)/((end+1)-b))+1),2)

 REM Check legal integer value.
 check:

 REM Get the contents of the memory address.
 number=PEEKB(tnum)

 REM Convert it to a hexadecimal string.
 intobase:(2)

 REM Store it in the file.
 B.byte$=number$
 APPEND
```

```
  REM Increment the memory address.
  start=start+1

REM Continue until all bytes stored.
UNTIL start>end

REM Close the file.
CLOSE

REM Finished.
RETURN

REM ******************************************************
REM         //// END OF SUBROUTINE "ORGSAVE" \\\\
REM ******************************************************
```

```
REM ****************************************************
REM              //// SUBROUTINE "ORGDIR" \\\\
REM ****************************************************

orgdir:

LOCAL file$(10),keypres$(1),onclear$(1)

REM Initialise variables.
onclear$=CHR$(1)
file$=DIR$("A")

CLS
DO

 REM Display title.
 central:("- ORGDIR -",1)

 REM Clear bottom line.
 PRINT CHR$(15)

 REM Display filename.
 central:(file$,2)

 REM Wait for keypress.
 keypres$=UPPER$(GET$)
 file$=DIR$("")

REM Continue until <ON/CLEAR> is pressed or end of files.
UNTIL keypres$=onclear$ OR file$=""

REM Finished.
RETURN

REM ****************************************************
REM         //// END OF SUBROUTINE "ORGDIR" \\\\
REM ****************************************************
```

```
REM ****************************************************
REM              //// SUBROUTINE "ORGKILL" \\\\
REM ****************************************************

orgkill:

LOCAL file$(8)
CLS

REM Get filename to be deleted, exiting if null string entered.
central:("- ORGKILL -",1)
PRINT"File: ";
INPUT file$
IF file$=""
 badnews:
 RETURN
ENDIF

CLS

REM IF file does not exist, issues a warning and exits.
IF NOT EXIST(file$)
 badnews:
 central:("-FILE "+file$+"-",1)
 central:("Doesn't exist",2)
 PAUSE 40
 RETURN

REM Otherwise, deletes the file.
ELSE
 central:("-FILE "+file$+"-",1)
 central:("Patience ...",2)
 DELETE"A:"+file$
ENDIF

REM Inform user of succesful file deletion.
central:("-KILL "+file$+"-",1)
central:("Deleted",2)
```

```
REM Wiat for 4 secs.
PAUSE 40

REM Finished.
RETURN

REM ***************************************************
REM          //// END OF SUBROUTINE "ORGKILL" \\\\
REM ***************************************************
```

```
REM ****************************************************
REM               //// SUBROUTINE "PCLOAD" \\\\
REM ****************************************************
pcload:
LOCAL rname$(100),lname$(8)
CLS

REM Get remote filename.
central:("- PCLOAD -",1)
AT 1,2
PRINT"Remote: ";
INPUT rname$

REM Get local filename.
central:("- PCLOAD -",1)
AT 1,2
PRINT"Local: ";
INPUT lname$

REM If remote or local filenames are null, beep and exit.
IF rname$="" OR lname$=""
  badnews:
  RETURN
ENDIF

REM Display ready to load warning and wait for key.
CLS
central:("-READY TO LOAD-",1)
central:("Press any key",2)
GET

REM Load file from PC.
XTRECV:(rname$,lname$,0)

REM Finished.
RETURN
REM ****************************************************
REM           //// END OF SUBROUTINE "PCLOAD" \\\\
REM ****************************************************
```

```
REM ********************************************************
REM                //// SUBROUTINE "PCSAVE" \\\\
REM ********************************************************

pcsave:

LOCAL rname$(100),lname$(8)
CLS

REM Get remote filename.
central:("- PCSAVE -",1)
AT 1,2
PRINT"Remote: ";
INPUT rname$

REM get local filename.
CLS
central:("- PCLOAD -",1)
AT 1,2
PRINT"Local: ";
INPUT lname$

REM If remote or local filename is null, exit.
IF rname$="" OR lname$=""
  badnews:
  RETURN

REM Otherwise, if no extension, add ".ODB".
ELSEIF LOC(rname$,".")=0
  rname$=rname$+".ODB"
ENDIF

CLS

REM Display ready to save warning and wait for key.
central:("-READY TO SAVE-",1)
central:("Press any key",2)
GET
```

```
REM Send file to PC.
XTSEND:(rname$,lname$,0)

REM Finished.
RETURN

REM ******************************************************
REM           //// END OF SUBROUTINE "PCSAVE" \\\\
REM ******************************************************
```

```
REM ****************************************************
REM             //// SUBROUTINE "SCREEN" \\\\
REM ****************************************************

screen:

LOCAL row%,cell%,start,ascii$(12)

REM Initialise variables.
row%=lines%-1
start=number-4*(row%-1)
ascii$=""

REM "Screen" loop.
DO
 cell%=0
 number=start
 check:

 REM Convert address to hexadecimal string.
 intobase:(4)

 REM Display address at beginning of line.
 AT 1,row%
 PRINT number$;

 REM "Line" loop.
 DO
  number=start

  REM Check for legal integer.
  check:

  REM Get memory contents, converting it into a hex string.
  number=PEEKB(tnum)
  intobase:(2)

  REM Display byte string.
  AT 6+cell%*3,row%
```

```
  PRINT number$;

  REM If byte is an alphanumeric character, add it to the ASCII    REM
string, otherwise add ".".
  IF number>31 AND number<127
   ascii$=ascii$+CHR$(number)
  ELSE
   ascii$=ascii$+"."
  ENDIF

  REM Increment the memory location.
  cell%=cell%+1
  start=start+1

 REM Continue until 4 bytes have been displayed.
 UNTIL cell%=4

 REM Decrement the line counter.
 row%=row%-1

REM Continue until all lines have been displayed.
UNTIL row%=0

REM Display the ASCII equivalent of the memory bytes on bottom REM
line.
central:(CHR$(91)+ascii$+CHR$(93),lines%)

REM Finished.
RETURN

REM ******************************************************
REM          //// END OF SUBROUTINE "SCREEN" \\\\
REM ******************************************************
```

```
REM *****************************************************
REM              //// SUBROUTINE "MODIFY" \\\\
REM *****************************************************

modify:

REM The ~LOCAL" statement which follows should all be on one REM
line. It is split by the wordprocessor line-wrapping.
LOCAL keypres$(1),legal$(5),up$(1),down$(1),lefft$(1),rite$(1),
    onclear$(1),exe$(1),arrow$(1),start,x%,y%

REM Initialise variables.
up$=CHR$(3)
down$=CHR$(4)
lefft$=CHR$(5)
rite$=CHR$(6)
exe$=CHR$(13)
legal$=up$+down$+lefft$+rite$+exe$
arrow$=CHR$(126)
x%=0
y%=1
start=number

REM "Modify" loop.
DO

 REM Display the arrow symbol at the cursor position.
 AT 5+x%*3,y%
 PRINT arrow$;

 REM Repeatedly get a key until it is a legal value.
 DO
  keypres$=UPPER$(GET$)
 UNTIL LOC(legal$,keypres$)>0

 REM Wipe the arrow symbol.
 AT 5+x%*3,y%
 PRINT" ";
```

```
 REM Alter cursor position.
 IF keypres$=up$ AND y%>1
  y%=y%-1
 ELSEIF keypres$=down$ AND y%<lines%-1
  y%=y%+1
 ELSEIF keypres$=lefft$ AND x%>0
  x%=x%-1
 ELSEIF keypres$=rite$ AND x%<3
  x%=x%+1
 ELSEIF keypres$=exe$

  REM Modify cell contents.
  CLS
  number=start+x%-((y%-1)*4)

  REM Check legal integer address value.
  check:

  REM get new value and POKE it in if it is not null.     getnum:("- NEW
CONTENTS -",2)
  IF number$<>""
   POKEB tnum,number
  ENDIF

 ENDIF

REM Continue until <EXE> is pressed.
UNTIL keypres$=exe$

REM Finished.
RETURN

REM ******************************************************
REM          //// END OF SUBROUTINE "MODIFY" \\\\
REM ******************************************************
```

```
REM ***************************************************
REM          //// PROGRAM "TYPEMNEM" \\\\
REM ***************************************************

typemnem:

LOCAL c%,k$(1)

REM Initialise variable.
c%=0

REM IF file already exists, delete it.
IF EXIST("A:MNEMONIC")
 DELETE "A:MNEMONIC"
ENDIF

REM Create new file.
CREATE "A:MNEMONIC",A,mode%,bytes%,mnem$

REM "Typemnem" loop.
DO
 DO
  CLS

  REM get address mode.
  PRINT"ADDRESSING MODE:";
  INPUT A.mode%
  CLS

  REM Get number of bytes in instruction.
  PRINT"NUMBER OF BYTES:";
  INPUT A.bytes%
  CLS

  REM Get mnemonic string.
  PRINT"MNEMONIC:"
  INPUT A.mnem$
  CLS
```

```
    REM Display entry and request confirmation.
    PRINT A.mode%,A.bytes%,A.mnem$
    PRINT" CONFIRM  <Y/N>";
    k$=GET$

  REM Repeat process until <Y> or <ON/CLEAR> pressed.
  UNTIL k$="Y" OR k$=CHR$(1)

  REM Add entry to file.
  APPEND

  REM Increment count.
  c%=c%+1

REM Continue until <ON/CLEAR> pressed or 256 entries made.
UNTIL c%=256 OR k$=CHR$(1)

REM Display terminal message.
PRINT"<<< FINISHED >>>";
REM Wait for key press.
GET

REM Close the file.
CLOSE

REM Finished.
RETURN

REM ******************************************************
REM           //// END OF PROGRAM "TYPEMNEM" \\\\
REM ******************************************************
```

HD6303 MNEMONICS

Instructions for entering the data:

a. On Microcomputer Disc. Each of the following codes consists of 2 digits, followed by a mnemonic string. Scan across the page, PRESSING TAB BETWEEN EACH ITEM FOR A CODE AND ENTER AT THE END OF EACH MNEMONIC. For example, the first entry should look like this:-

0<TAB>1<TAB>——<ENTER>.

You should end up with a long text file, holding 3 items on each line. Use the serial interface on the Organiser to load the file, which must have a ".ODB" extension.

b. USING TYPEMNEM. Each of the following codes consists of 2 digits, followed by a mnemonic string. Scan across the page, PRESSING ENTER OR EXE AFTER EACH ITEM. For example, the first entry should look like this:-

0<RET>1<RET>——<RET>.

0 1 ——	6 1 NOP	0 1 ——	0 1 ——
6 1 LSRD	6 1 ASLD	6 1 TAP	6 1 TPA
6 1 INX	6 1 DEX	6 1 CLV	6 1 SEV
6 1 CLC	6 1 SEC	6 1 CLI	6 1 SEI
6 1 SBA	6 1 CBA	0 1 ——	0 1 ——
0 1 ——	0 1 ——	6 1 TAB	6 1 TBA
6 1 XGDX	6 1 DAA	6 1 SLP	6 1 ABA
0 1 ——	0 1 ——	0 1 ——	0 1 ——

7 2 BRA	7 2 BRN	7 2 BHI	7 2 BLS
7 2 BCC	7 2 BCS	7 2 BNE	7 2 BEQ
7 2 BVC	7 2 BVS	7 2 BPL	7 2 BMI
7 2 BGE	7 2 BLT	7 2 BGT	7 2 BLE
6 1 TSX	6 1 INS	1 1 PUL A	1 1 PUL B
6 1 DES	6 1 TXS	1 1 PSH A	1 1 PSH B
6 1 PUL X	6 1 RTS	6 1 ABX	6 1 RTI
6 1 PSH X	6 1 MUL	6 1 WAI	6 1 SWI
1 1 NEG A	0 1 ——	0 1 ——	1 1 COM A
1 1 LSR A	0 1 ——	1 1 ROR A	1 1 ASR A
1 1 ASL A	1 1 ROL A	1 1 DEC A	0 1 ——
1 1 INC A	1 1 TST A	0 1 ——	1 1 CLR A
1 1 NEG B	0 1 ——	0 1 ——	1 1 COM B
1 1 LSR B	0 1 ——	1 1 ROR B	1 1 ASR B
1 1 ASL B	1 1 ROL B	1 1 DEC B	0 1 ——
1 1 INC B	1 1 TST B	0 1 ——	1 1 CLR B
5 2 NEG	5 3 ——	5 3 ——	5 2 COM
5 2 LSR	5 3 ——	5 2 ROR	5 2 ASR
5 2 ASL	5 2 ROL	5 2 DEC	5 3 ——
5 2 INC	5 2 TST	5 2 JMP	5 2 CLR

4 3 NEG	3 3 ——	3 3 ——	4 3 COM
4 3 LSR	3 3 ——	4 3 ROR	4 3 ASR
4 3 ASL	4 3 ROL	4 3 DEC	3 3 ——
4 3 INC	4 3 TST	4 3 JMP	4 3 CLR
2 2 SUB A	2 2 CMP A	2 2 SBC A	2 3 SUB D
2 2 AND A	2 2 BIT A	2 2 LDA A	0 1 ——
2 2 EOR A	2 2 ADC A	2 2 ORA A	2 2 ADD A
2 2 CPX	7 2 BSR	2 3 LDS	0 1 ——
3 2 SUB A	3 2 CMP A	3 2 SBC A	3 2 SUB D
3 2 AND A	3 2 BIT A	3 2 LDA A	3 2 STA
3 2 EOR A	3 2 ADC A	3 2 ORA A	3 2 ADD A
3 2 CPX	3 2 JSR	3 2 LDS	3 2 STS
5 2 SUB A	5 2 CMP A	5 2 SBC A	5 2 SUB D
5 2 AND A	5 2 BIT A	5 2 LDA A	5 2 STA A
5 2 EOR A	5 2 ADC A	5 2 ORA A	5 2 ADD A
5 2 CPX	5 2 JSR	5 2 LDS	5 2 STS
4 3 SUB A	4 3 CMP A	4 3 SBC A	4 3 SUB D
4 3 AND A	4 3 BIT A	4 3 LDA A	4 3 STA A
4 3 EOR A	4 3 ADC A	4 3 ORA A	4 3 ADD A

4 3 CPX	4 3 JSR	4 3 LDS	4 3 STS
2 2 SUB B	2 2 CMP B	2 2 SBC B	2 3 ADD D
2 2 AND B	2 2 BIT B	2 2 LDA B	0 1 ——
2 2 EOR B	2 2 ADC B	2 2 ORA B	2 2 ADD B
2 3 LDD	0 1 ——	2 3 LDX	0 1 ——
3 2 SUB B	3 2 CMP B	3 2 SBC B	3 2 ADD D
3 2 AND B	3 2 BIT B	3 2 LDA B	3 2 STA B
3 2 EOR B	3 2 ADC B	3 2 ORA B	3 2 ADD B
3 2 LDD	3 2 STD	3 2 LDX	3 2 STX
5 2 SUB B	5 2 CMP B	5 2 SBC B	5 2 ADD D
5 2 AND B	5 2 BIT B	5 2 LDA B	5 2 STA B
5 2 EOR B	5 2 ADC B	5 2 ORA B	5 2 ADD B
5 2 LDD	5 2 STD	5 2 LDX	5 2 STX
4 3 SUB B	4 3 CMP B	4 3 SBC B	4 3 ADD D
4 3 AND B	4 3 BIT B	4 3 LDA B	4 3 STA B
4 3 EOR B	4 3 ADC B	4 3 ORA B	4 3 ADD B
4 3 LDD	4 3 STD	4 3 LDX	4 3 STX

Annex G

The *Psion Organiser* Operating System

G:The *Psion Organiser* Operating System

G.1 INTRODUCTION. As you can see from a glance at the memory map in Annex C, the Organiser ROM starts at address $8000 and goes on to $FFFF. It is in this area, unalterable by the user, that the PSION code (the FIRMWARE) for the Operating System (OS), the Applications such as the Diary and OPL itself are stored. The OS is used a great deal by the other 2 since it is really a library of ready-made routines which affect the whole software environment of the computer. This Annex therefore aims to list the OS routines and describe how you can call them up.

G.2 CALLING AN OS ROUTINE. Calling system services is simplicity itself. You must first tell the computer that you are about to invoke an OS service. To do this, your machine code must call a Software Interrupt (SWI). The hexadecimal command for this is $3F. The number of the required OS service should immediately follow. Once the service has done its job, control is passed to the byte in your program following the service number. Thus, you can look upon OS services as subroutines of your own program.

G.3 PARAMETERS. Just as with OPL routines, you can (indeed, you may be required to) pass data to the OS service. However, instead of doing this via variables, the data is placed in the CPU registers (see Annex C), locations $0041/$0043 or the Run-time Buffer at $2188. Indeed, the OS may make use of any location between $0041-$005A as these are used as word-length variables. It would be prudent to assume that the registers will be trashed during a call, however in some cases data is passed back to the programmer via these same registers.

G.4 ERROR CODES. Although there are no actual error messages, some OS services can give error returns. In such cases the Carry Flag is set to indicate an error condition while the B register holds the error number. The error codes are as detailed on pages 127-133 of the Organiser Manual with the following exceptions:

CODE	MEANING
192	Device Write Fail
193	Device Read Fail
194	Battery Too Low

G.5 NEW SYSTEM SERVICES. The new OS vectors for the LZ have the numbers 128 to 179 inclusive. They are designed to be run ONLY on an LZ system and, if called using a 2-line Organiser, they will cause the machine to crash in a non-spectacular fashion.

VECTOR NUMBER: 0

TITLE: FREE A CELL

ENTRY REQUIREMENTS: THE TAG OF THE CELL MUST BE PLACED IN THE X REGISTER

OUTPUT: NIL

FUNCTION: The cell whose tag is held in the X Register is freed from memory. For a more complete description of cells, see Annex C. Note that if the tag is not in the correct range ($2000-$203E) disastrous results could occur unless the cell is already free.

VECTOR NUMBER: 1

TITLE: GRAB A CELL

ENTRY REQUIREMENTS: THE REQUIRED SIZE OF CELL (IN BYTES) MUST BE PLACED IN THE D REGISTER

OUTPUT: THE X REGISTER HOLDS THE TAG OF THE CELL

FUNCTION: This service is used to allocate a new cell. The base address of the cell is held at the location indicated by the X Register. Because constant shrinking and growing (not to mention grabbing and freeing) will inevitably change the base address of the cells, their respective addresses are held in a table starting at $2000.

VECTOR NUMBER: 2

TITLE: GROW A CELL

ENTRY REQUIREMENTS: THE TAG OF THE CELL TO BE ENLARGED IS PLACED IN THE X REGISTER
THE NUMBER OF BYTES TO BE ADDED TO THE CELL IS PLACED IN THE D REGISTER
THE POINT WITHIN THE CELL AT WHICH THE EXTRA BYTES ARE TO BE INSERTED IS PLACED IN THE VARIABLE AT $41

OUTPUT: NIL

FUNCTION: This service is called to enlarge an existing cell whose tag is held in the X Register. The number of bytes to be added is placed in the D Register while the point at which the insertion is to be made is held in the word variable at $41. Note that the correct tag must be used and the offset must be less than the size of the cell if interesting results are not to occur. Moreover, while the base of the target cell will not move, those above will change.

VECTOR NUMBER: 3

TITLE: REPLACE ITEM WITHIN A CELL

ENTRY REQUIREMENTS: THE TAG OF THE CELL IS HELD IN THE X REGISTER
THE SIZE OF THE ITEM TO BE REPLACED IS HELD IN THE D REGISTER
THE OFFSET WITHIN THE CELL IS HELD IN THE FIRST WORD VARIABLE AT $41
THE SIZE OF THE NEW ITEM IS HELD

IN THE SECOND WORD VARIABLE AT $43

OUTPUT: NIL

FUNCTION: This service will replace a byte length (held in the D Register) with a new byte length (held in the second word variable) at the offset (held in the first word variable) of the cell whose tag is held in the X Register. Be careful that the tag is in the correct range and that the offset is not bigger than the size of the cell.

VECTOR NUMBER: 4

TITLE: SHRINK A CELL

ENTRY REQUIREMENTS: THE TAG OF THE CELL IS HELD IN THE X REGISTER
THE NUMBER OF BYTES TO SHRINK THE CELL IS HELD IN THE D REGISTER
THE OFFSET WITHIN THE CELL IS HELD IN THE FIRST WORD VARIABLE AT $41

OUTPUT: NIL

FUNCTION: The cell whose tag is held in the X Register is shrunk by the number of bytes held in the D Register. The removal takes place at the point indicated by the offset held in the first word variable.

Note that the cell tag must be within range and that the offset must not be larger than the cell size.

VECTOR NUMBER: 5

TITLE: SIZE A CELL

ENTRY REQUIREMENTS: THE TAG OF THE CELL IS HELD IN THE X REGISTER

OUTPUT: THE SIZE OF THE CELL IS RETURNED IN THE D REGISTER

FUNCTION: The purpose of this service is to calculate the current size of the cell whose tag is held in the X Register. The required number is returned in the D Register.

VECTOR NUMBER: 6

TITLE: ZERO A CELL

ENTRY REQUIREMENTS: THE TAG OF THE CELL IS HELD IN THE X REGISTER

OUTPUT: NIL

FUNCTION: This service will reduce the size of a cell to zero but does not de-allocate it. Ensure that the cell tag is within the correct range.

VECTOR NUMBER: 7

TITLE: NON-MASKABLE INTERRUPTS (NMI) DISABLE

ENTRY REQUIREMENTS: NIL

OUTPUT: NIL

FUNCTION: NMIs to the CPU can be disabled by invoking this service. However, it should be noted that since the Organiser maintains its clocks (and thereby the Diary) by using the NMI as a time base, the accuracy of all time-related functions will be affected. Users who wish to disable NMIs and still maintain the clock should see Vector 9.

If Vector 7 is used to disable NMIs, they should be switched back on when required by means of Vector 8.

VECTOR NUMBER: 8

TITLE: NON-MASKABLE INTERRUPTS (NMI) ENABLE

ENTRY REQUIREMENTS: NIL
OUTPUT: NIL

FUNCTION: Re-activates NMIs disabled by Vector 7.

VECTOR NUMBER: 9

TITLE: DISABLE NMI - MAINTAIN CLOCK

ENTRY REQUIREMENTS: NIL

OUTPUT: NIL

FUNCTION: Vector 9 switches off the NMI in such a way as to preserve the Organiser's timekeeping. NMIs disabled in this fashion must be re-activated by calling Vector 10 within 2048 seconds if the clock is to maintain time.

When the NMI is restored, the Vector 10 service must wait for the first new NMI pulse to the clock before it can count the number of NMIs which have occurred in the NMI-disabled interval. Since NMIs occur once per second, a delay of 0-1 second can happen depending on when in the cycle Vector 10 is called. Moreover, since the counter which totals NMIs is also used to poll the keyboard, interrupts should be disabled before calling Vector 9 and no keyboard services should be called.

VECTOR NUMBER: 10

TITLE: RE-ENABLE NMI - MAINTAIN CLOCK

ENTRY REQUIREMENTS: NIL

OUTPUT: NIL
FUNCTION: This service is used to re-enable NMIs disabled by Vector 9.

VECTOR NUMBER: 11

TITLE: SAVE/RESTORE WORD-LENGTH VARIABLES

ENTRY REQUIREMENTS: NIL

OUTPUT: NIL

FUNCTION: The use of the 7 word-length variables were outlined in paragraph G.3. The service call must be followed by a byte which describes the exact operation required as detailed below:

Bit 0 - If set, operate on word variable number 0
Bit 1 - If set, operate on word variable number 1
Bit 2 - If set, operate on word variable number 2
Bit 3 - If set, operate on word variable number 3
Bit 4 - If set, operate on word variable number 4
Bit 5 - If set, operate on word variable number 5
Bit 6 - If set, operate on word variable number 6
Bit 7 - If set, then the operation on the variables detailed above will be to restore (pop) them to their position in memory. If it is clear, then those indicated will be saved (pushed) onto the stack.

Note that the higher variables are pushed first and the lower ones are popped first. If different combinations of pushing and popping are involved, the contents of the variables can be mixed up.

VECTOR NUMBER: 12

TITLE: SWITCH OFF

ENTRY REQUIREMENTS: NIL

OUTPUT: NIL

FUNCTION: The Organiser is switched off using this service. The entire status of the machine is saved so that, on power-up, everything is restore to the state immediately prior to calling the switch-off.

VECTOR NUMBER: 13

TITLE: SOUND THE ALARM

ENTRY REQUIREMENTS: NIL

OUTPUT: NIL

FUNCTION: This service emits the sound produced by the alarm. Note that it disables interrupts with an SEI.

VECTOR NUMBER: 14

TITLE: SOUND THE BEEP NOTE
ENTRY REQUIREMENTS: NIL

OUTPUT: NIL

FUNCTION: The beep produced by CHR$(16) is emitted by this service.

VECTOR NUMBER: 15

TITLE: SOUND A TONE

ENTRY REQUIREMENTS: THE DURATION OF THE NOTE IN MILLISECONDS IS HELD IN THE X REGISTER

THE PITCH OF THE NOTE IS HELD IN THE D REGISTER. THE NOTE IN HZ IS CALCULATED AS:
HZ=921600/(78 + 2 * D REGISTER)

OUTPUT: NIL

FUNCTION: This routine will emit a note of X milliseconds with a pitch determined by the D Register. Not that this routine disables interrupts with an SEI.

VECTOR NUMBER: 16

TITLE: OUTPUT A CHARACTER

ENTRY REQUIREMENTS: THE A REGISTER HOLDS THE CHARACTER TO BE OUTPUT

OUTPUT: NIL

FUNCTION: This service outputs a character to the display, including the UDGs. Control characters can also be called. While characters 8-16 have effects as detailed in pages 196-7 of the User Manual, 3 other ones are not documented:

a. Refresh Display - If character number 17 is used, the display will be refreshed from the line buffers. These hold the top and bottom lines, respectively (see Annex C).

b. Refresh Top Line - Character 18 refreshes only the top line.

c. Refresh Bottom Line - Character 19 refreshes the bottom line only.

As each printable character appears on the screen, the cursor position is updated and scrolling occurs as in the OPL PRINT statement.

VECTOR NUMBER: 17

TITLE: PRINT STRING

ENTRY REQUIREMENTS: THE B REGISTER HOLDS THE NUMBER OF CHARACTERS TO PRINT
THE X REGISTER HOLDS THE DOUBLE-BYTE ADDRESS OF THE STRING TO BE PRINTED

OUTPUT: NIL

FUNCTION: This service prints out the indicated string one character at a time by calling Service Number 16.

VECTOR NUMBER: 18

TITLE: RESTORE SCREEN

ENTRY REQUIREMENTS: NIL

OUTPUT: NIL

FUNCTION: This service restores a screen stored by a previous call to Service Number 19. Note that if such a previous call has not been made, the results may not be those expected! This is the case even when the LZ is being operated in 2-line mode. Similarly, Vector 18 will restore the screen from the 4-line buffer.

VECTOR NUMBER: 19

TITLE: SAVE SCREEN

ENTRY REQUIREMENTS: NIL

OUTPUT: NIL

FUNCTION: This service saves the screen display into the 32-byte buffer starting at $2090. The cursor position and status are stored in locations $67 and $68, respectively. LZ users should note that the 4-line buffer at

$7F62 is used instead of the 2-line variant at $2090. This is the case even when the LZ is being operated in 2-line mode. Similarly, Vector 18 will restore the screen from the 4-line buffer.

VECTOR NUMBER: 20

TITLE: CURSOR DISPLAY CONTROL

ENTRY REQUIREMENTS: THE A REGISTER HOLDS THE CURSOR POSITION
THE B REGISTER HOLDS DATA CONCERNING THE CURSOR APPEARANCE

OUTPUT: NIL

FUNCTION: The A Register holds the cursor position as a single- byte number in the range 0-31. The B Register controls 2 aspects of the cursor appearance:

a. ON/OFF - If bit 7 of the byte contained in Register B is set, the cursor is displayed. Otherwise it is concealed.

b. LINE/BLOCK - If bit 0 of the Register B byte is set then the cursor will be displayed as a line. Otherwise it is displayed as a block.

VECTOR NUMBER: 21

TITLE: VIEW STRING

ENTRY REQUIREMENTS: THE A REGISTER DETERMINES THE DISPLAY LINE AND TERMINATION CONDITIONS
THE B REGISTER HOLDS THE LENGTH OF THE STRING TO BE VIEWED
THE X REGISTER HOLDS THE DOUBLE-BYTE ADDRESS OF THE STRING TO BE VIEWED

	THE SCROLL DELAY, IN 1/20 SEC, IS HELD IN THE FIRST WORD VARIABLE AT $41
OUTPUT:	THE B REGISTER HOLDS THE KEY PRESS WHICH TERMINATED SCROLLING

FUNCTION: The A Register parameter should hold 0-1 for the Organiser II and 0-3 for the LZ variants when in 4-line mode, while a 1 uses the bottom line. In addition, if bit 7 of the A Register byte is set, this service will ignore the arrow keys and terminate scrolling on any key press.

The service stores the key press in the B Register but if this key is not of interest to the programmer the service can be called again, this time with the X register set to zero. This can be done as often as necessary but no other calls to the display driver should be made in between. Note that the initial call to the service must not be made with the X Register set to zero or unpredictable results could follow.

While the cursor is removed from the display during this service, it is returned to its state prior to the call but the original position will be trashed.

VECTOR NUMBER: 22

TITLE:	READY-TO-DISPLAY PAUSE
ENTRY REQUIREMENTS:	NIL
OUTPUT:	NIL

FUNCTION: This Service waits until the value in the Ready-to- Display counter ($6D/E) has decremented to zero. This counter is decremented by 1 on each keyboard interrupt and therefore provides a sort of 50 millisecond timer. It is used by the display driver to implement scrolling pauses. Note that this Service will still work even if interrupts have been disabled.

VECTOR NUMBER: 23

TITLE: BOOT DEVICES

ENTRY REQUIREMENTS: Nil.

OUTPUT: NIL.

FUNCTION: This function will boot all devices which are currently connected to the Organiser. Should any errors occur, the screen contents are first restored before the error message is displayed. Afterwards, the original screen is restored. LZ users should note that, unless 4-line mode has been set, this function will go to 2-line mode when running "REMOVE" and "INSTALL" vectors which print.

VECTOR NUMBER: 24

TITLE: UN-BOOT

ENTRY REQUIREMENTS: Nil.

OUTPUT: NIL.

FUNCTION: The reverse of Vector 23.

VECTOR NUMBER: 25

TITLE: LOOKUP

ENTRY REQUIREMENTS: THE X REGISTER HOLDS THE ADDRESS OF THE STRING.

OUTPUT: THE A REGISTER HOLDS THE DEVICE NUMBER.
THE B REGISTER HOLDS THE VECTOR NUMBER.

FUNCTION: The X Register holds the address of the name string of a procedure. This service calls the language vector of all devices booted in and offers the procedure. If a device is prepared to do so, the service returns with the A Register holding the device number and the B Register holding the vector of the procedure handling code.

VECTOR NUMBER: 26

TITLE: LOAD

ENTRY REQUIREMENTS: THE D REGISTER HOLDS THE ADDRESS TO LOAD THE OVERLAY. THE X REGISTER HOLDS THE ADDRESS ON PACK OF OVERLAY.

$41/$42 HOLDS THE RELOCATION ADDRESS.

OUTPUT: NIL.

FUNCTION: This service loads a relocatable program from a device into memory, applying any fix-ups. The relocated address is as held in $41/$42. The D Register holds the memory address for the load and the X Register the address on the pack where the code may be found. The execution address is held in $41/$42. NOTE THAT THE CORRECT SLOT SHOULD ALREADY BE SELECTED (USING VECTOR 98) BEFORE CALLING THIS SERVICE.

VECTOR NUMBER: 27

TITLE: GET VECTOR

ENTRY REQUIREMENTS: THE A REGISTER HOLDS THE NUMBER OF THE REQUIRED DEVICE.

THE B REGISTER HOLDS THE VECTOR NUMBER.
OUTPUT: NIL.

FUNCTION: This vector searches for the device whose number is held in the A Register. If found, it then checks to see that the vector number, as indicated by the B Register, is not greater than the maximum vector number supported by the device. If all is well, a jump will be made to the appropriate vector.

Note that the X Register and the contents of $41/$42 are passed to the device. The user can therefore use these as parameters.

VECTOR NUMBER: 28

TITLE: CALL EDIT

ENTRY REQUIREMENTS: THE A REGISTER SHOULD HOLD: BIT 0 CLEAR FOR SINGLE-LINE EDITS
BIT 0 SET FOR MULTI-LINE EDITS
BIT 7 CLEAR FOR EXIT ON MODE KEY BEING PRESSED
BIT 7 SET FOR NO EXIT ON MODE KEY BEING PRESSED.
THE B REGISTER HOLDS THE MAXIMUM INPUT LENGTH.

OUTPUT: THE B REGISTER HOLDS THE KEY RESPONSIBLE FOR TERMINATING THE EDIT.

FUNCTION: This service calls the line editor after setting the cursor on the first editable line using $41/$42. LZ users should note that if BIT 1 of the A register is set, the edit will terminate if the Up or Down arrow is pressed.

VECTOR NUMBER: 29

TITLE: LINE EDITOR

ENTRY REQUIREMENTS: THE A REGISTER SHOULD HOLD: BIT 0 CLEAR FOR SINGLE-LINE EDITS
BIT 0 SET FOR MULTI-LINE EDITS
BIT 7 CLEAR FOR EXIT ON MODE KEY BEING PRESSED.
BIT 7 SET FOR NO EXIT ON MODE KEY BEING PRESSED.
THE B REGISTER HOLDS THE MAXIMUM INPUT LENGTH.
MEMORY LOCATIONS $41/$42 HOLD THE POSITION WITHIN THE LINE TO START EDITING.

OUTPUT: THE B REGISTER HOLDS THE NUMBER OF THE KEY RESPONSIBLE FOR TERMINATING THE EDIT.

FUNCTION: This is the service used to edit lines. The maximum number of characters which can be edited is specified by the B Register. In single-line editing, using the UP/DOWN arrows will place the cursor at the beginning/end of the editable text. In multiple line editing, these keys retain their normal use.

The text held in the Editor Buffer is used as the default string for editing. Pressing the EXE key, or ON/CLEAR with an empty buffer, will exit the service. An occupied buffer can be cleared using the ON/CLEAR key. In the latter case, the routine will not exit. Note also that the user can decide to allow the MODE key to cause an exit. LZ users should note that if BIT 1 of the A register is set, the edit will terminate if the Up or Down arrow is pressed.

VECTOR NUMBER: 30

TITLE: VIEW

ENTRY REQUIREMENTS: THE X REGISTER HOLDS ZERO IF THE USER WISHES TO TAKE UP VIEWING WHERE HE LEFT OFF LAST TIME. OTHERWISE, IT IS NON-ZERO. MEMORY LOCATIONS $41/$42 HOLD THE DELAY BEFORE SCROLLING ACTION TAKES PLACE.

OUTPUT: NIL.

FUNCTION: Views the string held in the Run Time Buffer. The Run Time Buffer Length must also be specified. TABs cause NEWLINEs and the UP/DOWN arrows control which line is VIEWed. Pressing any other key will exit the routine, while preserving the offending key in the B Register.

VECTOR NUMBER: 31

TITLE: LOCATE ERROR MESSAGE

ENTRY REQUIREMENTS: THE B REGISTER HOLDS THE ERROR NUMBER.

OUTPUT: THE X REGISTER HOLDS THE ADDRESS OF THE APPROPRIATE ERROR MESSAGE.

FUNCTION: This service is used by the OPL function ERR$. Taking an error number in the B Register, the routine finds the address of the appropriate message. If there is no specific message for the number, the address of the string "*** ERROR ***" is given instead. The string starts with its byte count.

VECTOR NUMBER: 32

TITLE: DISPLAY ERROR MESSAGE

ENTRY REQUIREMENTS: THE B REGISTER HOLDS THE ERROR NUMBER.

OUTPUT: NIL.

FUNCTION: This routine displays the message associated with the error number held in the B Register. As in the case of Vector 31, the default "*** ERROR ***" is displayed in the case of unspecified errors. The routine waits for the SPACE or ON/CLEAR key to be pressed before continuing. Note that if the error number is 194, the message "BATTERY TOO LOW" will be displayed for 4 seconds before the Organiser switches off. LZ users should note that this function prints errors on four lines if the Organiser is being operated in 4-line mode.

VECTOR NUMBER: 33

TITLE: BACK

ENTRY REQUIREMENTS: Nil.

OUTPUT: THE X REGISTER HOLDS THE UPDATED RECORD NUMBER.

FUNCTION: Used by the OPL command. It makes the previous record the current one. It should not be called if the X register is 0 or 1 i.e. if there IS no previous record.

VECTOR NUMBER: 34

TITLE: BLOCK FILE CATALOGUE

ENTRY REQUIREMENTS: THE A REGISTER HOLDS 1 ON INTIAL CALL TO THE ROUTINE AND 0 ON SUBSEQUENT CALLS.
THE B REGISTER HOLDS THE DEVICE NUMBER (0-3).
THE X REGISTER HOLDS THE DESTINATION ADDRESS OF THE FILENAME.
MEMORY LOCATION $42 HOLDS THE FILE TYPE ($81- &8F).

OUTPUT: Nil.

FUNCTION: Functions similar to the OPL DIR$. Repeated calls store the names (count byte first) of block files of type as specified in $42, held on the device indicated by the B Register, at the address held in the X Register. When no more files of the specified type remain, the Carry flag is set and the B Register contains the END-OF-FILE error number.

VECTOR NUMBER: 35

TITLE: DELETE BLOCK FILE

ENTRY REQUIREMENTS: THE X REGISTER HOLDS THE ADDRESS OF THE FILENAME.
THE B REGISTER HOLDS THE BLOCK FILE TYPE ($82-$8F)

OUTPUT: Nil.

FUNCTION: This function deletes the block file whose name is stored at the location pointed to by the X Register. The name, stored count byte first, is in the form D:NAME.

VECTOR NUMBER: 36

TITLE: OPEN BLOCK FILE

ENTRY REQUIREMENTS: THE X REGISTER HOLDS THE LOCATION OF THE BLOCK FILENAME.
THE B REGISTER HOLDS THE BLOCK FILE TYPE.

OUTPUT: THE D REGISTER HOLDS THE LENGTH OF DATA IN THE BLOCK FILE.

FUNCTION: Opens a block file of type as specified by the B Register and name as pointed to by the X Register. The pack address is set to the beginning of the file and the D Register returns with the length of data.

VECTOR NUMBER: 37

TITLE: PREPARE TO SAVE

ENTRY REQUIREMENTS: THE B REGISTER HOLDS THE BLOCK FILE TYPE.
THE X REGISTER POINTS TO THE FILENAME.

LOCATIONS $41/$42 HOLD THE LENGTH OF CODE TO BE SAVED BY VECTOR 97.

OUTPUT: NIL.

FUNCTION: This routine is called in preparation for a block file save. It saves the filename, long record code $0280 and the code length as indicated by $41/$42. It also checks to see if there is enough room on the pack for the above data. The filename is preceded by is length byte and is in the form D:NAME. Vector 97 must then be called to actually save the code.

VECTOR NUMBER: 38

TITLE: FILE CATALOGUE

ENTRY REQUIREMENTS: THE A REGISTER CONTAINS 1 FOR A FIRST CALL AND 0 FOR SUBSEQUENT ONES
THE B REGISTER CONTAINS THE DEVICE NUMBER (0- 3)
THE X REGISTER CONTAINS THE DESTINATION ADDRESS FOR THE FILENAME (INCLUDING ITS LEADING COUNT BYTE)

OUTPUT: Nil.

FUNCTION: On being called repeatedly, this service outputs the names of each file on the device indicated by the B Register. When no more files remain, the Carry flag is set and the B Register returns with the "END_OF_FILE" error code. The operation of this vector is similar to the OPL function DIR$.

VECTOR NUMBER: 39

TITLE: COPY

ENTRY REQUIREMENTS: THE D REGISTER POINTS TO THE COPY-TO STRING.

THE X REGISTER POINTS TO THE COPY-FROM STRING.
LOCATIONS $41/$42 INDICATE THE TYPE OF COPY REQUIRED.

OUTPUT: Nil.

FUNCTION: This routine copies files from one device to another. The $41 must contain zero or a legal file type in the range $82 to $8F. If the copy-to string contains only the device name, the file will be copied with the same name. If both names are omitted, all files on the copy- from device will be copied to the target device.

The copy-to device must be different from the copy-from device. Moreover, the copy-to filename can be different to the copy-from. However, in the latter case, the first line of any procedure file will remain with its copy-from name and this will show up on any subsequent printout.

If a the copy-to filename already exists, the copy-from will be appended to it.

VECTOR NUMBER: 40

TITLE: CREATE FILE

ENTRY REQUIREMENTS: THE X REGISTER POINTS TO THE FILENAME LOCATION.

OUTPUT: IF NO ERROR HAS OCCURRED, THE A REGISTER WILL RETURN WITH THE DATA RECORD TYPE TO BE USED.

FUNCTION: Creates a file whose name, leading count byte first, is held at the location pointed to by the X Register.

VECTOR NUMBER: 41

TITLE: DELETE FILE

ENTRY REQUIREMENTS: THE X REGISTER CONTAINS THE ADDRESS OF THE FILENAME STRING.

OUTPUT: NIL.

FUNCTION: This routine deletes the file whose name is held at the location (leading count byte first) stored in the X Register.

VECTOR NUMBER: 42

TITLE: ERASE RECORD

ENTRY REQUIREMENTS: Nil.

OUTPUT: NIL.

FUNCTION: This service erases the current record in the current file, maintaining the current position but pulling up the next record in the file. In RAM files, the space is recovered but in DATAPACKs only the top bit of the file type is cleared.

VECTOR NUMBER: 43

TITLE: FIND

ENTRY REQUIREMENTS: THE X REGISTER HOLDS THE ADDRESS OF THE SEARCH STRING.
THE A REGISTER HOLDS THE LENGTH OF THE SEARCH STRING.
THE B REGISTER HOLDS THE RECORD TYPE TO BE SEARCHED FOR.

OUTPUT: NIL.

FUNCTION: This service searches through the current pack for a record of the type indicated by the B Register which BEGINS with the string indicated by the X Register. If found, the match is placed in the RUN TIME BUFFER starting at $2187 as a leading length count byte string.

VECTOR NUMBER: 44

TITLE: NEXT FIND

ENTRY REQUIREMENTS: THE D REGISTER HOLDS THE ADDRESS OF THE SEARCH STRING.
THE X REGISTER IS THE DESTINATION ADDRESS OF THE MATCH.

OUTPUT: THE A REGISTER HOLDS THE RECORD TYPE OF THE MATCH.

FUNCTION: This service finds the next record of the current type on the current datapack which CONTAINS the search string. The matching record is placed at the location pointed to by the X Register and the A Register will return with the record type of the match.

VECTOR NUMBER: 45

TITLE: LOCATE RECORD

ENTRY REQUIREMENTS: THE D REGISTER HOLDS THE RECORD NUMBER TO BE FOUND.
OUTPUT: THE A REGISTER HOLDS THE LENGTH OF THE RECORD.
THE B REGISTER HOLDS THE TYPE OF RECORD.
LOCATION $41 HOLDS THE MOST SIGNIFICANT BYTE OF THE 3- BYTE PACK ADDRESS.
THE X REGISTER HOLDS THE LOWER 2 BYTES OF THE PACK ADDRESS.

FUNCTION: This routine returns information concerning the record specified by the D Register in the current record on the current pack. If found, the A Register returns with the length of the record,the B Register with the record type while location $41 and the X Register combine to indicate the 3-byte pack address of the record.

VECTOR NUMBER: 46

TITLE: NEXT

ENTRY REQUIREMENTS: Nil.

OUTPUT: NIL.

FUNCTION: Increments the current record number. Note that this vector does not check for end of file. Any subsequent READ will return the "END OF FILE" error.

VECTOR NUMBER: 47

TITLE: OPEN FILE

ENTRY REQUIREMENTS: THE X REGISTER HOLDS THE ADDRESS OF THE FILENAME.

OUTPUT: THE A REGISTER RETURNS THE RECORD TYPE OF THE DATA (IF THE FILE IS FOUND)

FUNCTION: This routine opens a previously existing file whose name is held, leading count byte first, at the location indicated by the X Register. If the device name is omitted from the filename, the device number held at location $97 is assumed.

VECTOR NUMBER: 48

TITLE: CHECK FILENAME

ENTRY REQUIREMENTS: THE X REGISTER HOLDS THE ADDRESS OF THE FILENAME TO BE CHECKED.
THE D REGISTER HOLDS THE

DESTINATION ADDRESS OF THE CHECKED ADDRESS.
LOCATION $41 HOLDS THE DEFAULT DEVICE NUMBER.

OUTPUT: NIL.

FUNCTION: This service checks that the filename indicated by the X Register is legal and adds the default device if the user omitted it from the filename. The finished product, padded with spaces to make 8 characters, is stored at the address indicated by the D Register. OPL users will be familiar with the naming conventions of the Organiser.

VECTOR NUMBER: 49

TITLE: READ RECORD

ENTRY REQUIREMENTS: THE X REGISTER HOLDS THE DESTINATION ADDRESS OF THE RECORD TO BE READ.

OUTPUT: THE B REGISTER HOLDS THE RECORD TYPE.

FUNCTION: This routine reads the current record in the current file into the memory address (leading count byte first) indicated by the X Register, leaving the record number unchanged.

VECTOR NUMBER: 50

TITLE: SET CURRENT RECORD TYPE

ENTRYREQUIREMENTS: THE B REGISTER HOLDS THE REQUIRED RECORD TYPE.

OUTPUT: NIL.

FUNCTION: This service sets the current record type to the value in Register B. This value should be between $80-$FE.

VECTOR NUMBER: 51

TITLE: RENAME

ENTRY REQUIREMENTS: THE X REGISTER HOLDS THE ADDRESS OF THE CURRENT FILENAME.
THE D REGISTER HOLDS THE ADDRESS OF THE NEW FILENAME.

OUTPUT: NIL.

FUNCTION: Renames an already existing file. Note that a file can only be renamed onto the same pack. The filenames are stored leading count byte first.

VECTOR NUMBER: 52

TITLE: SET CURRENT RECORD NUMBER

ENTRY REQUIREMENTS: THE D REGISTER HOLDS THE REQUIRED RECORD NUMBER.

OUTPUT: NIL.

FUNCTION: This service sets the current record number the that held in the D Register.

VECTOR NUMBER: 53

TITLE: SELECT PACK

ENTRY REQUIREMENTS: THE B REGISTER HOLDS THE NUMBER OF PACK TO BE SELECTED - THIS MUST BE BETWEEN 0 AND 3.

OUTPUT: NIL.

FUNCTION: This service selects the pack indicated by the B Register. It is ESSENTIAL that this number lies in the range 0-3, since this service does not check the legality of the number. The selected pack then becomes the current one.

VECTOR NUMBER: 54

TITLE: SIZE PACK

ENTRY REQUIREMENTS: Nil.

OUTPUT: LOCATION $43 AND THE D REGISTER HOLD THE NUMBER OF BYTES FREE ON THE DATAPACK AS A 3-BYTE NUMBER, THE MOST SIGNIFICANT BYTE BEING HELD IN $43.
THE X REGISTER HOLDS THE NUMBER OF RECORDS OF THE CURRENT RECORD TYPE HELD ON THE PACK.
LOCATIONS $44,$41,$42 HOLD THE ADDRESS OF THE FIRST FREE BYTE ON THE PACK AS A 3-BYTE NUMBER.

FUNCTION: This service returns general information about the currently selected datapack, file type and record type.

VECTOR NUMBER: 55

TITLE: APPEND

ENTRY REQUIREMENTS: THE X REGISTER HOLDS THE ADDRESS OF THE RECORD TO BE WRITTEN TO THE CURRENT DEVICE.

OUTPUT: NIL.

FUNCTION: This service adds the record, stored leading count byte first, indicated by the X Register to the current device. The record length must be no more than 254 characters and the routine checks to see if there is sufficient room before appending the record. Note that a write failure on an EPROM will result in the loss of the record. The current record number becomes the number of the appended record.

VECTOR NUMBER: 56

TITLE: ARCTANGENT

ENTRY REQUIREMENTS: THE FLOATING POINT ARGUMENT MUST FIRST BE STACKED.

OUTPUT: THE FLOATING POINT RESULT IS STACKED.

FUNCTION: This routine returns the arctangent of the argument, in radians, on the run-time stack.

VECTOR NUMBER: 57

TITLE: COSINE

ENTRY REQUIREMENTS: THE FLOATING POINT ARGUMENT MUST FIRST BE STACKED.

OUTPUT: THE FLOATING POINT RESULT IS STACKED.

FUNCTION: This service returns the Cosine of the floating point argument, which must be in radians, on the run-time stack.

VECTOR NUMBER: 58

TITLE: EXPONENT

ENTRY REQUIREMENTS: THE FLOATING POINT ARGUMENT MUST FIRST BE STACKED.

OUTPUT: THE FLOATING POINT RESULT IS STACKED.

FUNCTION: This service returns the floating point exponent on the run-time stack.

VECTOR NUMBER: 59

TITLE: LOG (e)

ENTRY REQUIREMENTS: THE FLOATING POINT ARGUMENT MUST FIRST BE STACKED.

OUTPUT: THE FLOATING POINT RESULT IS STACKED.

FUNCTION: This service returns LOG e of the floating point argument on the run-time stack.

VECTOR NUMBER: 60

TITLE: LOG (10)

ENTRY REQUIREMENTS: THE FLOATING POINT ARGUMENT MUST FIRST BE STACKED.

OUTPUT: THE FLOATING POINT RESULT IS STACKED.

FUNCTION: This service returns the floating point argument to LOG(10) on the run-time stack.

VECTOR NUMBER: 61

TITLE: POWER

ENTRY REQUIREMENTS: THE TWO FLOATING POINT ARGUMENTS MUST FIRST BE STACKED.

OUTPUT: THE FLOATING POINT RESULT IS STACKED.

FUNCTION: This service returns the floating point result of the first argument raised to the power of the second. The result is stacked on the run-time stack. Note that the stack pointer will have incremented by 8 after this service.

VECTOR NUMBER: 62

TITLE: RANDOM

ENTRY REQUIREMENTS: Nil.

OUTPUT: THE FLOATING POINT RANDOM NUMBER IS STACKED

FUNCTION: This service returns a floating point random number on the run-time stack. As in OPL, this number lies between 0 and 0.999999999999 inclusive. Note that the stack pointer will then be decremented by 8. Note also that the sequence of numbers produced by this service are always the same. To alter the sequence to a new one, the 7-byte random number seed at $23AE will have to be altered.

VECTOR NUMBER: 63

TITLE: SINE

ENTRY REQUIREMENTS: THE FLOATING POINT ARGUMENT MUST FIRST BE STACKED.

OUTPUT: THE FLOATING POINT RESULT IS STACKED.

FUNCTION: This function returns the floating point SIN of the argument, assumed to be in radians, on the run-time stack.

VECTOR NUMBER: 64

TITLE: SQUARE ROOT

ENTRY REQUIREMENTS: THE FLOATING POINT ARGUMENT MUST FIRST BE STACKED

OUTPUT: THE FLOATING POINT RESULT IS STACKED.

FUNCTION: This service returns the floating point square root of the argument on the run-time stack.

VECTOR NUMBER: 65

TITLE: TANGENT

ENTRY REQUIREMENTS: THE FLOATING POINT ARGUMENT MUST FIRST BE STACKED.

OUTPUT: THE FLOATING POINT RESULT IS STACKED.

FUNCTION: This service returns the floating point TANGENT of the argument, assumed to be in radians, on the run-time stack.

VECTOR NUMBER: 66

TITLE: ACTION PARAMETER OFFSET

ENTRY REQUIREMENTS: THE B REGISTER HOLDS THE OFFSET TO THE ACTION PARAMETER.

OUTPUT: THE B REGISTER HOLDS THE VALUE OF THE ACTION PARAMETER.

FUNCTION: This service returns the value of the ACTION PARAMETER by using the B Register as an offset.

VECTOR NUMBER: 67

TITLE: ACTION PARAMETER REGISTER OFFSET

ENTRY REQUIREMENTS: THE B REGISTER HOLDS THE OFFSET TO ACTION PARAMETER SPECIFYING A REGISTER.

OUTPUT: THE X REGISTER HOLDS THE ADDRESS OF THE TABLE REGISTER.

FUNCTION: This service causes the X Register to point to the table register by using the B Register as an offset.

VECTOR NUMBER: 68

TITLE: TABLE START

ENTRY REQUIREMENTS: THE D REGISTER HOLDS THE ADDRESS OF THE TABLE TO BE INTERPRETED.

OUTPUT: THE B REGISTER IS SET TO 0 IF THE END ACTION IS PERFORMED LAST.THE Z FLAG IS SET IF THE END ACTION IS PERFORMED LAST.

FUNCTION: This service interprets the table whose base address is held in the D Register. This is not discussed further.

VECTOR NUMBER: 69

TITLE: TABLE ADD

ENTRY REQUIREMENTS: THE B REGISTER IS SET TO HOLD THE OFFSET TO THE ACTION PARAMETER.

OUTPUT: THE D REGISTER HOLDS THE WORD WHICH IS LOCATED B BYTES FROM THE TABLE PROGRAM COUNTER.

FUNCTION: This service adds the contents of the B Register to the table program counter and places the word at that location in the D Register.

VECTOR NUMBER: 70

TITLE: BREAK TEST

ENTRY REQUIREMENTS: NIL

OUTPUT: IF THE ON/CLEAR KEY IS PRESSED, THE CARRY FLAG IS SET

FUNCTION: This Service checks to see if the ON/CLEAR key is being pressed, both by reading the keyboard and checking in the Keyboard Buffer. If found, the Service waits for the key to be released, flushes the Keyboard Buffer and sets the Carry Flag of the CCR. Otherwise, the Carry Flag is cleared.

VECTOR NUMBER: 71

TITLE: FLUSH KEYBOARD BUFFER

ENTRY REQUIREMENTS: NIL

OUTPUT: NIL

FUNCTION: The contents of the Keyboard Buffer. along with all the associated variables, are flushed.

VECTOR NUMBER: 72

TITLE: GET KEY

ENTRY REQUIREMENTS: NIL

OUTPUT: THE B REGISTER HOLDS THE ASCII CODE OF THE CHARACTER REMOVED FROM THE KEYBOARD BUFFER

FUNCTION: The routine waits for a key to be pressed and puts it in the B Register. If there are no keys in the Buffer, the machine executes a SLP instruction to save power until a keypress is detected. Note that the Auto Switchoff Counter at $7D is reset to the value in the Auto Switchoff Constant at $20CD at the beginning of a call to this Service to give the maximum possible time to get a key before a machine switch-off.

VECTOR NUMBER: 73

TITLE: INITIALISE KEYBOARD INTERRUPTS

ENTRY REQUIREMENTS: NIL

OUTPUT: NIL

FUNCTION: This Service initialises the keyboard interrupts by:

a. Flushing the Keyboard Buffer.
b. Setting the value of the Keyboard Interrupt Rate variable to $B3DD.
c. Setting the value of the Keyboard Delay variable to 14.
d. Setting the value of the Keyboard Repeat Rate variable to 0.
e. Clearing the flags in the Keyboard Status Byte to 0.
f. Setting the value of the Keyboard Click variable to 1.
g. The interrupts are enabled.
h. The Free Running Counter is reset.
i. The Timer 1 Output Compare Register is set to $B3DD.
j. Bit 3 of Timer 1 Control Status Register 1 is set.
k. The I mask of the CCR is cleared.

VECTOR NUMBER: 74

TITLE: SET THE KEYBOARD STATE

ENTRY REQUIREMENTS: THE B REGISTER HOLDS THE REQUIRED KEYBOARD STATE

OUTPUT: THE B REGISTER IS PRESERVED

FUNCTION: This service acts in the same way as the OPL KSTAT command. The contents of the B Register are stored in the Keyboard Status variable at $7B. The byte is constructed as follows:

a. If Bit 0 of the byte is set then Lower Case is selected, otherwise Upper Case is in force.

b. If Bit 6 is set then Numeric Lock is selected otherwise Numeric Lock is de-selected.

Note that the other bits of the byte are used by the Operating System for other purposes and should not be changed. For this reason, users wishing to employ Vector 74 should read the byte from the Keyboard Status variable and deal with bits 0 or 6 before calling the routine. This service also affects the cursor display, since it varies according to the keyboard state. Any change will be effected at the next display refresh.

VECTOR NUMBER: 75

TITLE: TEST KEYBOARD BUFFER

ENTRY REQUIREMENTS: NIL

OUTPUT: ASCII NUMBER OF NEXT KEY IN BUFFER OR 0 IF NO KEY

FUNCTION: This is a surprisingly complex Service. It looks into the Keyboard Buffer and, if it has something in it, puts the ASCII number of the first character into the B
Register. It also looks into the Unget Buffer at $76. If it is empty and there is something in the Keyboard Buffer, the first key of the Keyboard Buffer is transferred into the Unget Buffer. However, if no keys are found, things become more complicated:

a. If the Pack Switch-off flag at $20C1 is not 0, the Pack will switch off.
b. If the Auto Switch-off flag at $7C is not 0 and the Auto-switchoff Countdown Counter at $7D is 0, the Organiser will switch off.
c. If a Battery Low condition is detected, the machine will display "BATTERY TOO LOW" for 4 seconds before switching off.

VECTOR NUMBER: 76

TITLE:

ENTRY REQUIREMENTS: THE KEY TO BE PLACED IN THE BUFFER IS HELD IN THE B REGISTER

OUTPUT: NIL

FUNCTION: This Service puts the key held in the B Register into the Unget Buffer at $75 if the Buffer is empty.

VECTOR NUMBER: 77

TITLE: NEW PROCEDURE

ENTRY REQUIREMENTS: Nil.

OUTPUT: NIL.

FUNCTION: This service gives the user access to the RUN,LIST, EDIT and DELETE commands found in the PROGRAM Menu. Note that while LIST, EDIT and DELETE can be used on any text file, only OPL procedures can be the subject of a RUN command. The name of the file must first be placed in the Find Buffer at $22C9. The length of the name is held in the preceding byte. Moreover, the actual function required must be entered into location $A3:-

FUNCTION REQUIRED	VALUE FOR $A3
A. EDIT	3
B. LIST	4
C. RUN	7
D. DELETE	8

An area specially created for the Editor is set up and all entries are placed in it. The keys function as for the OPL versions and the block file type must be indicated at location $23E0 for all operations using this vector. If the user is manipulating a text-only file, the TRANSLATE option can be suppressed by inserting any non-zero number in the menu option location at $23E1.

VECTOR NUMBER: 78

TITLE: PROCESS PROCEDURE

ENTRY REQUIREMENTS: Nil.

OUTPUT: NIL.

FUNCTION: This service is similar to the preceding in that it allows the user to employ the PROGRAM Menu functions on an already existing file. All circumstances are as for vector 77 except that the file is brought into the editing are for work.

VECTOR NUMBER: 79

TITLE: TRANSLATE

ENTRY REQUIREMENTS: THE B REGISTER IS SET TO :
0 TO TRANSLATE LANGUAGE PROCEDURES.
1 TO TRANSLATE CALC EXPRESSIONS.
2 TO LOCATE CALC ERRORS.
3 TO LOCATE LANGUAGE ERRORS.
THE X REGISTER HOLDS THE Q-CODE OFFSET TO THE RUN-TIME ERROR. HOWEVER, IF THE B REGISTER IS SET TO TRANSLATE, THE X REGISTER IS IGNORED.

OUTPUT: ERROR: THE X REGISTER CONATINS THE TEXTCELL OFFSET TO THE ERROR. THE B REGISTER HOLDS THE ERROR NUMBER.

NO ERROR: THE TRANSLATED PRODUCT IS HELD IN THE Q-CODE OUTPUT CELL.

FUNCTION: This service runs the TRANSLATOR. LZ users should note that this function will translate the OPL in 2- or 4-line mode, as specified by the "display mode" variable at $2184.

VECTOR NUMBER: 80

TITLE: MENU

ENTRY REQUIREMENTS: THE D REGISTER HOLDS THE BIT MASK REQUIRED TO TERMINATE THE SERVICE.
THE X REGISTER HOLDS THE ADDRESS OF THE MENU LIST.

OUTPUT: IF THE A REGISTER IS ZERO, THE X REGISTER HOLDS THE ADDRESS OF THE SELECTED ROUTINE.
OTHERWISE, THE X REGISTER POINTS TO THE NAME OF THE SELECTED ITEM IN THE MENU LIST.
THE B REGISTER HOLDS THE TERMINATING KEY PRESS.
LOCATION $41 HOLDS THE NUMBER OF THE MENU ITEM SELECTED. NOTE THAT THE FIRST ELEMENT IS NUMBER 0.

FUNCTION: This service operates in the same way as the OPL MENU function. The menu list is held in memory at the address pointed to by the X Register. Each name is stored, leading byte count first, followed by the address of the corresponding routine or zero where appropriate. The list is completed by a name of zero length. The service operates as for the MENU command. LZ users should note that menus are aligned in three columns when operating in 4-line mode. Furthermore, spaces within menu items are changed to hard spaces (character 254) to avoid confusion.

The terminating mask allows the user to select those keys which will terminate the service. Each bit of Register D controls a key. If set, it will terminate when the key with the corresponding number+1 is pressed. Thus, if bit 0 is set, the ON/CLEAR key, which has an ASCII code of 1, will terminate the menu when pressed.

When the routine terminates, the X Register will contain the address of the routine indicated after the item in the menu list. If this address was entered as zero, the X Register will hold the address of the menu item in the menu list. The A register indicates which of the 2 cases is in force. The B Register returns the terminating key press. Note that this will be the EXE key if the routine is terminated by pressing the initial letter of the menu item. Location $41 returns the number of the menu item.

VECTOR NUMBER: 81

TITLE: STRING TO FLOATING POINT

ENTRY REQUIREMENTS: THE X REGISTER HOLDS THE ADDRESS OF THE STRING TO BE CONVERTED.
THE D REGISTER CONTAINS THE DESTINATION ADDRESS OF THE FLOATING POINT NUMBER.

OUTPUT: THE FLOATING POINT NUMBER IS PLACED AT THE PREVIOUSLY INDICATED ADDRESS.
THE X REGISTER POINTS TO THE END OF THE STRING.

FUNCTION: This service converts the string held at the address indicated by the X Register into a floating point number and places the number at the address indicated by the D Register. The string may be terminated by any non-numeric character. Moreover, the characters "E", "e" and "." are illegal unless they have already occurred within the string.

Note that although the D Register indicates the start address for the result, a copy of this address should be kept BEFORE calling the service, as the Register is subsequently trashed.

VECTOR NUMBER: 82

TITLE: FLOATING POINT ADDITION

ENTRY REQUIREMENTS: THE TWO FLOATING POINTNUMBERS ARE PLACED IN THE FLOATING POINT REGISTERS.

OUTPUT: THE FLOATING POINT ACCUMULATOR HOLDS ITS PREVIOUS VALUE PLUS THE CONTENTS OF THE FLOATING POINT OPERAND.

FUNCTION: This service adds the operand register to the accumulator register and places the result in the accumulator register.

VECTOR NUMBER: 83

TITLE: FLOATING POINT TO DECIMAL

ENTRY REQUIREMENTS: THE FLOATING POINT ACCUMULATOR HOLDS THE FLOATING POINT NUMBER TO BE CONVERTED.
THE A REGISTER HOLDS THE FILED WIDTH OF THE STRING TO BE OUTPUT.
THE B REGISTER HOLDS THE NUMBER OF DECIMAL PLACES REQUIRED.
THE X REGISTER HOLDS THE DESTINATION ADDRESS OF THE DECIMAL STRING.

OUTPUT: THE B REGISTER HOLDS THE LENGTH OF THE DECIMAL STRING.

FUNCTION: This service converts the floating point number held in the floating point accumulator to decimal-format ASCII text and stores it at the address held in the X Register.

VECTOR NUMBER: 84

TITLE:	FLOATING POINT TO ASCII EXPONENTIAL
ENTRY REQUIREMENTS:	THE NUMBER TO BE EXPRESSED IS STORED IN THE FLOATING POINT ACCUMULATOR. THE A REGISTER HOLDS THE FIELD WIDTH OF THE RESULT. THE B REGISTER HOLDS THE NUMBER OF DECIMAL PLACES REQUIRED. THE X REGISTER HOLDS THE DESTINATION ADDRESS OF THE RESULT.
OUTPUT:	THE B REGISTER HOLDS THE LENGTH OF THE RESULT.

FUNCTION: This service takes the BCD-format floating point number held in the accumulator and converts it into ASCII exponential, storing it at the address indicated by the X Register.

VECTOR NUMBER: 85

TITLE:	FLOATING POINT TO NUMERIC ASCII
ENTRY REQUIREMENTS:	THE A REGISTER HOLDS THE REQUIRED FIELD WIDTH. THE B REGISTER HOLDS THE NUMBER OF DECIMAL PLACES. THE X REGISTER HOLDS THE DESTINATION ADDRESS FOR THE STRING.
OUTPUT:	THE B REGISTER HOLDS THE LENGTH OF THE RESULTANT STRING.

FUNCTION: This service converts the number in the floating point accumulator into a numeric ASCII string, stored at the address indicated by the X Register.

The number will be converted into an integer, decimal or exponential as appropriate. The number of decimal points can be set using the B Register. A negative number in the B Register will disable this facility.

VECTOR NUMBER: 86

TITLE: FLOATING POINT TO INTEGER ASCII

ENTRY REQUIREMENTS: THE A REGISTER INDICATES THE FIELD WIDTH REQUIRED.
THE X REGISTER INDICATES THE DESTINATION BUFFER FOR THE STRING.

OUTPUT: THE B REGISTER CONTAINS THE LENGTH OF THE RESULTANT STRING.

FUNCTION: This service converts the number in the floating point accumulator and stores it as an ASCII integer at the address indicated by the X Register, rounding to the nearest integer if necessary.

VECTOR NUMBER: 87

TITLE: FLOATING POINT DIVISION

ENTRY REQUIREMENTS: THE DIVIDEND IS PLACED IN THE FIRST FLOATING POINT ACCUMULATOR, THE DIVISOR IN THE SECOND.

OUTPUT: THE FLOATING POINT ACCUMULATOR HOLDS THE RESULT.

FUNCTION: This service performs a floating point division on the two numbers as indicated above.

VECTOR NUMBER: 88

TITLE: FLOATING POINT MULTIPLICATION.

ENTRY REQUIREMENTS: THE TWO FLOATING POINT ACCUMULATORS CONTAIN THE NUMBERS TO BE MULTIPLIED.

OUTPUT: THE FLOATING POINT ACCUMULATOR CONTAINS THE RESULT.

FUNCTION: This service performs a floating point multiplication on the two numbers indicated above.

VECTOR NUMBER: 89

TITLE: FLOATING POINT NEGATION

ENTRY REQUIREMENTS: THE X REGISTER HOLDS THE ADDRESS OF THE REGISTER WHOSE CONTENTS IS TO BE NEGATED.

OUTPUT: NIL.

FUNCTION: This service negates the floating point number held in the address pointed to by the X Register. Note that an already negative number will become positive. Moreover, the routine expects a 7-digit mantissa. If the number is BCD, the user should set the X Register to indicate the byte below the first byte of the target number.

VECTOR NUMBER: 90

TITLE: FLOATING POINT SUBTRACTION

ENTRY REQUIREMENTS: THE TWO FLOATING POINT ACCUMULATORS HOLD THE NUMBERS TO BE SUBTRACTED.

OUTPUT: THE FIRST ACCUMULATOR HOLDS THE RESULT.

FUNCTION: This service subtracts the two floating point numbers indicated above, placing the result in the first accumulator.

VECTOR NUMBER: 91

TITLE: PACK TURN OFF

ENTRY REQUIREMENTS: NIL.

OUTPUT: NIL.

FUNCTION: This service turns off all slots.

VECTOR NUMBER: 92

TITLE: CURRENT PACK

ENTRY REQUIREMENTS: NIL.

OUTPUT: THE B REGISTER HOLDS THE UPPER BYTE OF THE PACK ADDRESS.
THE X REGISTER HOLDS THE LOWER TWO BYTES OF THE PACK ADDRESS.

FUNCTION: This service returns the address of the current pack as a 3-byte word in the B and X Registers. Note that the B Register will return zero if the machine is a CM version.

VECTOR NUMBER: 93

TITLE: PACK READ BYTE

ENTRY REQUIREMENTS: NIL.

OUTPUT: THE B REGISTER CONTAINS THE BYTE READ BY THE ROUTINE.

FUNCTION: Reads a byte at the current location in the current pack and stores it in the B Register, incrementing the pack address by one. DO NOT ATTEMPT TO READ BEYOND THE PACK.

VECTOR NUMBER: 94

TITLE: PACK READ SERIES

ENTRY REQUIREMENTS: THE D REGISTER HOLDS THE NUMBER OF BYTES TO BE READ.

OUTPUT: THE X REGISTER HOLDS THE DESTINATION ADDRESS OF THE SERIES.

FUNCTION: Reads a number of bytes, as indicated by the D Register, FORM THE CURRENT POSITION and stores them at the address indicated by the X Register.

VECTOR NUMBER: 95

TITLE: PACK READ WORD

ENTRY REQUIREMENTS: NIL.

OUTPUT: THE D REGISTER HOLDS THE WORD READ.

FUNCTION: This service reads a word from the current position in the current pack and returns it in the D Register,
incrementing the pack address by two. DO NOT ATTEMPT TO READ BEYOND THE PACK.

VECTOR NUMBER: 96

TITLE: SET PACK ADDRESS

ENTRY REQUIREMENTS: THE B REGISTER HOLDS THE UPPER BYTE OF THE PACK ADDRESS.
THE X REGISTER HOLDS THE LOWER 2 BYTES OF THE ADDRESS.

OUTPUT: NIL.

FUNCTION: This service sets up the address indicated by the B and X Registers.

VECTOR NUMBER: 97

TITLE: PACK SAVE BYTES

ENTRY REQUIREMENTS: THE D REGISTER HOLDS THE NUMBER OF BYTES TO BE SAVED.

THE X REGISTER HOLDS THE SOURCE ADDRESS.

OUTPUT: NIL.

FUNCTION: This routine saves a series of bytes, as indicated by the D Register, from the current address on the current pack. If a failure occurs, the pack counter will indicate the offending byte.

VECTOR NUMBER: 98

TITLE: SET PACK

ENTRY REQUIREMENTS: THE A REGISTER IS MADE NON-ZERO IF A PACK CHANGE IS TO BE REPORTED AS AN ERROR.
THE B REGISTER INDICATES WHICH PACK TO CHANGE.

OUTPUT: THE A REGISTER INDICATES THE PACK TYPE.
THE X REGISTER INDICATES THE PACK SIZE IN 8K BLOCKS.

FUNCTION: *THIS SERVICE MUST BE CALLED PRIOR TO ANY OTHER PACK ROUTINES IF THE PACKS HAVE BEEN TURNED OFF.* The current pack becomes as indicated by the B Register and the operating system configured to access it.

VECTOR NUMBER: 99

TITLE: PACK SKIP BYTES

ENTRY REQUIREMENTS: THE D REGISTER CONTAINS THE NUMBER OF BYTES TO BE SKIPPED.

OUTPUT: NIL.

FUNCTION: Adds the contents of the D Register to the pack address.

VECTOR NUMBER: 100

TITLE: RUN PROCEDURE

ENTRY REQUIREMENTS: THE X REGISTER INDICATES THE ADDRESS OF THE PROCEDURE NAME. IF THE B REGISTER IS SET, THE CALCULATOR IS RUN.

OUTPUT: NIL.

FUNCTION: Runs the OPL procedure whose name is indicated by the X Register. Note that the procedure must not contain parameters. LZ users should note that this Vector will revert to 2-line mode when running OPL which was translated on an Organiser II model.

VECTOR NUMBER: 101

TITLE: TOP MENU INSERT

ENTRY REQUIREMENTS: THE B REGISTER CONTAINS THE POSITION IN THE MENU LIST AT WHICH THE INSERTED TEXT IS TO BE PLACED.

OUTPUT: NIL.

FUNCTION: This routine inserts an item into the top level menu at the position indicated by the B Register, "0" meaning at the beginning of the list, "1" after the first item and "$FF" before "OFF".

The item to be inserted is stored in the run time buffer at $2187. It starts with a leading count byte, the item text and its execution address (or zero, if appropriate). Refer to the Organiser Manual for further details of the top level menu customising procedure.

VECTOR NUMBER: 102

TITLE: COPY

ENTRY REQUIREMENTS: NIL.

OUTPUT: NIL.

FUNCTION: This service performs all the functions of the OPL "COPY" command.

VECTOR NUMBER: 103

TITLE: TOP MENU DELETE

ENTRY REQUIREMENTS: THE X REGISTER HOLDS THE ADDRESS OF THE ITEM NAME.

OUTPUT: NIL.

FUNCTION: This service deletes the item indicated by the X Register (the name begins with a leading count byte) from the top level menu.

VECTOR NUMBER: 104

TITLE: EDIT FILENAME.

ENTRY REQUIREMENTS: BIT 0 OF THE A REGISTER IS SET FOR SINGLE- LINE EDITING, CLEARED FOR MULTI-LINE. NOTE THAT BIT 7 MUST BE CLEAR FOR THIS SERVICE TO WORK .
THE B REGISTER HOLDS THE MAXIMUM INPUT LENGTH.
THE X REGISTER HOLDS THE ADDRESS OF THE PROMPT (WITH LEADING COUNT BYTE) EXCLUDING THE PACK INDICATOR.

OUTPUT: THE CARRY FLAG IS SET IF THE ON/CLEAR WAS PRESSED.

FUNCTION: This service clears the screen and prints the prompt pointed to by the X Register, followed by the pack letter+":". Normal editing is then allowed.

VECTOR NUMBER: 105

TITLE: CALCULATE DAY

ENTRY REQUIREMENTS: THE X REGISTER INDICATES THE ADDRESS OF THE TIME BUFFER.

OUTPUT: THE B REGISTER HOLDS THE DAY VALUE.
THE X REGISTER HOLDS THE ADDRESS OF THE 3-BYTE DAY NAME.

FUNCTION: This service takes the date stored in the time buffer indicated by the X Register and returns the day as a B Register byte in the range 0 to 6 and the address of the 3-letter day in the X Register. The date must be in the range 1 JAN 1900 to 31 DEC 1999 for Organiser II owners and 31 DEC2155 for those with LZ variants.

VECTOR NUMBER: 106

TITLE: GET TIME

ENTRY REQUIREMENTS: THE X REGISTER CONTAINS THE DESTINATION ADDRES FOR THE TIME VALUE.

OUTPUT: NIL.

FUNCTION: This service gets a copy of the real-time clock and places it in the buffer indicated by the X Register.

VECTOR NUMBER: 107

TITLE: UPDATE TIME

ENTRY REQUIREMENTS: THE A MINUTES CONTAINS THE NUMBER OF MINUTES TO UPDATE THE TIME.

THE B REGISTER HOLDS THE NUMBER OF SECONDS TO UPDATE THE TIME.
THE X REGISTER HOLDS THE ADDRESS OF THE 6- BYTE BUFFER HOLDING THE TIME.

OUTPUT: NIL.

FUNCTION: This service updates the time stored in at the address indicated by the X Register(pointing to the year field) by the minutes and seconds stored in the A and B Registers.

VECTOR NUMBER: 108

TITLE: WAIT

ENTRY REQUIREMENTS: THE D REGISTER HOLDS THE DEGREE OF PAUSE.

OUTPUT: NIL.

FUNCTION: This service pauses for the number of ticks indicated by the D Register. Note that a tick is the interval between successive keyboard interrupts, normally 50ms.

VECTOR NUMBER: 109

TITLE: COPY BUFFER

ENTRY REQUIREMENTS: THE X REGISTER CONTAINS THE ADDRESS OF THE SOURCE BUFFER.
THE D REGISTER CONTAINS THE ADDRESS OF THE DESTINATION BUFFER.
LOCATIONS $41/$42 INDICATE THE LENGTH OF BUFFER TO BE COPIED.

OUTPUT: NIL.

FUNCTION: This service copies the first buffer, indicated by the X Register into the buffer pointed to by the D Register. The two buffers may overlap. The routine caters for this.

VECTOR NUMBER: 110

TITLE: DATA DISPLAY 1

ENTRY REQUIREMENTS: THE D REGISTER CONTAINS THE ADDRESS OF THE FORMAT CONTROL STRING.
THE MACHINE CODE CONTAINS THE VARIABLES TO BE DISPLAYED.

OUTPUT: NIL.

FUNCTION: Displays text/variables as governed by the control string. The display is not pre-cleared.

VECTOR NUMBER: 111

TITLE: DATA DISPLAY 2

ENTRY REQUIREMENTS: THE MACHINE STACK CONTAINS THE VARIABLES TO BE DISPLAYED.

OUTPUT: NIL.

FUNCTION: As for service 110, except that the control string is held on the stack instead of in a discrete buffer. LZ users have a further control code - ASCII 31. When used, the next string to be displayed will be printed centred on the screen with the line on either side cleared of old text.

VECTOR NUMBER: 112

TITLE: ENTER ROUTINE

ENTRY REQUIREMENTS: THE X REGISTER CONTAINS THE ADDRESS OF THE ROUTINE.
THE D REGISTER CONTAINS THE PARAMETER TO BE PASSED TO THE ROUTINE.

OUTPUT: THE B REGISTER CONTAINS A CODE

	NUMBER. THE CARRY FLAG IS CLEARED IS THE B REGISTER IS EMPTY. SET OTHERWISE.

FUNCTION: This service allows the routine indicated by the X Register to be called in a way which allows it to be exited from any routines nested within it. A very useful application of this service in in the ON ERROR and RAISE commands.

VECTOR NUMBER: 113

TITLE:	FILL BUFFER
ENTRY REQUIREMENTS:	THE X REGISTER CONTAINS THE ADDRESS OF THE BUFFER TO BE FILLED. THE A REGISTER CONTAINS THE BYTE TO BE USED AS A FILLER. THE B REGISTER INDICATES THE LENGTH OF THE FILL.
OUTPUT:	NIL.

FUNCTION: This service fills the buffer pointed to by the X Register with the byte indicated by the A Register.

VECTOR NUMBER: 114

TITLE:	INDEPENDENT BUFFER COMPARE
ENTRY REQUIREMENTS:	THE X REGISTER CONTAINS THE ADDRESS OF THE FIRST STRING. LOCATIONS $41/$42 INDICATE THE ADDRESS OF THE SECOND STRING. THE A REGISTER INDICATES THE LENGTH OF THE FIRST STRING. THE B REGISTER CONTAINS THE LENGTH OF THE SECOND STRING.
OUTPUT:	THE B REGISTER WILL BE ZERO IF THE STRINGS ARE IDENTICAL, LESS

THAN ZERO IF THE FIRST STRING IS FIRST ALPHABETICALLY AND GREATER THAN ZERO IF THE SECOND STRING IS FIRST ALPHABETICALLY. THE Z AND N FLAGS ARE SET TO REFLECT THE CONTENTS OF THE B REGISTER.

FUNCTION: This service compares the two strings, independent of case.

VECTOR NUMBER: 115

TITLE: BUFFER INSTRING

ENTRY REQUIREMENTS: THE X REGISTER INDICATES THE MAJOR STRING.
LOCATIONS $41/$42 INDICATE THE MINOR STRING.
THE A REGISTER CONTAINS THE LENGTH OF THE MAJOR STRING.
THE B REGISTER CONTAINS THE LENGTH OF THE MINOR STRING.

OUTPUT: THE B REGISTER INDICATES THE POSITION OF OCCURRENCE OF THE MINOR STRING WITHIN THE MAJOR STRING IF A MATCH WAS FOUND. THE LENGTH OF THE MAJOR STRING OTHERWISE.

FUNCTION: This service returns the position within the major string that the minor string occurs. Note that the first position is "0". If no match is found, the B Register returns with the length of the major string.

VECTOR NUMBER: 116

TITLE: LEAVE ROUTINE

ENTRY REQUIREMENTS: THE B REGISTER CONTAINS THE CODE NUMBER TO BE RETURND BY SERVICE 112.

OUTPUT: THE B REGISTER CONTAINS THE REQUIRED CODE.
THE CARRY FLAG IS CLEAR IF THE B REGISTER IS CLEAR, SET OTHERWISE.

FUNCTION: This service allows early termination from a routine set up using service 112.

VECTOR NUMBER: 117

TITLE: INTEGER DIVISION

ENTRY REQUIREMENTS: THE X REGISTER CONTAINS THE NUMERATOR.
THE D REGISTER CONTAINS THE DENOMINATOR.

OUTPUT: THE X REGISTER CONTAINS THE RESULT.

FUNCTION: This service carries out a signed integer division of the two numbers indicated above.

VECTOR NUMBER: 118

TITLE: INTEGER MULTIPLICATION

ENTRY REQUIREMENTS: THE X REGISTER HOLDS THE FIRST SIGNED INTEGER.
THE D REGISTER HOLDS THE SECOND SIGNED INTEGER.

OUTPUT:	THE X REGISTER HOLDS THE LESS SIGNIFICANT WORD OF THE PRODUCT. THE D REGISTER CONTAINS THE MORE SIGNIFICANT WORD OF THE PRODUCT.

FUNCTION: This service carries out a signed integer multiplication of the two numbers indicated above, placing the less significant word of the 4-byte result in the X Register and the more significant in the D Register.

VECTOR NUMBER: 119

TITLE:	SPLIT OUT FIELD
ENTRY REQUIREMENTS:	THE X REGISTER CONTAINS THE ADDRESS OF THE BUFFER FROM WHICH THE FIELD IS TO BE EXTRACTED. LOCATIONS $41/$42 INDICATE THE LENGTH OF THE BUFFER. THE A REGISTER CONTAINS THE CHARACTER SEPARATOR. THE B REGISTER CONTAINS THE FIELD NUMBER REQUIRED.
OUTPUT:	IF THE FIELD WAS FOUND, THE X REGISTER WILL CONTAIN THE ADDRESS OF THE FIELD, THE D REGISTER WILL INDICATE THE LENGTH OF THE FIELD AND THE CARRY FLAG WILL BE CLEAR. OTHERWISE, LOCATIONS $41/$42 WILL CONTAIN THE B REGISTER MINUS THE NUMBER OF FIELDS FOUND AND THE CARRY FLAG WILL BE SET.

FUNCTION: Finds a specific field within the record held at the location indicated by the X Register. The length of the record is indicated by locations $41/$42. The field separator is held in the A register, while the field number is stated by the B Register. Note that the first filed is numbered 0.

VECTOR NUMBER: 120

TITLE: UNSIGNED INTEGER DIVISION

ENTRY REQUIREMENTS: THE X REGISTER CONTAINS THE NUMERATOR.
THE D REGISTER CONTAINS THE DENOMINATOR.

OUTPUT: THE X REGISTER CONTAINS THE QUOTIENT.
THE D REGISTER CONTAINS THE REMAINDER.
LOCATIONS $45/$46 CONTAIN A COPY OF THE X REGISTER.

FUNCTION: This service carries out an unsigned integer division. The DIV goes to the X Register, while the MOD goes to the D Register.

VECTOR NUMBER: 121

TITLE: UNSIGNED INTEGER MULTIPLICATION

ENTRY REQUIREMENTS: THE D REGISTER CONTAINS THE FIRST INTEGER.
THE X REGISTER CONTAINS THE SECOND INTEGER.

OUTPUT: THE X REGISTER HOLDS THE LESS SIGNIFICANT WORD OF THE RESULT.
THE D REGISTER HOLDS THE MORE SIGNIFICANT WORD OF THE RESULT.
LOCATIONS $45/$46 CONTAINS A COPY OF THE X REGISTER.
LOCATIONS $43/$44 CONTAINS A COPY OF THE D REGISTER.

FUNCTION: This service carries out an unsigned integer multiplication of the two numbers indicated above. The product is placed in the D and X Registers with copies in locations $43-$46.

VECTOR NUMBER: 122

TITLE: BINARY TO DECIMAL

ENTRY REQUIREMENTS: THE X REGISTER INDICATES THE DESTINATION BUFFER.
THE D REGISTER CONTAINS THE UNSIGNED BINARY NUMBER TO BE CONVERTED.

OUTPUT: THE B REGISTER CONTAINS THE LENGTH OF THE RESULTANT STRING.

FUNCTION: This routine converts the unsigned binary number held in the D Register into an ASCII decimal at the location pointed to by the X Register. The length of the result is placed in the B Register.

VECTOR NUMBER: 123

TITLE: DEVICE CATALOGUE

ENTRY REQUIREMENTS: LOCATION $42 INDICATES THE RECORD TYPE.

OUTPUT: NIL.

FUNCTION: This service displays all the records of record type, as indicated by location $42, on the current device. Displays each record after EXE is pressed until "END OF PACK" or the ON/CLEAR key is pressed.

VECTOR NUMBER: 124

TITLE: BINARY TO HEX

ENTRY REQUIREMENTS: THE X REGISTER POINTS TO THE DESTINATION BUFFER.
THE D REGISTER HOLDS THE UNSIGNED BINARY NUMBER.

OUTPUT: THE B REGISTER INDICATES THE LENGTH OF THE STRING RESULT.

FUNCTION: This service takes the unsigned binary number held in the D Register and converts it to ASCII hex, storing it in the buffer pointed to by the X Register and returning its length in the B Register.

VECTOR NUMBER: 125

TITLE: CONFIRM

ENTRY REQUIREMENTS: NIL.

OUTPUT: THE B REGISTER CONTAINS THE VALUE OF THE KEY PRESSED.
THE CARRY FLAG IS SET FOR "n", "N" OR "ON/CLEAR".

FUNCTION: This service waits until "Y", "y", "N", "n" or "ON/CLEAR" is pressed and returns the key in the B Register, setting the Carry flag if any of the last 3 are the cause. Note that this routine first does the equivalent of a KSTAT 1, destroying the previous keyboard condition.

VECTOR NUMBER: 126

TITLE: UT$CDSP

FUNCTION: This function is a general utility display facility which is available only on versions 2.5 and above. No further information is presented here.

VECTOR NUMBER: 127

TITLE: TL$RSTR

FUNCTION: This facility is a translation function and is only available on versions 2.7 and above. It is not discussed further here.

VECTOR NUMBER: 128

TITLE: SET LANGUAGE

ENTRY REQUIREMENTS: THE B REGISTER HOLDS THE CODE OF THE LANGUAGE TO BE USED BY THE LZ. CODES ARE:

0 = ENGLISH
1 = FRENCH
2 = GERMAN
3 = SPANISH
4 = ITALIAN
5 = PORTUGUESE
6 = SWEDISH
7 = DANISH
8 = NORWEGIAN
9 = DUTCH
10 = TURKISH

OUTPUT: SETS LANGUAGE VARIABLE ($2186) TO CODE SELECTED.

FUNCTION: This function is available only on multi-lingual Organisers. It sets the language to that indicated by the code in the B Register, unless the language is not available. In the latter case, English is used by default. The top level menu is reset, which means that any user-inserted menu items will be lost. Note that in cases of restricted memory, there may be insufficient RAM space for the new menu, since different languages require different space. Should this occur, the language will remain unchanged. The language variable can be read but must not be set directly.

LZ users should note that the range of languages offered is, sadly, not as extensive as multi-lingual CM/XP models and is currently limited to English, French and German.

NEW CALLS PECULIAR TO THE LZ VERSION

VECTOR NUMBER: 129

TITLE: TEMPORARY SWITCH OFF

ENTRY REQUIREMENTS: THE D REGISTER IS SET TO HOLD SWITCH OFF PERIOD IN SECONDS (IN THE RANGE 2-1800).

OUTPUT: NIL

FUNCTION: This function allows the user to make the LZ switch off for a number of seconds, as specified by the D Register. When this period is over, the machine will switch back on automatically. Since the Organiser must periodically update its clock, the maximum time it can be switched off using this function is 30 minutes, or 1800 seconds. Longer periods can be simulated by repeatedly calling this vector. Note that if an out-of-range value is set in the D Register, incorrect results will follow.

VECTOR NUMBER: 130

TITLE: SET LINE MODE

ENTRY REQUIREMENTS: THE A REGISTER IS SET AT '0' FOR 2-LINE MODE AND '1' FOR 4-LINE. BIT 7 IS SET TO LEAVE UDG CLOCK UNAFFECTED AND CLEARED TO KILL IT

OUTPUT: THE A REGISTER HOLDS THE PREVIOUS MODE.

FUNCTION: This function is called to convert the display to/from 2-/4-line mode. It first checks to see if the top bit of the A Register is clear, disabling the UDG Clock if this is the case. The variable DPB-MCHK is cleared and the routine exits at this point if the mode called is already in force. If no exit is made, the system clears a 2x16 window with border (for 2-line mode) or the entire 4x20 screen. The variables holding the address of the screen buffer ($2090), the number of screen lines ($2092) and the screen width ($2093) are initialised.

VECTOR NUMBER: 131

TITLE: SET CLOCK DISPLAY STATUS

ENTRY REQUIREMENTS: THE B REGISTER HOLDS THE POSITION OF THE CLOCK ON SCREEN. BIT 7 IS SET TO SWITCH OFF CLOCK DISPLAY.

OUTPUT: THE B REGISTER HOLDS THE PREVIOUS CLOCK POSITION AND STATUS.

FUNCTION: This function sets the clock display position and status. Since the clock is printed right-justified in a 6-character field, this gives a B Register range of 0-74 (0-26 in 2-line mode). No clock will be displayed if the top bit of the B Register is set. UDGs 3-7 are used to display the clock in 24-hour mode and UDG 1 is additionally used as an am/pm indicator in 12-hour. These will overwrite previous definitions.

VECTOR NUMBER: 132

TITLE: RE-DEFINE CLOCK UDGs

ENTRY REQUIREMENTS: IF THE A REGISTER HOLDS '0', ONLY UDG 5 WILL BE RE-DEFINED.

OUTPUT: NIL

FUNCTION: This function re-defines the UDGs used to display the current time. If the A Register holds '0', UDG 5 will be defined as a flashing colon, otherwise as the underscore symbol. The screen status and all scratch registers ($41-$4B) are preserved.

VECTOR NUMBER: 133

TITLE: READ/WRITE UDG

ENTRY REQUIREMENTS: THE A REGISTER HOLDS '0' FOR 8-BYTE PATTERN AND '1' FOR A 5-BYTE ONE. THE TOP BIT IS SET TO READ THE UDG AND CLEAR TO WRITE.
THE B REGISTER HOLDS THE UDG NUMBER.
THE X REGISTER POINTS TO THE ADDRESS WHERE THE DEFINITION IS LOCATED.

OUTPUT: NIL

FUNCTION: This function allows the user to define a UDG or to read the bit pattern of an existing definition. If bit 7 of the A Register is clear, the call will define a UDG whose number is held in B and whose data is held at the location pointed to by the X Register. Normally, a UDG would be stored as 8 bytes of data. However, since the actual appearance of the character is 5x8 pixels, this call allows the user to retrieve definitions which have been stored in 5-byte formats. To do this, the A Register must hold '1'. The definition of a UDG can be read into the location specified at the X Register (always in 8-byte format) if the top bit of the A Register is set. Users should note that this call disables interrupts.

VECTOR NUMBER: 134

TITLE: TITLED MENU DISPLAY

ENTRY REQUIREMENTS: THE D REGISTER HOLDS THE TERMINATING BIT MASK.
THE X REGISTER POINTS TO THE LOCATION OF THE MENU LIST.

OUTPUT: THE A REGISTER ACTS AS A FLAG TO INDICATE THE NATURE OF THE

CONTENTS OF THE X REGISTER. IF A IS ZERO, THE X REGISTER WILL HOLD THE ADDRESS OF THE ROUTINE WHICH IS ASSOCIATED WITH THE ITEM SELECTED FROM THE MENU LIST. IF IT IS NON-ZERO, THE X REGISTER WILL POINT TO THE NAME OF THE SELECTED ITEM IN THE MENU LIST BUFFER.
THE B REGISTER HOLDS THE TERMINATING KEY PRESS.
THE GENERAL WORD VARIABLE 0 ($41) HOLDS THE NUMBER OF THE MENU ITEM SELECTED (STARTING AT ZERO).

FUNCTION: This function works in the same way as the normal menu call except that it treats any text already on the screen as a title. The menu is then displayed on the next clear line. If the title text occupies more than 3 lines, the 4th will be wiped and the menu located at that position. Users should note that if the D Register is specified as '0' for the call, the routine will never terminate - there will be no valid terminating character. In addition, this call automatically puts the keyboard into alpha shift.

VECTOR NUMBER: 135

TITLE: SINGLE-LINE MENU DISPLAY

ENTRY REQUIREMENTS: THE D REGISTER HOLDS THE TERMINATING BIT MASK.
THE X REGISTER HOLDS THE ADDRESS OF THE MENU LIST.

OUTPUT: THE A REGISTER ACTS AS A FLAG TO INDICATE THE NATURE OF THE CONTENTS OF THE X REGISTER. IF A IS ZERO, THE X REGISTER WILL POINT TO THE ADDRESS OF THE ROUTINE LINKED TO THE ITEM WHICH HAS

BEEN SELECTED FROM THE MENU. IF IT IS NON-ZERO, THE X REGISTER WILL POINT TO THE NAME OF THE ITEM IN THE MENU LIST.
THE B REGISTER HOLDS THE TERMINATING KEYPRESS.
GENERAL WORD VARIABLE 0 ($41) HOLDS THE NUMBER OF THE SELECTED MENU ITEM (STARTING AT 0).

FUNCTION: This function operates like the normal menu display call except that the menu is displayed on a single, scrolling line. The remaining 3 lines of the display are left untouched. The line used by the menu will be the one containing the cursor in its current position, as specified by the cursor position variable at $62. Users should note that if the D Register is passed as '0', the routine will never terminate, having no valid terminating character. In addition, the call puts the keyboard into alpha shift.

VECTOR NUMBER: 136

TITLE: DISPLAY MENU WITH ICON

ENTRY REQUIREMENTS: THE D REGISTER HOLDS THE TERMINATING BIT MASK.
THE X REGISTER HOLDS THE ADDRESS OF THE MENU LIST.

OUTPUT: THE A REGISTER INDICATES THE NATURE OF THE X REGISTER. IF A IS ZERO, THE X REGISTER WILL POINT TO THE ROUTINE WHICH IS LINKED WITH THE ITEM SELECTED FROM THE MENU. OTHERWISE, IT POINTS TO THE NAME OF THE SELECTED ITEM IN THE MENU LIST.
THE B REGISTER HOLDS THE TERMINATING KEYPRESS.

THE GENERAL WORD VARIABLE 0 ($41) HOLDS THE NUMBER OF THE SELECTED ITEM (STARTING AT ZERO).

FUNCTION: This function operates much like the other menu functions except that the top line is used to display an icon at the left and the clock on the right. UDG 0 is always used at the top left. Users should note that if the D Register is passed with zero contents, the routine will never terminate, having no valid terminating character. In addition, this function puts the keyboard into alpha shift.

VECTOR NUMBER: 137

TITLE: FLOATING POINT SUM

ENTRY REQUIREMENTS: THE POINTER TO THE ADDRESS OF THE FIRST FLOATING POINT NUMBER IS PUSHED ON THE STACK, FOLLOWED BY THE LENGTH OF THE SERIES TO BE SUMMED.

OUTPUT: THE FLOATING POINT RESULT IS LEFT ON THE STACK.

FUNCTION: The address of the series of numbers is pushed onto the runtime stack, followed by a word-length number denoting the length of the series to be summed. The result is placed on the stack and the original input parameters are left unchanged.

VECTOR NUMBER: 138

TITLE: FLOATING POINT MEAN

ENTRY REQUIREMENTS: THE ADDRESS OF THE SERIES OF FLOATING POINT NUMBERS IS PLACED ON THE STACK FOLLOWED BY A WORD DESCRIBING THE LENGTH OF THE SERIES.

OUTPUT: THE FLOATING POINT MEAN IS LEFT ON THE STACK.

FUNCTION: This function takes the address of the series of number from the stack, together with the length of the series, and calculates the mean. This result is then left on the stack, leaving the input parameters unchanged.

VECTOR NUMBER: 139

TITLE: FLOATING POINT VARIANCE

ENTRY REQUIREMENTS: THE ADDRESS OF THE SERIES OF NUMBERS S PUSHED ONTO THE STACK, FOLLOWED BY A WORD-LENGTH NUMBER DESCRIBING THE LENGTH OF THE SERIES.

OUTPUT: THE FLOATING POINT RESULT IS PLACED ON THE STACK.

FUNCTION: This function takes the address and length of the series from the stack and calculates the sample variance using the formula:

```
                          N
var(Xi) = (Sigma (Xi-Xm)**2)/(N-1)
                         i=1
```

where Xm is the arithmetic mean.

Users should note that this is the sample variance. If the population variance is required, it can be arrived at by multiplying the sample variance by (N-1)/N.

VECTOR NUMBER: 140

TITLE: FLOATING POINT STANDARD DEVIATION

ENTRY REQUIREMENTS: THE ADDRESS OF THE SERIES IS PLACED ON THE STACK, TOGETHER WITH A WORD-LENGTH NUMBER DESCRIBING THE LENGTH OF THE SERIES.

OUTPUT: THE FLOATING POINT RESULT IS LEFT ON THE STACK.

FUNCTION: This function takes the address of the floating point series, together with its length, from the stack and calculates the sample standard deviation, using the formula:

```
                        N
std(Xi) = sqrt((Sigma (Xi-Xm)**2)/(N-1)) = sqrt(var(Xi))
                       i=1
```

The floating point result is left on the stack with the original parameters. This assumes that the data set is only a sample and not the complete population. If it IS, in fact, the complete set, the population standard deviation can be calculated by multiplying the sample deviation by sqrt((N-1)/N).

VECTOR NUMBER: 141

TITLE: FLOATING POINT MIN

ENTRY REQUIREMENTS: THE ADDRESS OF THE SERIES OF FLOATS IS STACKED, TOGETHER WITH THE LENGTH OF THE SERIES.

OUTPUT: THE FLOATING POINT RESULT IS LEFT ON THE STACK.

FUNCTION: This function finds the series of floating point numbers and, knowing the length, finds the minimum of the series. This number is placed on the stack, leaving the original parameters unchanged.

VECTOR NUMBER: 142

TITLE: FLOATING POINT MAX

ENTRY REQUIREMENTS: THE ADDRESS OF THE SERIES, TOGETHER WITH THE LENGTH OF THE SERIES, IS PLACED ON THE STACK.

OUTPUT: THE FLOATING POINT RESULT IS PLACED ON THE STACK.

FUNCTION: This function finds the address of the series indicated by the stack and calculates the maximum of the series. This number is placed on the stack, leaving the original parameters unchanged.

VECTOR NUMBER: 143

TITLE: VALIDATE WILD CARD FILENAME.

ENTRY REQUIREMENTS: THE B REGISTER CONTAINS THE LENGTH OF THE FILENAME. THE X REGISTER POINTS TO THE FILENAME. NULL FILENAMES ARE ILLEGAL.

OUTPUT: THE A REGISTER HOLDS THE FILE TYPE OF THE FILENAME. THIS WILL BE 0 IF THE EXTENSION IS ".*" AND $FF IF NO EXTENSION IS SPECIFIED. FURTHERMORE, IF THE EXTENSION IS ".OPO" OR ".OPT" THE FILETYPE WILL BE RETURNED AS "$83", WHICH IS THE CODE FOR ".OPL" FILES. IF THIS IS THE CASE, LOCATION $43 (THE

LOW BYTE OF GENERAL WORD VARIABLE 0) WILL BE SET ACCORDINGLY.
THE B REGISTER HOLDS THE LENGTH OF THE FILENAME BEFORE THE "." CHARACTER. THIS MUST BE NO LONGER THAN 8 CHARACTERS AND EXTENSIONS MUST BY 3 CHARACTERS LONG OR ".*".
ADDRESS $42 HOLDS 1 IF THE EXTENSION IS ".OPO", 2 IF IT IS "OPT" AND 0 IN ANY OTHER CASE.

FUNCTION: This function retrieves the wild card filename pointed to by the X Register, validates it and returns with its length and filetype.

VECTOR NUMBER: 144

TITLE: WILD CARD CATALOGUE.

ENTRY REQUIREMENTS: THE A REGISTER IS SET TO 1 FOR THE INITIAL CALL TO THE ROUTINE AND 0 THEREAFTER. THE TOP BIT IS SET IF THE USER WISHES THE SIZES OF THE FILE TO BE DISPLAYED.
THE B REGISTER CONTAINS A CODE INDICATING THE DEVICE:
0 = DEVICE A
1 = DEVICE B
2 = DEVICE C
3 = DEVICE D
THE X REGISTER INDICATES THE BUFFER TO HOLD THE FILENAME AFTER THE CALL. NOTE THAT THE BUFFER WILL HOLD THE LEADING COUNT BYTE FIRST.
THE LOW BYTE OF GENERAL WORD VARIABLE 0 ($42) INDICATES THE LENGTH OF THE MATCH STRING. SET

	THE TOP BIT TO INDICATE THAT THE FILETYPE OF THE MATCH HAS BEEN PLACED IN THE HIGH BYTE OF THE VARIABLE ($41). THE HIGH BYTE OF THE GENERAL WORD VARIABLE 0 ($41) HOLDS THE FILETYPE OF THE MATCH IF BIT 7 OF LOCATION $42 HAS BEEN SET. GENERAL WORD VARIABLE 1 ($43) POINTS TO THE MATCH STRING.
OUTPUT:	THE A REGISTER HOLDS THE TYPE OF THE FILE FOUND. THE B REGISTER HOLDS 1 IF ".OPO", 2 IF ".OPT" AND 0 OTHERWISE. GENERAL WORD VARIABLE 0 ($41) HOLDS THE NUMBER OF BYTES IN A BLOCK FILE OR THE NUMBER OF RECORDS IN A ".ODB" FILE, IF THE TOP BIT OF THE A REGISTER WAS SET.

FUNCTION: This function provides the user with a facility to call a catalogue of a specified device using wild card matches. The initial call to the function must see the A register non-zero and subsequent require it to be zero. In the latter case, only the X register need be passed. The match string can contain "*" to indicate any number of wild characters and "+" to indicate a single one. In addition, file extensions from the following list may also be specified:

.ODB	TEXT OR DATABASE FILES
.OPL	TEXT OR PROCEDURE FILES
.DIA	CM/XP DIARY SAVE FILES
.COM	COMMS LINK SETUP FILES
.PLN	SPREADSHEET FILES
.PAG	PAGER SETUP FILES
.NTS	NOTEPAD FILES
.TY8-TYF	FILE TYPES IN THE RANGE $88-$8F
.OPT	TEXT-ONLY OPL PROCEDURES
.OPO	OBJECT-ONLY OPL PROCEDURES

Users should note that only "*" may be used in the extension and that ".OPL" will match a text OR object file, and that ".OPO" and ".OPT" operate in the same way.

VECTOR NUMBER: 145

TITLE: WILD CARD COPY.

ENTRY REQUIREMENTS: THE D REGISTER CONTAINS THE ADDRESS OF THE "COPY-TO" FILENAME.
THE X REGISTER CONTAINS THE ADDRESS OF THE "COPY-FROM" FILENAME.
GENERAL WORD VARIABLE 0 ($41) CONTAINS THE ADDRESS OF ANY USER ROUTINE WHICH SHOULD BE CALLED EACH TIME A FILE IS COPIED. IF NO SUCH ROUTINE EXISTS, THIS VARIABLE SHOULD CONTAIN $0000.

OUTPUT: NIL.

FUNCTION: This function allows the user to copy files from one device to another. Copying to the same device is not permitted but a different filename may be specified when performing legal copies. Note, however, that a ".OPL" file copied in this way will NOT have the name of the first line changed. Subsequent printing of this file will reveal this disparity. If the device alone is specified in the "copy-to" string, the file will be copied with the same name. Wildcards ("*" for any number of wild characters and "+" for a single one) can be used in the "copy-from" string but not, for obvious reasons, in the "copy-to". In such a case, the "copy-to" string must specify ONLY the device e.g. "C:". Extensions, as specified in Vector 144, may also be used. If the General Word Variable 0 ($41) indicates a user routine address, the routine will be called each time a file is copied. On the call, the X register will be set to indicate the filename just copied and the A register will indicate its filetype.

VECTOR NUMBER: 146

TITLE: WILD CARD DELETE.

ENTRY REQUIREMENTS: THE X REGISTER CONTAINS THE ADDRESS OF THE FILENAME TO BE DELETED (LEADING BYTE COUNT). GENERAL WORD VARIABLE 0 CONTAINS THE ADDRESS OF ANY USER ROUTINE TO BE CALLED EACH TIME A DELETION IS COMPLETED. THIS SHOULD HOLD $0000 IF NO ROUTINE IS TO BE CALLED.

OUTPUT: NIL.

FUNCTION: This function allows the user to delete the file whose name is indicated by the X register. Wildcards are allowed ("*" to indicate any number of wild characters and "+" to indicate a single one). Only the "*" may be used in the extension of the filename, which must be in the form "A:BBBBBBBB.CCC".

VECTOR NUMBER: 147

TITLE: WILD CARD FIND.

ENTRY REQUIREMENTS: THE D REGISTER HOLDS THE ADDRESS OF THE SEARCH STRING, LEADING BYTE COUNT. THE X REGISTER INDICATES THE BUFFER TO HOLD THE "FOUND" RECORD, LEADING BYTE COUNT.

OUTPUT: THE A REGISTER CONTAINS THE RECORD TYPE OF THE "FOUND" RECORD.

FUNCTION: This function works like the normal FIND call except that wildcards are permitted ("*" for any number of wild characters and "+"

for a single one). Note that the call works from the CURRENT position in the file and that, if the user wishes the search to start from the beginning of the file, Vector 52 must be called with the D register set to 1.

VECTOR NUMBER: 148

TITLE: WILD INSTRING.

ENTRY REQUIREMENTS: THE A REGISTER HOLDS THE LENGTH OF THE MAJOR STRING.
THE B REGISTER HOLDS THE ADDRESS OF THE MINOR STRING.
THE X REGISTER POINTS TO THE LOCATION OF THE MAJOR STRING.
GENERAL WORD VARIABLE 0 POINTS TO THE LOCATION OF THE MINOR STRING.

OUTPUT: THE B REGISTER HOLDS THE POSITION OF THE MATCH OF THE MINOR STRING WITHIN THE MAJOR.
THE CARRY FLAG IS CLEAR IF A MATCH WAS FOUND AND SET OTHERWISE.

FUNCTION: This function works much in the same way as Vector 115, except that wildcards are permitted ("*" to mean any number of wild characters and "+" to indicate a single one). However, note the following, where null strings are involved:

MAJOR	MINOR	MATCH
"ABC"	""	FALSE
""	""	TRUE
""	"*"	TRUE
""	"+"	FALSE

VECTOR NUMBER: 149

TITLE: NUMBER OF DAYS.

ENTRY REQUIREMENTS: THE X REGISTER HOLDS THE ADDRESS OF THE 3-BYTE DATE IN THE FORMAT "YEAR:MONTH:DAY".

OUTPUT: THE B REGISTER HOLDS THE MOST SIGNIFICANT BYTE OF THE RESULT.
THE X REGISTER HOLDS THE 2 LESS SIGNIFICANT BYTES OF THE RESULT.
THE CARRY FLAG IS SET IF THE DATE IS INVALID.

FUNCTION: This function returns the number of days which have passed from 01 Jan 1900 to the date indicated by the X register. The "year" byte can be any number in the range 0-255, while the "month" and "day" bytes must hold valid calendar values.

VECTOR NUMBER: 150

TITLE: WEEK NUMBER.

ENTRY REQUIREMENTS: THE X REGISTER HOLDS THE ADDRESS OF THE 3-BYTE DATE IN THE FORMAT "YEAR:MONTH:DAY".

OUTPUT: THE B REGISTER HOLDS THE WEEK NUMBER.
THE CARRY FLAG IS SET IF THE DATE WAS INVALID.

FUNCTION: This function returns the week number of the date indicated by the X register. Week number 1 (which is actually returned as 0) is assumed to start with the first Monday of the year. Any days prior to this are assumed to be part of the last week of the previous year. Note that applications convert the range 0-53, which is returned by this function, to range 0-255, while the "month" and "day" bytes must hold valid calendar values.

VECTOR NUMBER: 151

TITLE: DAY NAME.

ENTRY REQUIREMENTS: THE B REGISTER HOLDS THE DAY NUMBER IN THE WEEK (0-6, WITH MONDAY AS 0).

OUTPUT: THE X REGISTER POINTS TO THE 3-LETTER DAY NAME STRING.

FUNCTION: This function returns a 3-letter day name string for a given day-of-the-week number. Note that this string is in the selected language and that if numbers outside the 0-6 range are passed to the routine, garbage will be assiduously handed back.

VECTOR NUMBER: 152

TITLE: GET EXTENSION.

ENTRY REQUIREMENTS: THE A REGISTER HOLDS THE FILETYPE.
THE X REGISTER INDICATES WHERE TO STORE THE FILE EXTENSION.
THE LESS SIGNIFICANT BYTE OF GENERAL WORD VARIABLE 0 ($42) HOLDS THE OPL FILETYPE IF THE A REGISTER HOLDS $83.

OUTPUT: THE B REGISTER HOLDS THE LENGTH OF THE EXTENSION.

FUNCTION: This function will retrieve the file extension for a specified filetype. The string, including the ".", is stored at the location indicated by the X register.

VECTOR NUMBER: 153

TITLE: GET TYPE.

ENTRY REQUIREMENTS: THE X REGISTER POINTS TO THE LOCATION OF THE EXTENSION STRING.
THE B REGISTER HOLDS THE LENGTH OF THE EXTENSION. LEGAL VALUES ARE 0,2,4.

OUTPUT: THE A REGISTER HOLDS THE FILETYPE FOR THE EXTENSION INDICATED BY THE X REGISTER.
THE LOW BYTE OF GENERAL WORD VARIABLE 0 ($42) HOLDS "1" IF THE FILE IS ".OPO", "2" IF IT IS ".OPT" AND "0" OTHERWISE.

FUNCTION: This function is the reverse of Vector 152. The X register points to the location of the "." of the extension in memory while the B register specifies its length. If the extension is ".*" the A register will return "0". If the length is passed as "0", the A register will return "$FF".

VECTOR NUMBER: 154

TITLE: LZ-ONLY TRANSLATE.

ENTRY REQUIREMENTS: THE B REGISTER HOLDS:
0 TO TRANSLATE LANGUAGE PROCEDURE.
1 TO TRANSLATE CALC EXPRESSIONS.
2 TO LOCATE ERRORS IN CALC.
3 TO LOCATE ERRORS IN LANGUAGE PROCEDURES.
THE X REGISTER HOLDS THE OFFSET IN Q CODE TO RUNTIME ERROR. THIS IS IGNORED IF THE B REGISTER HOLDS 0 OR 1.

	THE A REGISTER HOLDS: 0 TO PERFORM TRANSLATION AS FOR 2-LINE MACHINE. 1 TO PERFORM TRANSLATION AS FOR 4-LINE MACHINE.
OUTPUT:	IF AN ERROR OCCURS: THE X REGISTER HOLDS THE OFFSET IN SOURCE CODE TO ERROR. THE B REGISTER HOLDS THE ERROR CODE.

FUNCTION: This function operates much like the Translate routine at Vector 79 except that the user can specify, via the A register, whether the code is to be translated as if the machine was a 2-line version OR a 4-line. This allows 4-line code to take advantage of the increased facilities of the LZ family. Users should note that object code generated in 4-line mode is 2 bytes longer than identical source code translated under 2-line mode. Thus, LZ code will be recognized as such by a 2-line machine and will not run.

VECTOR NUMBER: 155

TITLE:	DIRTY EDIT FILENAME.
ENTRY REQUIREMENTS:	THE X REGISTER HOLDS THE ADDRESS OF THE PROMPT STRING. THE A REGISTER HOLDS THE PARAMETER FOR VECTOR 28. THE B REGISTER HOLDS THE MAXIMUM INPUT LENGTH. THE LOW BYTE OF GENERAL WORD VARIABLE 0 ($42) INDICATES THE LINE NUMBER FOR THE PROMPT.
OUTPUT:	THE B REGISTER HOLDS THE KEY WHICH CAUSED EXIT.

FUNCTION: This function performs much like Vector 104 except that the screen is not cleared. The key causing exit from the routine is returned in the B register. In addition, the Carry Flag is set if the <ON/CLEAR> key was used to terminate the edit.

VECTOR NUMBER: 156

TITLE: SPECIAL DIRECTORY.

ENTRY REQUIREMENTS: THE X REGISTER POINTS TO THE LOCATION OF THE PROMPT STRING WHICH IS STORED WITH A LEADING COUNT BYTE.
THE B REGISTER HOLDS THE MAXIMUM LENGTH OF THE INPUT STRING.
THE A REGISTER HOLDS THE FILE TYPE FOR THE DIRECTORY ($81-$8F OR $00 FOR ALL).
THE RUN-TIME BUFFER AT $2188 HOLDS THE DEFAULT FILENAME. THE LENGTH IS STORED AT $2187.
THE HIGH BYTE OF THE GENERAL WORD VARIABLE 0 ($41) HOLDS:
0 FOR PROMPT ON TOP LINE.
1 FOR PROMPT ON SECOND LINE.
THE LOW BYTE HOLDS:
0 TO PRODUCE NO DIRECTORY (IN WHICH CASE, IT JUST CALLS VECTOR 155).
1 FOR DIRECTORY OF FILES.
2 TO DISPLAY FILE SIZES AT RIGHT.
4 TO DISPLAY FILETYPES AT LEFT.
8 TO PUT "*" AS ENTRY 1 FOR "COPY" ETC.
16 TO INSERT FILETYPE AFTER PROMPT.
32 TO DISABLE <EXE> KEY FROM EXITING.
64 TO DISABLE <MODE> FROM SWITCHING PACKS.

OUTPUT: THE A REGISTER RETURNS THE FILETYPE OF THE FILE SELECTED, PROVIDING $42 IS NON-ZERO.
IF <ON/CLEAR> WAS PRESSED, CARRY FLAG SET.
ELSE
THE RUNTIME BUFFER AT $2188 HOLDS THE SELECTED FILENAME AND THE "SELECTED PACK" VARIABLE AT $A2 HOLDS THE DEVICE SELECTED.

FUNCTION: This function displays a directory of files with a prompt. The user can select a file using the <EXE> key, after which the lower 2 or 3 lines of screen will be cleared when the function terminates.

VECTOR NUMBER: 157

TITLE: N'TH WILD CARD CATALOGUE.

ENTRY REQUIREMENTS: THE A REGISTER HOLDS "1" ON INITIAL CALL AND "0" THEREAFTER.
THE TOP BIT IS SET TO DISPLAY FILE SIZES.
THE B REGISTER HOLDS THE DEVICE TYPE (0,1,2, ETC).
THE X REGISTER POINTS TO THE FILENAME BUFFER.
THE TOP BYTE OF GENERAL WORD VARIABLE 0 ($41) HOLDS THE FILETYPE IF THE TOP BIT OF THE LOW BYTE IS SET.
THE LOW BYTE OF GENERAL WORD VARIABLE 0 ($42) HOLDS THE LENGTH OF THE STRING POINTED TO BY THE GENERAL WORD VARIABLE 1 ($43).
THE GENERAL WORD VARIABLE 1 ($43) POINTS TO THE MATCH STRING.
GENERAL WORD VARIABLE 2 ($45)

	INDICATES THE N'TH MATCH REQUIRED.
OUTPUT:	THE A REGISTER INDICATES THE FILETYPE FOUND. THE B REGISTER HOLDS "1" FOR ".OPO", 2 FOR ".OPT" AND "0" OTHERWISE. THE GENERAL WORD VARIABLE 0 ($41) INDICATES THE NUMBER OF BYTES IF A BLOCK FILE OR THE NUMBER OF RECORDS IF A ".ODB" FILE (IF THE TOP BIT OF THE A REGISTER WAS SET).

FUNCTION: This function is similar to Vector 144 except that it gets the nth match as held in the General Word Variable 2 ($45).

VECTOR NUMBER: 158

TITLE:	ALARM ENTRY.
ENTRY REQUIREMENTS:	THE B REGISTER HOLDS THE FUNCTION NUMBER INTHE RANGE 0-6.
OUTPUT:	NIL.

FUNCTION: This function provides a user with a means to enter the alarm routines. The functions available are:

Function 0 - Initialise. This function clears all alarms and allows the alarm to be checked by setting the "alarm-check" variable at $2335.

Function 1 - Call Alarm Application. This function calls the alarm application as is it were from the top-level and sets the screen to 4-line mode. It then allows the alarms to be viewed and modified. When the routine is exited, the display is returned to its previous mode.

Function 2 - Check For Time-out Alarms. If the "alarm-check" variable at $2335 is set, this function checks for diary and ordinary alarms which are due to sound within the next 34 mins 08 secs and sets them off. The maximum likely to sound is 1 diary and 2 ordinary alarms. Alarms which are due to sound within the next 2048 secs are then examined. If any are in fact due, the routine exits with the Carry Flag set and the D register indicating the number of seconds before the first of the alarms is due. The contents of the D register in such cases will be greater than or equal to 2 and less than 2048.

Function 3 - Check For Alarms Due Now. If the "alarm-check" variable at $2335 is set, this function checks for alarms due now and sounds them (maximum of 1 diary and 2 ordinary).

Function 4 - Check For Unacknowledged Alarms. If the "alarm-check" variable at $2335 is set, this function activates the "Review Missed Alarms" on switch-on. Any Diary alarms which were not cleared by the <ON/CLEAR> key are reviewed, preserving the existing screen.

Function 5 - Turn Alarms Off. This function clears the "alarm-check" variable at $2335 after copying its previous state to another storage location. Users should exercise some degree of care in using this apparently simple call. If it is called again without restoring the state of the "alarm-check" variable, all alarms will be disabled until the variable is set by POKEing it.

Function 6 - Restore Alarms. This is the reverse of Function 5. It copies the preserved alarm status into the "alarm-check" variable at $2335.

VECTOR NUMBER: 159

TITLE: NOTEPAD ENTRY.

ENTRY REQUIREMENTS: THE B REGISTER HOLDS THE FUNCTION NUMBER.

OUTPUT: NIL.

FUNCTION: This function provides the user with an entry point to the Notepad facilities. There are 5 functions, all of which begin by flushing the Diary Paste Buffer. This buffer is used by the Notepad application to save the current find string. The block file type and cell type are initialised for Notepad editing and, after the function has terminated, they are restored to OPL editing values. The functions are:

Function 0 - Initialise Notepad. This function is called on cold booting the LZ. It inserts the name "Notepad:" into the cell, sets the cursor to the first editable character and clears the "password status" variable at $7EFB to indicate that no password exists. In addition, it sets the "Notepad Flags" variable at $7FEA to 8, which indicates that the Notepad is not to be numbered, the name is not capitalized, a title line is required and exit is permitted on <ON/CLEAR>.

Function 1 - Call Notepad. This function calls the Notepad application as if it had been selected from the top level menu "Notes".

Function 2 - Find String. This function is also called by the "Search" option in the "Utils" menu. It searches all Notepads not password-protected, starting with the current and then all the saved Notepads in "A:", "B:", "C:" order. The find string must be stored in the run-time find buffer at $22C9. When a match is located, it will be displayed on the bottom line of the screen. Pressing:

<MODE>	will allow editing at that point.
<EXE>	will search for the next match.
<ON/CLEAR>	will exit from the search.

Function 3 - Edit Notepad. Allows the user to edit a named notepad as if from a top-level Notepad menu item. The General Word Variable 0 ($41) points to the location of the Notepad name. If this name does not match that in the Notepad cell, the packs are searched in "A:", "B:", "C:" order until the match is made. The file is then loaded into the Notepad cell. Any errors are displayed immediately. No error codes are returned. However, on exit, the following can be true:

Carry Set	= search went past end.
Carry Clear + B Register Clear	= <ON/CLEAR> pressed.
Carry Clear + B Register Set	= <MODE> pressed.

Function 4 - Check Password Status. This function ascertains whether a Notepad file is password protected. The General Word Variable 0 ($41) points to the location of the Notepad name. On exit, the B register returns "1" if the Notepad is protected and "0", otherwise.

VECTOR NUMBER: 160

TITLE: ENTER CALCULATOR.

ENTRY REQUIREMENTS:NIL.

OUTPUT: NIL.

FUNCTION: This function enters the calculator in exactly the same way as from the top level menu. Users should note that this facility must not be called from within an OPL procedure. This is due to the fact that, unless all variables are preserved, OPL is not re-entrant.

VECTOR NUMBER: 161

TITLE: CALL UTILITY APPLICATION.

ENTRY REQUIREMENTS: THE B REGISTER HOLDS FUNCTION NUMBER (0-11).

OUTPUT: NIL.

FUNCTION: This function allows the user to call any of the options in the top level "UTILS" menu. Twelve functions are available:

Function 0 - Initialises the system password.
Function 1 - Calls the "UTILS" menu.
Function 2 - Calls the Utils "Search" option.
Function 3 - Calls the Utils "Info" option.
Function 4 - Calls the Utils "Passw" option.
Function 5 - Calls the Utils "Lang" option.
Function 6 - Checks the system password if set "ON".
Function 7 - RESETS the machine.
Function 8 - Formats the RAMPAK whose code is passed in the A Register (1="B:", 2="C:").
Function 9 - Calls the Utils "Dir" option.
Function 10 - Calls the Utils "Copy" option.
Function 11 - Calls the Utils "Delete" option.

VECTOR NUMBER: 162

TITLE: CREATE BAR UDGs

ENTRY REQUIREMENTS: THE A REGISTER SPECIFIES THE % BLACK ON LEFT.
THE B REGISTER SPECIFIES THE % GREY ON RIGHT.

OUTPUT: PLACES THE BAR CHARACTERS IN THE RUNTIME BUFFER AT $2188.
SETS THE RUNTIME BUFFER LENGTH AT $2187 TO 20.

FUNCTION: This function sets up the UDGs for drawing the bar graph and stores them in the runtime buffer.

VECTOR NUMBER: 163

TITLE: PARTIAL VIEW STRING.

ENTRY REQUIREMENTS: THE TOP BIT OF THE A REGISTER IS SET IF EXIT ON ARROW KEYS IS REQUIRED.
THE B REGISTER HOLDS THE LENGTH OF THE STRING TO VIEW.
THE X REGISTER POINTS TO THE LOCATION OF THE STRING.
GENERAL WORD VARIABLE 0 HOLDS THE TIME DELAY BEFORE SCROLLING BEGINS.

OUTPUT: NIL.

FUNCTION: This function operates in the same way as Vector 21 but at the current cursor position, as specified by the "Cursor Position" variable at $62. Characters before the cursor position will not be scrolled but the rest of the string will scroll on the remainder of the line.

VECTOR NUMBER: 164

TITLE: ENTER TIME.

ENTRY REQUIREMENTS: THE B REGISTER CONTAINS THE FUNCTION NUMBER.

OUTPUT: NIL.

FUNCTION: This function allows the user to enter the TIME application as from the top level menu. There are 2 functions:

Function 0 - Initialise. This function actually does nothing at all.

Function 1 - Calls the TIME application as if from the top level menu.

VECTOR NUMBER: 165

TITLE: QUICK SORT.

ENTRY REQUIREMENTS: THE D REGISTER HOLDS THE NUMBER OF ITEMS TO BE SORTED. THE X REGISTER CONTAINS THE ADDRESS OF THE USER-SUPPLIED ROUTINE.

OUTPUT: NIL.

FUNCTION: This function provides the basis for a Quick Sort by assigning space for a tag for each of the items to be sorted. The user's routine is called for each of these items to obtain the tag. Using the user's routine, these are sorted and passed (again to the user's routine). The user's routine must not use the runtime variables at $4D, $4F and $51 unless their contents are preserved on each call. Furthermore, the runtime buffer at $2188 is also used by the Vector and should therefore be avoided.

The user's routine can be called by the Vector, giving a parameter with 3 possible values:

> Register B = 0. When the call to the User's routine is made with this value, the X register indicates the number of the record (0 to n-1), leaving it as the tag for that record.
>
> Register B = 1. This indicates that the X register holds the tag for the left hand record and the General Word Variable 0 ($41) the right. The routine should leave the condition flags as for "CMP X,UTW_S0".
>
> Register B = 2. This means that the X register holds the tag for the next SORTED record.

As this is a rather complex subject, users should study the assembler example below which is reproduced courtesy of PSION PLC.

EXAMPLE

Sorts the qwerty alphabet into order

```
   LDD  #26
   LDX  #MYROUTINE
   OS   UT$SORT
   BCC  OKRTS
   OS   ER$MESS
OKRTS:  RTS

MYROUTINE:
   TST  B
   BNE  1$
   XGDX          ; returns address of letter
   ADDD #ORIGINAL
   XGDX
   RTS

1$: DEC  B
   BNE  2$
   LDA  A,0,X
   LDX  UTW_S0:
   LDA  B,0,x
   CBA           ; does comparison
   RTS

2$: LDA  A,0,X         ; copies sorted letters in order
   LDX  SRTTAG
   STA  A,0,X
   INX
   STX  SRTTAG
   RTS

SRTTAG:
   .word    SORTED
ORIGINAL:
   .ascii "QWERTYUIOPASDFGHJKLZXCVBNM"
SORTED:
   .ascii "00000000000000000000000000"
```

VECTOR NUMBER: 166

TITLE: ENTER WORLD.

ENTRY REQUIREMENTS: THE B REGISTER HOLDS THE FUNCTION NUMBER.

OUTPUT: NIL.

FUNCTION: This Vector allows the user to enter the "WORLD" application as from the top level menu. It has 3 functions:

Function 0 - Initialise. This sets the base to London, Bonn or Paris according to the language in force (indicated by the "language" variable at $2186) and sets the initial city to Manhattan.

Function 1 - Enters the "WORLD" application as if from the top level menu.

Function 2 - Places the base city and country name into the runtime buffer at $2188. The function then returns the city name at $2188+100 and the country name at $2188+120 unless there IS no city. In such a case the country name is placed in the city location and the country location is left blank. Both strings are byte length.

VECTOR NUMBER: 167

TITLE: ENTER DIARY.

ENTRY REQUIREMENTS: THE B REGISTER HOLDS THE FUNCTION NUMBER.

OUTPUT: NIL.

FUNCTION: This Vector provides the user with a means of entering the Diary application. there are 4 functions, each of which begins by enabling <SHIFT-EXE>, clearing the Diary paste buffer, setting the time in the

Diary to the system time and defining the Diary UDGs. All Functions end by disabling <SHIFT-EXE>. The functions are as follows:

Function 0 - Initialise. This works as per cold boot, clearing the diary, setting the "slot boundary" variables ($20A9-$20AB) to 48,56 and 72 respectively. It also enables Diary alarm prompts by setting the "alarm prompt" variable at $20AC to a non-zero value.

Function 1 - Call Diary. This function enters the Diary week-view as if from the top level menu.

Function 2 - Find String. This searches the current Diary for a given string which must be located in the find buffer at $22C9. If a match is found, it will be displayed on the bottom 2 lines, allowing the user to press:

<MODE> to enter the Diary at that point in page mode.

<EXE> to search for the next match.

<ON/CLEAR> to abort.

On exit from this function, one of the following conditions will be set:

Carry Flag Set. This means that the search went past the end of the Diary.

Carry Set + B Register Clear. The <ON/CLEAR> key was pressed, aborting the search.

Carry Set + B Register Set. The <MODE> key was pressed, the Diary entered and subsequently left.

Function 3 - Display Monthly Calendar. This is as per top level option "Month". The day page can be entered by pressing <EXE>.

VECTOR NUMBER: 168

TITLE: ENTER XFILES.

ENTRY REQUIREMENTS: THE B REGISTER CONTAINS THE FUNCTION NUMBER.

OUTPUT: NIL.

FUNCTION: This Vector allows the user to enter the "XFILES" application. there are 6 functions available:

Function 0 - Initialise. This function initialises the current XFILES file to "MAIN".

Function 1 - This function allows the user to enter the XFILES application as from the top level menu.

Function 2 - Find String. This function searches files on all devices for the string stored in the find buffer at $22C9, whose length is held at the "find buffer length" variable at $22C8. On exit:

Carry Set. This means that the string was not found or that it WAS found but that <EXE> was then pressed.

Carry Clear and B Register Set. This indicates that <MODE> was pressed.

Carry Clear and B Register Clear. This means that <ON/CLEAR> was pressed or an error occurred.

Function 3 - Find File. This function searches for the file whose name string is pointed to by the General Word Variable 0 ($41). The search examines packs in the order "A:", "B:" and "C:". If the file is found, it is made the current XFILES file.

Function 4 - FIND Function. This function runs the top level FIND function.

Function 5 - SAVE Function. This function runs the top level SAVE function.

VECTOR NUMBER: 169

TITLE: DISPLAY ERROR.

ENTRY REQUIREMENTS: THE X REGISTER POINTS TO THE ERROR STRING.

OUTPUT: NIL.

FUNCTION: This function displays the string which is stored, leading byte count, at the address pointed to by the X register in error message format. Note that the string must be less than 21 characters for 4-line displays and less than 17 for 2-line.

VECTOR NUMBER: 170

TITLE: MONTH NAME.

ENTRY REQUIREMENTS: THE B REGISTER HOLDS THE MONTH NUMBER (0-11).

OUTPUT: THE X REGISTER POINTS TO THE MONTH NAME.

FUNCTION: This function returns the 3-letter, capitalized month name in the current language. The B register value does not appear to be checked. Values outside the range 0-11 will return garbage.

VECTOR NUMBER: 171

TITLE: ENTER EDITOR.

ENTRY REQUIREMENTS: THE B REGISTER HOLDS THE FUNCTION NUMBER.

OUTPUT: THE X REGISTER INDICATES THE CURRENT LINE.
THE A REGISTER CONTAINS THE FOLLOWING FLAGS:

BIT 7 - TRUE IF NUMBERED.
BIT 2 - TRUE IF PROMPT TO BE CAPITALIZED.
BIT 1 - TRUE IF NO TITLE REQUIRED.
BIT 0 - TRUE IF CHANGED.
THE B REGISTER HOLDS THE POSITION IN THE LINE INDICATED BY THE X REGISTER.

FUNCTION: This Vector allows the user to enter the Editor. The Register A flags which are passed to Function 2 can be ignored by passing 0 in the MSB of the General Word Variable 0 ($41) before calling "EDIT". This will cause editing, as in the Organiser II, to be enforced. This Vector does not handle files but offers the following functions:

Function 0 - Initialise. This function initialises the parameters. The A register should holds the block file type and the General Word Variable 0 ($41) the cell address*2.

Function 1 - New. This function requires the name string of the new file to be pointed to by the X register. It will insert the name at the start of an existing cell.

Function 2 - Edit Cell. This function allows editing of an existing cell which must have a name terminated by a colon at the start. The function requires the following input data:

The X Register to indicate the current line (starting at 0).

The A Register to indicate the position in the current line.

The MSB of the General Word Variable 0 ($41) to hold these flags:

BIT 7 - True if numbered.
BIT 2 - True if prompt to be capitalized.
BIT 1 - True if no title required.
BIT 0 - True if changed.

Function 3 - Find.

Function 4 - Zap.

Function 5 - Top.

Function 6 - Bottom.

Function 7 - Print.

Function 8 - Restore Editor Status. This function must be called when finished with the editor.

VECTOR NUMBER: 172

TITLE: ARCSIN.

ENTRY REQUIREMENTS: FLOATING POINT ARGUMENT MUST BE STACKED.

OUTPUT: FLOATING POINT RESULT IS RETURNED ON THE STACK.

FUNCTION: This function returns the arcsine in radians of the floating point argument on the stack, leaving the stack pointer ($A5) unchanged.

VECTOR NUMBER: 173

TITLE: ARCCOS.

ENTRY REQUIREMENTS: THE FLOATING POINT ARGUMENT MUST BE STACKED.

OUTPUT: FLOATING POINT RESULT IS LEFT ON THE STACK.

FUNCTION: This function takes the floating point argument from the stack and returns the floating point arccosine again on the stack. The stack pointer ($A5) is left unchanged.

VECTOR NUMBER: 174

TITLE: SORT FILE.

ENTRY REQUIREMENTS: THE X REGISTER POINTS TO THE FILENAME TO BE SORTED.
THE D REGISTER HOLDS THE ADDRESS OF THE USER ROUTINE TO BE CALLED OR $0000 FOR NO ROUTINE.

OUTPUT: NIL.

FUNCTION: This function is similar to Vector 165, except that the X register indicates the name string (leading count byte in form "A:NNNNNNNN") of the file to be sorted. The D register points to the user routine which will be given a value in the A register at each pass (1,2,3). In addition, the X register will contain the record number/number of comparisons during the sort. There are 3 passes, First the tag list is generated, then the list is sorted and, finally, the file is re-constructed from the sorted tag list. If there is insufficient space in memory for the tag list, the file will be left unsorted.

VECTOR NUMBER: 175

TITLE: ENTER PROG.

ENTRY REQUIREMENTS: THE B REGISTER HOLDS THE FUNCTION NUMBER.
OUTPUT: NIL.

FUNCTION: This Vector provides the user with a means by which he can enter the top level PROG application. There are 2 functions:

> Function 1 - Call PROG. This calls the PROG application as if from the top level menu.
>
> Function 2 - Find String. Searches the block files, whose type is held in variable $23E0, for the string held in the runtime

find buffer at $22C9 and whose length is stored in the "runtime find buffer length" variable at $22C8. On exit, one of the following will be true:

Carry Set. This means that the string was not found or that it WAS found but that <EXE> was subsequently pressed.

Carry Clear + B Register Set. This means that <MODE> was pressed.

Carry Clear + B Register Clear. This means that either <ON/CLEAR> was pressed or that an error occurred.

VECTOR NUMBER: 176

TITLE: FAST DELETE.

ENTRY REQUIREMENTS: THE D REGISTER INDICATES THE RECORD TO DELETE FROM.
THE X REGISTER INDICATES EITHER THE NUMBER OF RECORDS TO DELETE OR "$FFFF" TO DELETE TO END OF FILE.

OUTPUT: NIL.

FUNCTION: This function "fast deletes" the number of records specified in the X register of the type indicated by the "current record type variable" at $96, starting at the record stated in the D register (or to the end of the file, if the X register holds $FFFF).

VECTOR NUMBER: 177

TITLE: CURSOR-ON GET KEY.

ENTRY REQUIREMENTS: NIL.

OUTPUT: THE B REGISTER HOLDS THE ASCII VALUE OF THE KEY PRESS.

FUNCTION: This function is similar to Vector 72 except that the cursor is turned ON before the key is "GOT" and OFF afterwards.

VECTOR NUMBER: 178

TITLE: CASE DEPENDENT BUFFER COMPARE.

ENTRY REQUIREMENTS: THE X REGISTER POINTS TO THE LEFT HAND STRING.
THE GENERAL WORD VARIABLE 0 ($41) POINTS TO THE RIGHT HAND STRING.
THE A REGISTER HOLDS THE LENGTH OF THE LEFT HAND STRING.
THE B REGISTER HOLDS THE LENGTH OF THE RIGHT HAND STRING.

OUTPUT: THE B REGISTER WILL BE:

a. EQUAL TO ZERO IF THEY STRINGS ARE IDENTICAL.

b. LESS THAN ZERO IF THE LEFT HAND STRING IS FIRST ALPHABETICALLY.

c. GREATER THAN ZERO IF THE RIGHT HAND STRING IS FIRST ALPHABETICALLY.
THE Z FLAG WILL BE SET ACCORDING TO THE CONTENTS OF THE B REGISTER.
THE N FLAG WILL BE SET ACCORDING TO THE CONTENTS OF THE B REGISTER.

FUNCTION: This function compares 2 buffers and is similar to Vector 114 except that the comparison is case dependent.

VECTOR NUMBER: 179

TITLE: SET TIME.

ENTRY REQUIREMENTS: THE X REGISTER POINTS TO THE DATE AND TIME.

OUTPUT: NIL.

FUNCTION: This function sets the time indicated by the X register. The data must be 6 bytes in length and cannot be directly POKEd into memory, since the system time might be undergoing an update by the NMI.

Index